The best guide on estate planning that I have ever come across is a book called Plan Your Estate: Wills, Probate Avoidance, Trusts & Taxes. *It suggests how to reduce death taxes, reduce probate fees and costs, provide prompt cash for your survivors and transfer your estate in exactly the way you choose. And — an unlooked-for blessing — it is easy to read.*

Carol Mathews
Money Watch

Plan Your Estate *is particularly helpful to the layperson who does not want to consult a lawyer — a clear, comprehensive and even charming book. . . .*

The Book Review
Los Angeles Times

Nolo Press has published a book on dying that is designed for the living. Written in a clear, concise format that cuts through the mass of legal gobbledygook which usually surrounds probate, death taxes, trusts, etc. The book is designed to help persons with small and moderate estates understand the nuts and bolts of estate planning.

Lee Smith
Sacramento Bee

Clifford's book provides practical advice on how to keep death taxes and probate fees as low as possible, insure that survivors receive the money due them quickly and be certain that your overall wishes are carried out. He writes simply, avoids legal jargon and includes many of the forms necessary. . . .

Stephen Fox
Associated Press

An excellent book . . . a thorough reading of this book would be a wise initial step.
Pat Dunn
Orange Coast Daily Pilot

Plan Your Estate:
WILLS, PROBATE AVOIDANCE, TRUSTS & TAXES

Plan Your Estate:
WILLS, PROBATE AVOIDANCE, TRUSTS & TAXES

California Third Edition

By Attorney Denis Clifford

Editor: Ralph Warner

NOLO PRESS

950 Parker St.   Berkeley, CA 94710

PRINTING HISTORY

Nolo Press is committed to keeping its books up-to-date. Each new printing, whether or not it is called a new edition, has been completely revised to reflect latest law changes. If this book is ''out-of-date,'' do not rely on the information without checking it in a new edition.

First Edition:	January 1980
Second Edition:	April 1981
Third Edition:	September 1982
Editorial Assistance:	David Brown
Production:	Keija Kimura
Book Design & Layout:	Toni Ihara
Contemporary Line Drawings:	Linda Allison
Typesetting:	Aardvark Type
Cover Illustration:	Elizabeth Delphey

ISBN 0-917316-53-3

Acknowledgments

My thanks and gratitude to all those friends who helped work on this book: people who read the manuscript—Dave Brown, Peter Jan Honigsberg, Robert Wood of Athearn, Chandler & Hoffman, San Francisco, members of the Bay Area Funeral Society, Walter Warner, and especially Marilyn Putnam, a real wizard in estate planning; people who helped prepare the manuscript—Sandy Wieker, Christy Rigg, Cathy Cummings and Bethany Korwin-Pawloski; all the people of Nolo Press—Keija Kimura, Carol Pladsen, Linda Allison, a fine artist, Jake Warner, a superb editor, and Toni Ihara, who started it all.

Table of Contents

Introduction
How to Use This Book

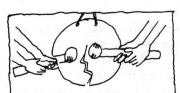

IN LAOS A LAMEN TAN VILLAGE MAN IS BURIED WITH HIS CROSSBOW, RAIN COAT, WALLET AND BASKETS. IF HE DIES WITHOUT A MALE HEIR, RELATIVES BEAT THE GONG UNTIL IT SHATTERS. THE BROKEN BITS ARE LAID ON TOP OF THE GRAVE.

This book is designed to assist non-lawyers in understanding and coping with both the legal and the practical consequences of a person's death. I'm aware that legal matters may often be of minor concern in the face of the overwhelming emotional force and mystery of death, but I don't deal with the larger meanings; they are appropriately left for philosophers, clergy, poets, and ultimately to you. Death is a difficult subject to think about, to talk about, and (often) to plan for. The ancient Greeks believed the inevitability of death could best be faced by performing great deeds. Christian religions offer the promise of eternal life; preparing for death means preparing to "meet your maker." Other cultures have prepared for death in a wide variety of ways.

However anyone chooses to prepare, emotionally, for death, their own or someone's they care for, there are also practical matters that must be dealt with. If no practical planning has been done, the normal result is that the survivors, normally upset and confused, turn everything over to so-called "professionals." A body must suddenly be disposed of, so a funeral parlor is called. Property must be handled, bills paid and tax returns prepared, so a lawyer is hired. Many other problems inevitably arise. Some are immediate: How does a surviving family member get money to eat? What about flowers at a funeral? Others are long-term: What happens now to the family house? How are family heirlooms to be distributed? Who pays inheritance taxes?

While trying to deal with the emotional trauma and the physical reality of death, it's easy for thousands of dollars to be consumed in the excessive or unneeded fees of professionals, or needlessly wasted on taxes. Invariably, the wasted money will ultimately be provided from the assets — the "estate" — of the person who died. That is, money that would otherwise be available for the family, friends or other inheritors.

"Estate planning" means sensibly preparing for these types of problems. The term "estate planning" can be used to describe only the transfer of your property to your inheritors. However, in this book I use the term more broadly to describe as well all sorts of other practical matters and choices, that surround death. What are your choices regarding body disposition? What about cremation, funeral societies, donating a body to medical school, or your heart for a heart transplant? How do you actually obtain the property of someone who died? How do you collect insurance proceeds, a bank account, or transfer title to a car, after a death? What transfer methods are the most economical and save the most on taxes and fees?

The need for some system of inheritance responds to a basic human urge. Every civilization has had some means of transferring property upon death. Rightly or wrongly, the peculiarities of the American system of inheritance mean that substantial amounts of money can often be saved, if property is labelled and/or transferred by certain legal means rather than others.

This book is especially designed for small and moderate estates, which, in estate planner's terms, means estates worth less than, roughly $500,000. In this financial range there is a great deal that people can safely do for themselves. Those with larger estates may benefit from complicated techniques that are beyond the scope of this book, especially certain types of trusts that I do not cover in detail. However, even those with large estates will find much valuable material here as a good understanding of the basic concepts of estate planning is essential to anyone with an estate, no matter what its size. Whether your estate is moderate or immense, if you eventually decide to seek professional help on some aspect of your estate plan, you will benefit greatly by comprehending the issues and objectives involved and the information in this book will enable you to deal with a professional to get the help you really need, as opposed to what he feels like providing.

There is one point I would like to make loud and clear—all the technical details and options of estate planning should never be allowed to obscure your main goal which is to distribute your property as you think best. This goal is private, and personal, and it cannot be dictated to you by another person or book. Each individual must take stock of their own situation, financial and emotional, and determine what these goals are. Only **after** you decide what persons or organizations you wish to leave your property to should the techniques of estate planning be considered. Equally obvious and no less important, all estate planning should be discussed with those closest to you, those who will be most affected by that plan. Dealing with the pain and grief of the death of a loved person is hard enough without adding confusion over how financial and practical matters are to be handled.

The actual process of planning your estate can be complicated, but for most moderate estates it doesn't have to be nearly as forbidding as professionals often seem to make it. But as different aspects of estate planning are intertwined, you must get a good overview of the whole field before you make your plan. So, read through the entire book once before you actually start to make your estate plan, skipping only the parts that obviously don't apply to your situation. For example, you could draft a competent, legally sufficient will simply by using the forms and information provided in Wills, Chapter 12. However, before you can sensibly draft a will, you must understand what the probate process is and why it is often sensible to pass property outside of a will. Mastering the handling of the practical aspects of a death does take some attention, but it is a task that laymen can readily do. The benefits—both in terms of peace of mind, and assets conserved for inheritors—can be substantial. Estate planning is musty stuff, not heroic work, but anyone concerned with the effect their death will have on those they love should be knowledgeable about it.

This book is divided into four basic sections:
Introduction to Estate Planning
Choices Regarding Body Disposition—Funerals, Cremation, Body Donations
Estate Taxes
Probate and Estate Planning Methods, Including Wills.

THE BAVENDA OF S. AFRICA HAVE SENTIMENTAL FEELINGS TOWARD HEIRLOOMS NO MATTER HOW VALUELESS. OLD OBJECTS ARE CONSIDERED LINKS BY WHICH THE LIVING CAN CONTACT THE DEAD OWNERS.

Not every topic in these sections is necessary for every person. For example, if you're not married, there's no reason to study the chapter on Community Property carefully. If your "taxable estate" (once you learn how to calculate that) is less than roughly **$275,000,** you **can't** owe federal estate taxes, and won't have to spend time learning how reduce or avoid them. However, you might still read the chapter on federal taxes, because that shows you how to calculate the taxable estate which can be useful knowledge for other purposes.

The laws of wills and estate planning are one of the more jargon-ridden areas of law (rather a feat). I've tried to keep the jargon to a minimum,* but there are words that anyone who wants to learn about these subjects should know. Many are euphemisms; for examples, a dead person is referred to as a "decedent." I've defined the major terms when they are first used in the text. There's also a glossary in the back, where you can look up the definition of a term that puzzles you. Here's one that's important, and puzzled me for a while: "real property" is land, and buildings on it; "personal property" is **every** other kind of property, from stocks to cash to furniture to wedding rings to your pet canary and the dust under your bed.

And one final, but important, point—this book does not claim to present definitive advice on all aspects of estate planning. The subjects covered, such as estate taxes, or life insurance, or probate avoidance, or will drafting, or burial options, are large matters; there are volumes of books on each topic in any good sized law library. Here I provide only basic information needed for handling problems and making choices in these areas. For example, the possible intricacies with trusts are endless, and learned experts will always be debating the fine points. But, fortunately, in most cases where a relatively simple trust is needed (to avoid probate) for people with a moderate estate, a standard form of trust will suffice for that need. I've tried to describe both the uses, and the limits, of these standard forms, but finally only you can decide if they cover your needs and desires, or if you want more specialized (and expensive) work done. Make this judgment carefully, of course, but do remember that lawyers aren't magicians, and the costs of hiring an expensive estate planner, for persons with a moderate estate, is often far greater than any savings or certainty they can achieve, beyond what you accomplish yourself by the methods presented here. As is discussed in Chapter 1, if you're nervous at the idea of doing all your own estate planning, you can consider hiring a lawyer to review the plan you've prepared. This should be much cheaper than having an attorney prepare the plan from scratch and, because you have educated yourself and done much of the work yourself, you are much more likely to end up with something that fully expresses your desires.

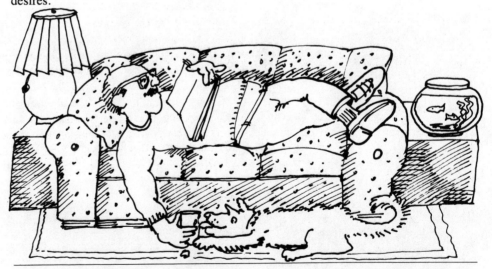

* A note on writing style. After several cumbersome attempts to use both masculine and feminine identifiers — "his/her," "executor/executrix," etc. — the author decided brevity was preferable to participating in the fight against (possible) verbal chauvinism. Accordingly, abstract individuals have usually been identified either as "he" or "her," rather than commingling both sexes.

1
What's Estate Planning?

A. What Estate Planning Covers

Estate planning covers many problems. The major ones include:
1. Having a practical plan for body disposition;
2. Reducing death taxes as low as possible;
3. Reducing probate costs and fees as low as possible;
4. Providing prompt cash to dependent survivors (usually family); and
5. Transferring the property of your estate to those you want to have it.

The phrase "estate planning" has many meanings. When rich folks' lawyers, accountants, and their ilk talk about "estate planning" they are using one of the many dignified-sounding terms they have invented for that grand old American game of "beat-the-taxman." You may wonder, as I do, why a civilization should set up the rules so that property transferred, or owned, under certain labels and forms is taxed less than if held in other ways. It is rather puzzling, but that's how it works. The Anglo-American legal system has a (warped) genius for protecting property of the wealthy, and that genius has produced many types of "estate planning" to minimize the impact of death taxes. These can often be so esoteric and involved that only a handful of tax lawyers understand them. For example, the nuances of new tax rules governing "generation skipping transfers" — e.g., where wealth is left in "trust" for grandchildren, with the children receiving only the income produced by the trust property — are now being explored and created by prosperous tax lawyers.* Most of these intricacies aren't covered here. Fortunately, however, estate planning can have meaning for average folks too. These are safe and understandable ways for the average person to save substantial sums of money while passing his or her property in ways that make sense.

---

* Similarly, many advantageous alternatives are made available only to those in the upper reaches of corporate hierarchies. Thus, executives can receive some of their pay in the form of "split dollar" insurance, special stock options, delayed compensation, and in a number of other tax—dodging ways.

One pillar of estate planning is respect for forms. I imagine most people know that oral wills aren't valid in California, and realize that a formal, written will must be properly prepared. That's true — the written form must be honored. But what can be surprising is how simple it often is to learn how to use the written forms correctly. The forms are not as demanding as you might fear.

B.   What Is An Estate?

In order to actually plan your estate, you have to first determine how much the estate is worth. This is more difficult than it appears. In common sense terms, a person's "estate" includes all the property he owns. Its worth is simply its total market value.* But, in estate planning terms, the valuation of an estate gets more complicated. **There are two different valuations of a person's estate that are vital for estate planning purposes:**

1. **The taxable estate:** all property of the decedent that is subject to federal estate taxes; this is normally about the same as the net worth of all the decedent's property.

2. **The probate estate:** whatever portion of the decedent's estate that is transferred by means of his will** as opposed to other possible transfer mechanisms. This is normally considerably less than all of a person's property.

The rules for calculating the value of an estate vary greatly, depending on whether it's the "taxable" estate or the "probate" estate. These rules are set out in subsequent chapters; but remember, as you read on, that the distinction between probate and taxable estate is crucial.

C.   What Is Probate?

"Probate" is the name given to the legal process of carrying out the terms of a will (or the transferring, according to state law, of the decedent's property, if there was no will). To "probate" an estate, legal proceedings must be held in Superior Court. Although these proceedings are usually a formality, since there is rarely any contest of the will, they are still cumbersome and lengthy. The average probate proceeding in California takes at least a year before the estate can actually be distributed to the inheritors. In a probate proceeding, the assets of the decedent are collected, all debts and death taxes paid, and the remaining property is finally distributed to the inheritors. Unless **all** property has been transferred by other means, which (as explained in subsequent chapters) is usually not desirable, some form of probate is inescapable. Every will must be probated.*** **However, and this is an extremely important point, much of a person's property does not have to pass through probate, even if there is a will. It is difficult and usually not wise to escape probate altogether, but it is very sensible to greatly reduce the costs, and impact of probate, by the estate planning and probate avoidance methods set out in the following chapters.**

---

* "Net worth," which is the amount you actually have for your estate, is market value less any amounts owed on the property.

** Or, if there is no will, by "intestate" probate proceedings. See Chapter 5, *Probate,* §G.

*** Probate of a will cannot be avoided even if the will writer and all the heirs and inheritors agree to dispense with it. In certain cases, summary methods are available which greatly simplify the probate process. See Chapter 6, *Simple Probate Methods* and Chapter 7, *Community Property.*

IN POLAND THE ESTATE IS SETTLED ON THE EIGHTH DAY AFTER THE FUNERAL. THE SOUL OF THE DEPARTED IS FELT TO BE WATCHING WHICH DOESN'T NECESSARILY PREVENT SQUABBLES AMONG THE HEIRS

The very word "probate" has acquired a notorious aura. Probate in California does not, from my experience, involve evil officials, bribery, or outright corruption. Rather, probate has institutionalized the rip-off of a dead person's estate by lawyers, and executors, for large fees for what in most cases is routine, albeit tedious, paperwork. By state law, the lawyer's fee for a probate case is set at a percentage of the worth of the gross probate estate, rather than as compensation for the time he or she actually works. The catch here is basing fees on a percentage of the gross estate. Thus, if there is a house in the estate that has a market value of $200,000, with a $150,000 mortgage, the value of that house, for the purpose of determining the lawyer's fee, is $200,000, not the actual equity of $50,000.*

Since probate is costly and time-consuming, one question that is often asked is whether you should do it yourself, either handling the estate of someone who has died, or arranging in advance for a layperson to handle your estate? The answer is NO. I don't recommend doing probate without any attorney. Legally, it's permissible for the executor named in a will to act "in pro per" for the estate and to appear in probate court and handle the proceedings without an attorney. But probate is a very technical and tedious area of the law. There are many complicated forms to fill out, and proceedings to attend. The forms are far from self-explanatory. Learning how to do probate yourself would take a great deal of time. Even then, the courts and clerks would undoubtedly be unhelpful, or even hostile, to laymen in probate proceedings, so it would probably take you much longer than if you'd hired a lawyer.

The wiser approach is to greatly reduce the size of the estate that is subject to probate. This will correspondingly reduce the lawyer's fees. After death the probate attorney (more realistically, his staff) will complete all the paperwork required by the death and subsequent transfer of property, charging a reasonable fee for the service. And as you'll see, many estates can avoid probate entirely with some planning. There are several probate avoidance transfer methods to consider, including simplified probate for estates under $30,000 (Chapter 6), community property (Chapter 7), trusts (Chapter 9) and joint tenancy (Chapter 10). There are two principal reasons why an estate will become enmeshed in probate. First, if you want to use a will to transfer at least some of your property, which is often desirable for many reasons (see Chapter 12, Wills), a will must be probated. ** Secondly, in cases where estate taxes must be paid, and/or estate tax returns filed (see Chapter 3, Estate Taxes), it is usually wiser to have a probate lawyer, experienced in these tax matters, do the paperwork. Where estate taxes are involved, try to keep the estate transferred by probate small (transferring the bulk of your property outside of probate) and you should receive a fair amount of service for the attorney's fee charged.

D.   How Is Planning An Estate Valuable?

One important objective of estate planning is the avoidance of probate of much of your property. This means transferring a large part of the estate property by using methods that simply avoid probate altogether (such as gifts or joint tenancy), thus reducing probate costs, and, in addition, transferring property speedily, insuring that cash is available for the survivors soon after the decedent's death. But there's a lot more to estate planning than probate avoidance. Good estate planning covers all the assets a person has, including those not subject to probate, such as:

1. Life insurance payable to a named beneficiary (or trustee of an insurance trust);

---

* For this reason, it is often very important to transfer real property outside of probate.

** Except in very unusual cases, e.g., where all property is placed in irrevocable trusts before death, etc.

2. Property held in joint tenancy (including "Totten trust" bank acounts);*
3. Savings bonds, payable on death to another;
4. Inter vivos trust, gifts, Survivors' pension or social security rights; and
5. Community property left to a surviving spouse.

Estate planning also involves an understanding of how our tax laws work. Estate taxes may be assessed on all of the forms of property in the decedent's estate, however it is transferred. But (in many cases) there are methods of avoiding or reducing such taxes which can result in considerable savings. To take but one example, there are ways to transfer life insurance policies to another person that will avoid all estate taxes on the proceeds of the life insurance policy while other methods of ownership can result in heavy taxation (See Chapter 8).

Another important goal of estate planning is to provide ready cash (called "liquidity" in estate planner's terms) for the family, and estate, of a decedent. Particularly if the decedent was the family provider, the survivors will need cash for living expenses. Limited amounts for family necessities can normally be obtained by petitioning the probate court for a "family allowance," but it's easier, cheaper, and wiser to plan to have sources of money available without having to go to court and pay attorneys fees. Since there will be a delay of many months, possibly years, before the full probate estate is distributed, you can see that this sort of planning is important. Cash will also be needed for the immediate "costs of dying"—funeral, burial and hospitalization expenses and to pay immediate debts. Obviously, it is not desirable to risk a foreclosure on secured interest in the family home, furniture or automobile as a result of all the money in an estate being tied up in probate.**

Life insurance is one traditional means of providing ready cash. It isn't the only possible means though. For example, money held in a joint bank account can usually be released in a few days, if you understand the practicalities of obtaining the release. How much cash will be needed by your survivor? What's the best way to have this cash available? Should it all come from life insurance, or should you use other methods? Once again, a reminder: this book will show you what the choices you have are, but only you can decide what's the wisest plan. These methods shouldn't, of course, be used mechanically. Personal and emotional considerations should be respected and given serious weight even where following their dictates may cost a few extra dollars or more. What will best provide for peace of mind? Who do you believe would most need financial help? Who do you want to discuss your "estate plan" with? If your personal goals are kept in mind, the estate planning methods discussed here will be very useful in achieving them.

Practical estate planning also includes understanding several types of simple legal forms and formalities as well as how property transfers are carried out. Even if probate is avoided altogether, the actual title to assets—a house, a car, a boat, stocks, etc.—must somehow be transferred to the new owner. How? Here I describe that "how" so that it can be done without a lawyer. I include how you get tax clearances, how to get money released from a bank account, how to get a safety deposit box inventoried, etc. If you plan your estate to include non-probate transfers, it's wise to show those who will inherit the property how they can actually obtain it, legally and speedily.

Some authorities have attempted to codify estate planning by drafting sample plans for certain allegedly standard situations. If there's a "husband and wife with minor children and an estate of approximately $200,000," Plan A is proposed, whereas "husband and wife with no minor children and an estate over $200,000," should use Plan B, and so on. I don't think these codified estate plans are very helpful. There are simply too many variables in each person's, and family's, situation for these kinds of sample plans to have much practical use. This book describes basic estate planning methods, including presenting the information and forms necessary so you can do them yourself. You can then put the pieces of your over-all estate plan together yourself.

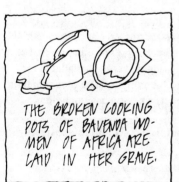

THE BROKEN COOKING POTS OF BAVENDA WOMEN OF AFRICA ARE LAID IN HER GRAVE.

---

* A "Totten trust" bank account is a simple passbook savings trust. See Chapter 10, *Joint Tenancy,* §C.

**A Foreclosure will rarely result, since the Probate Court can be petitioned to release some funds for such emergencies, but it's one more costly hassle.

E.   Will I Need A Lawyer?

Professionals of all sorts are in bad repute these days, yet somehow the mystique of professionalism survives. Lawyers may be under attack, but none of the big law firms seem likely to reduce their fees soon. "Estate planning" has been a particularly lucrative field for professionals; the subject seems complex and forbidding, yet many people accurately sense that behind some of the mumbo-jumbo are techniques that can save an estate a lot of money. By buying this book, you've demonstrated that you aren't willing to turn your estate planning over, carte blanche, to a professional. You have made some commitment to learn the mumbo-jumbo yourself, at least some of it. For instance, despite all the lawyers' propaganda, most people can draft a will themselves that fully meets their needs and desires. There is no reason to pay a lawyer $75 or $100 to prepare a will when all that is involved is his secretary typing up a standard form. Many lawyers are not even very knowledgeable about wills; those who specialize in will drafting are likely to charge an exhorbitant amount for esoteric knowledge, which may well benefit a DuPont or Rockfeller, but isn't likely to be of any help to someone with a small to moderate estate.

Still, there may be a time when you'll need a lawyer. Perhaps there are one of two problems you can't quite understand, or solve. Or, maybe you want the reassurance of having a lawyer review the estate plan you've adopted. In some cases, there will be no feasible way to solve a problem without consulting a lawyer or estate planner. At the least, after reading this book, you should be able to explain what you want, and determine if the lawyer can give it to you. Don't act the passive "client" (the Latin root of the word 'client' translates as 'to obey' 'to hear'). Approach lawyers and other estate planning professionals with a thorough knowledge of how they can help you and how much it will cost.

1. How To Find A Lawyer

By the time in life that most people are concerned with estate planning, they've acquired a lawyer. Ours is such a lawyer-ridden society that few property owners can escape without using one at times. But for those who don't have "their" lawyer, either because they've never needed one or never found one they liked and trusted, a few words of advice may be helpful.

It's important to feel personal rapport with your lawyer. If you pick one in a fancy downtown office, remember that you're paying a lot for that impressive view and repressed demeanor. Also remember that your case is likely to seem minor compared to those corporate clients who pay $100 or $150 per hour, hour after hour.

Personal routes are the traditional, and probably the best means for locating a lawyer. If a good friend found a lawyer he liked, chances are you'll like him too. Otherwise, you've got a problem. There are an awful lot of lawyers in California, but finding a good, and inexpensive one can be difficult. Some suggestions:

◑ Avoid referral panels of local bar associations. There's often a charge, up to $25, for the referral. Also, any lawyer can get on the referral panels, and you have no control over who you're sent to;

◑ Check with a local consumer organization to see if they can recommend someone;

◑ Check the ads in the paper usually listed under "Business Personals" in the classified section. Often younger attorneys just starting out advertise low rates to build up a practice. Sometimes they offer the first half hour consultation free of charge. Also, I know several semi-retired attorneys who advertise very reasonable rates for consultations with the understanding that they will not take cases to court. This could be just what you need.

◑ Shop around by calling different law offices and stating your problem. Ask them how much it would cost for a visit. Try to talk to a lawyer personally so you can get an idea of how friendly and sympathetic he is to your concerns. If you want advice on a specific area as opposed to turning your whole legal life over to the lawyer, make this clear from the beginning. Don't be afraid to fire a lawyer if you feel your problems are not getting sufficient attention. There is a growing surplus of lawyers; one out of every 400 americans will be one by 1980. (If we just look at white males, the figure is one out of 100).

You should decide whether you want expert help or competent legal assistance. "Estate planning" is a field where there are very expensive specialists, particularly in areas of federal taxation. Unless your estate will be subject to substantial taxation, (which you can determine yourself), there is no reason to pay the high fees these experts charge. If all you want is a general review to make sure you haven't committed any glaring legal mistakes, many lawyers will suffice.

When talking to the lawyer on the phone, or at the first conference, ask some specific questions. If the lawyer answers them clearly and concisely—explaining, but not talking down to you—fine. If he acts wise, but says little except to ask that the problem be placed in his hands (with the appropriate fee, of course), watch out. You are either talking with someone who doesn't know the answer and won't admit it (common), or someone who finds it impossible to let go of the "me expert, you peasant" way of looking at the world (even more common).

In some instances, you will need a lawyer. If you become involved in a contested court proceeding, such as a challenge to a will, you surely need an attorney. Also, I strongly urge a lawyer for all probate proceedings, after you have reduced the amount to be probated to a sensible level. If you understand their uses and you want to create an irrevocable trust or a testamentary trust (one established by a will), I recommend a lawyer do the drafting. Otherwise, it's up to you. One **caution:** Congress continues making yearly changes in federal estate tax laws. Every reasonable effort will be made to keep this book up-to-date, but I cannot guarantee that the law won't be altered after the book is published. If you have a complicated federal tax matter, it's wise to review the tax laws with a knowledgeable attorney.

2. Further Research—Law Libraries

Lawyers are experts at recycling information and charging enormous amounts for this limited service. I say limited because lawyers (or their paralegal assistants or secretaries) are often doing no more than opening a book of legal forms or information and copying out the answers. For example, most wills are copied directly out of standard legal form books. Even in more complicated situations of estate planning, all lawyers do in many cases is to check the standard legal resources for the answer. Why can't you do this for yourself? Often you can if you know which book to look in. They are all in your county law library which is free and open to the public (it ought to be as your court filing fees pay for it). Also, the law libraries of many law schools can be used for research.

If you decide you want to do more research yourself, either to resolve a problem or to prepare yourself to understand what a lawyer is talking about, try reading the source books at the County Law Library.* In many cases, the most useful books will be those prepared by the C.E.B.—the California Continuing Education of the Bar. These are clear and practical how-to-do-books, for lawyers. The major books for estate planning include: *California Decedent Estate Administration* (Vols. I and II); *Drafting California Irrevocable Inter Vivos Trusts; Drafting California Revocable Inter Vivos Trusts; California Will Drafting;* and *Estate Planning for the General Practitioner.*

---

* For an excellent explanation of how to conduct your own legal research, see Honigsberg, *Cluing Into Legal Research* distributed by Nolo Press. (Ordering information located at the back of this book.)

There are many other research sources that could be useful. The *Annotated California Probate Code* contains all the state statues on probate and wills, and excerpts from relevant judicial decisions and cross-references to related articles and laws. The judicial decisions are kept in books that are arranged according to a simple code which your law librarian can quickly explain. Federal tax statutes are located in the United States Code, Title 26; however, the tax code is so abstruse and dense it is often functionally impossible to determine its meaning, at least not without hours and hours of grueling effort. Also, ask your librarian to show you any legal encyclopedia which explains your problem. These are indexed by subject and are much like any other encyclopedia. You may want to check out the "Form" books. These are collections (often in many volumes) of sample legal forms designed to accomplish many thousands of legal tasks; using these form books is the foundation of most small practitioners' legal "expertise."

F. How To Determine The Value of Your Estate.

The first practical step in determining your estate plan is to calculate the value of your estate. If you don't know how much you're worth, it's difficult to determine a wise estate plan. Many people are surprised when they compute the worth of their estate. It's usually more than they thought.

Completing the following form should give you a rough idea of the value of your estate. This will **only** be a rough idea as you will be making estimates and calculating the value of your estate on a common sense basis. Of course, this will only tell you what you are worth today—what the value of your estate will be at the time of death is much less clear. The estate valuation form is printed three times with three separate headings:

❷ The first form, "Net Estate," can be used as a work sheet for you to add up the value of your assets. This can be done now. Keep these figures in mind as you read on; it helps to have a rough estimate of how many chips you have even while learning to play the game.

❷ The second form, labelled "Taxable Estate," shouldn't be completed until you understand how a taxable estate is calculated (See Chapter 3). Then you use this form to determine the actual worth of your taxable estate. The death taxes due, if any, can then be determined from the tax tables provided in Chapter 3, Estates Taxes.

❷ The third form, "Probate Estate," shouldn't be completed until you understand how a probate estate is calculated and what other transfer methods are feasible for you to eliminate property from the probate estate. (Chapters 4 through 10).

A Few Things To Understand Prior To Sharpening Your Pencil.

■ **California is a community property state.** Generally, all property acquired during marriage, except by one person receiving an inheritance or gift, is co-owned by both spouses. Thus, for your estate, count one-half (½) the worth of the total community property.

■ The amount you contributed towards property held in joint tenancy is part of your estate,* even though (as explained in Chapter 10) you can not control who receives that property because the surviving joint tenant automatically owns the property.

■ The ''worth'' of property is, generally, its **current** market value. To determine net worth, deduct all amounts owed on the property. If you own property that you expect will increase drastically in price before your death (this means an increase of far more than the rate of inflation) estimate that **increased** worth.

■ **If your net worth is less than $275,000** in 1983, there will be **no** federal taxes payable (unless federal estate tax credits have been used for gift taxes earlier. See Chapter 4).

Now fill out the check list. It isn't an exhaustive list, but it does cover the usual major items or property. Simply write in the estimate of market value, include any other property you have, add the figures up, and deduct liabilities.

NET ESTATE

A. Personal Property

cash (dividends, etc.)   _____

savings accounts   _____

checking accounts   _____

government bonds   _____

listed (private corporation) stocks and
bonds   _____

unlisted stocks and bonds   _____

money owed you including promissory
notes and accounts receivable (including
mortgages owed you, leases, etc.)   _____

vested interest in profit sharing plan,
pension rights, stock options, etc.   _____

automobile and other vehicles (include
boats and recreation vehicles; deduct any
amounts owed)   _____

household goods, net total   _____

art works and jewelry   _____

miscellaneous   _____

---

* Only part of the taxable, not the probate, estate.

B. Real Estate (do separately for each piece owned)

current market value _____

mortgages and other liens that you owe on
the property _____

equity (current market value less money
owed) _____

your share of that equity if you have less
than sole ownership _____

C. Business/Property Interests (including patents & copyrights)

1) name & type of business _____

2) percentage you own _____

3) when acquired _____

4) estimate of present (market) value of
your interest _____

D. Life Insurance (for each policy list)

1) company and type (or number) of
policy _____

2) name of insured _____

3) owner of policy _____

4) beneficiary of policy _____

5) amount collectable _____

6) cash surrender value, if any _____

Total Value of Assets _____

Deduct All Liabilities

Debts (including all mortgages, loans,
etc.) _____

Taxes (excluding estate taxes) _____

Other Liabilities _____

Total Liabilities _____

Total Net Worth _____

TAXABLE ESTATE

A. Personal Property

cash (dividends, etc.)   _____

savings accounts   _____

checking accounts   _____

government bonds   _____

listed (private corporation) stocks and bonds   _____

unlisted stocks and bonds   _____

money owed you including promissory notes and accounts receivable (including mortgages owed you, leases, etc.)   _____

vested interest in profit sharing plan or pension rights   _____

automobile and other vehicles (include boats and recreation vehicles; deduct any amount owed)   _____

household goods, net total   _____

art works and jewelry   _____

miscellaneous   _____

B. Real Estate (do separately for each piece owned)

current market value   _____

mortgages and other liens that you owe on the property   _____

equity (current market value less money owed)   _____

your share of that equity if you have less than sole ownership   _____

C. Business/Property Interests (including patents & copyrights)

1) name & type of business   _____

2) percentage you own   _____

3) when acquired   _____

4) estimate of present (market) value of your interest   _____

D. Life Insurance (for each policy list)
(if you are **neither** the owner nor beneficiary of a policy, exclude it. See Chapter 8 Insurance)

1) company and type (or number) of policy   _____

2) name of insured   _____

3) owner of policy   _____

4) beneficiary of policy   _____

5) amount collectable   _____

6) cash surrender value, if any   _____

Total Value of Assets   _____

Deduct All Liabilities

Debts   _____

Taxes (excluding estate taxes)   _____

Other Liabilities   _____

Total Liabilities   _____

Total Net Worth of Taxable Estate   _____

PROBATE ESTATE

(List only property passing by will and subject to probate.)

A. **Personal Property**

cash (dividends, etc.)   _____

savings accounts   _____

checking accounts   _____

government bonds   _____

listed (private corporation) stocks and bonds   _____

unlisted stocks and bonds   _____

money owed you including promissory notes and accounts receivable (including mortgages owed you, leases, etc.)   _____

vested interest in profit sharing plan or pension rights   _____

automobile and other vehicles (include boats and recreation vehicles; deduct amounts owed)   _____

household goods, net total   _____

art works and jewelry   _____

miscellaneous   _____

B. Real Estate (do separately for each piece owned)

current market value   _____

your share of that value if you have less
than sole ownership   _____

C. Business/Property Interest (including patents & copyrights)

1) name & type of business   _____

2) percentage you own   _____

3) when acquired   _____

4) estimate of present (market) value of
your interest   _____

D. Life Insurance
(list **only** if proceeds of policy are payable to your estate)

1) company and type (or number) of
policy   _____

2) name of insured   _____

3) owner of policy   _____

4) beneficiary of policy   _____

5) amount collectable   _____

6) cash surrender value, if any   _____

Total Value of Assets   _____

Deduct All Liabilities

Debts   _____

Taxes (excluding estate taxes)   _____

Other Liabilities   _____

Total Liabilities   _____

Total Net Worth of Probate Estate   _____

2
Practical Matters — Funeral, Burial, Body Donations and Choices

A. Introduction

People facing the grief and reality that someone they love has died face another immediate problem simultaneously—the disposition of the body. It's hard even to talk directly about this; using the word ''corpse'' sounds unfeeling and ''cadaver'' is worse. California law refers to the reality of a dead body as ''the remains,'' a word technically accurate and almost as disturbing. Perhaps its because we don't like to think about death that the language we have invented for it is so awkward. However, it is described, the reality is the same: a dead body must, somehow, be removed from the place of death and taken care of, rapidly. Most people die in hospitals, or in nursing homes. Hospitals, especially, want a dead body removed—fast and legally. So it's near-inevitable, if no planning has been done, for family or friends to turn (or be turned) uncritically to the ''professionals,'' i.e. funeral parlors. Often this is done without reflection, or even much knowledge, of what the ''traditional'' funeral parlor burial is, or what it costs.

Death is powerful. The ceremonies and rituals accompanying the disposition of the body of someone who has died are (or should be) intimately involved with the emotions the living feel for their deceased family member or friend. The reality, and sudden immediacy of these emotions—grief, sorrow, religious conviction, doubt, or whatever else they may be—often leave the very people who must deal with all the practical details feeling distraught and confused. In this condition, handling practical problems can seem trivial, or meaningless. However, I feel it is certainly no slight to the deceased, or to the feelings of those who survive, to suggest that nothing is gained by needless expenses. Funerals are expensive. The ''traditional'' funeral is the third most expensive item (after a house and a car) normally purchased by the average American family. It can easily cost many thousand dollars. To many, including this author, this is a huge and unnecessary cost to comply with the biblical injunction ''Remember, man, thou art dust and to dust thou shall return.''

Some people remain confident that turning matters over to a commercial funeral parlor must be correct—''the right sort of person doesn't consider money at a time like

IN WESTERN AUSTRALIA THE ABORIGINES WILL SHOW THEIR CHILDREN THEIR BIRTHPLACE SO THE CHILDREN KNOW WHERE THE PARENTS WISH TO BE BURIED.

FUNERALS AMONG THE IKONGO FOLK OF MADAGASCAR IS NEITHER SOLEMN NOR SAD. THE DEAD ARE CARRIED TO THE FOREST IN A LOG COFFIN AND BURIED. A NOTCH ON A TREE IS THE ONLY MARKER. THE PROCESSION STOPS ALONG THE WAY FOR GAMES AND WRESTLING MATCHES WITH LOTS OF SHOUTING AND HIGH SPIRITS.

this.'' More and more people, though, are reflecting and making decisions based on what choice will have the most emotional meaning, as well as considering the cost of the various alternatives.

Broadly viewed, there are three alternatives available:

(1) a ''traditional'' service by a commercial funeral parlor;

(2) a more simple burial and memorial service, without embalming of the dead body, provided through membership in a cooperative funeral society;

(3) donating the body to medical school, or organs to an organ bank. If a body's organs are donated to an organ bank, the body is normally returned (sans the removed organs) to the next-of-kin for burial.

As this chapter explains, there are many different possibilities within these three broad areas. For instance, inexpensive cremation can now be obtained from traditional funeral parlors, cooperative funeral societies, and newly-established commercial enterprises specializing in low cost cremations (irreverently called ''burn and scatter outfits'' in the trade). Some options are too esoteric to be covered here. Those interested in cryonics (body freezing) should seek information elsewhere.

A great deal of money, and probably some peace of mind as well, can be gained by planning for the immediate, practical aspects of death. Unless you decide on a commercial funeral, you must plan for other choices. You must be a member of a funeral society to utilize its low-cost services. You must have authorized a body or organ donation for it to be done. Even for a ''traditional'' commercial funeral, planning is usually desirable. Funeral parlors no longer, as they once did, effectively maintain price-fixing. Costs can vary widely. There's really no sensible reason to plan how to save money on estate taxes and probate fees, and then turn around and toss a large chunk of it away on an over-priced funeral. Equally important, there's no reason to dread thinking about what kind of service will be fitting.

Funerals and burials are only one, though the most expensive, of the choices that will have to be made when a person is dying. Other problems can include whether life should be artificially prolonged by mechanical means, autopsies, notifying relatives and friends, or obtaining death certificates. This chapter is designed to provide an overview of all the major practical aspects that may be involved when a person dies, so that all possible choices may be considered.

B.   Things to be Done When Death Occurs

A WHITE PAPER BIRD HUNG FROM A TALL BAMBOO POLE IN FRONT OF A HOUSE ANNOUNCES A DEATH IN BALI. A PAPER LANTERN IS LIT EACH NIGHT AS LONG AS THE BODY REMAINS IN THE HOUSE.

There are a lot of practical matters to attend to upon a death. The following list isn't definitive, but it may prove helpful. I discuss the details of many of these steps later in this chapter:

1. Immediate matters: notify funeral parlor, funeral society, or other institution responsible for removing the body from the hospital; obtain and begin to implement any instructions the decedent left regarding his disposition.

2. Contact appropriate religious officials; proceed with funeral service or other planned disposition.

3. Notify executor and estate lawyer; locate will.

4. Make a list of immediate family, close friends, and employer or business colleagues and notify each of them by phone.

5. If flowers are to be omitted, decide on appropriate memorial to which gifts may be made. (As a church, library, school, or some other charity.)

6. Prepare an obituary, including the deceased's place of birth, cause of death, occupation, college degrees, memberships held, military service, outstanding work, list of survivors in immediate family, and any other matter you (or the deceased) wanted included. Give time and place of services, and deliver the obituary to local newspapers.

7. Arrange for care for members of family or close friends, including appropriate child care, having people at the deceased's house, etc.

8. Notify concerned persons too far away to attend funeral.

9. Notify insurance companies, including automobile insurance for immediate cancellation and available refund.

10. Cancel all credit cards.

11. Check carefully all life and casualty insurance and death benefits, including Social Security, credit union, trade union, fraternal, military and other benefits. Check also on income for survivors from these sources.

12. Check promptly on all debts and installment payments. Some may carry insurance clauses that will cancel them. If there is to be a delay in meeting payments, consult with creditors and ask for more time before the payments are due.

13. If the decedent was living alone, notify utilities and landlord and tell post office where to send mail.

Many of these tasks overlap those that are done by the executor under a will, and the probate attorney, so, as soon as feasible, the executor should begin performing his responsibilities. There will still be plenty for others to do.

C. Leaving Funeral Instructions

NOODLES, POPPY SEEDS, PEAS, AND HONEY ARE FOODS OF THE POLISH FUNERAL FEAST. MUSIC AND DANCING OFTEN OCCUR. FOOD IS GIVEN AWAY TO BEGGARS.

Whatever decisions a person makes regarding the disposition of his body, it's highly desirable to leave written instructions. By state law the written burial instructions of a deceased person "shall be faithfully and promptly performed."* Written instructions should be kept in a safe and readily ascertainable place, and their existence should be known by the next of kin, or whoever is to have the responsibility (and trust) for implementing them.** If the directions are contained in a will, they must be immediately carried out, even if no probate proceeding has been commenced and regardless of the validity of other provisions in the will.

IMPORTANT: The written instructions do not **have** to be in a will, nor do they have to be witnessed or notarized. A will, if it will be readily available at death, is one possible place to put instructions. If, for some reason, you decide not to have a will or the will may be in a place difficult to get access to, such as a safe deposit box, it's still wise to leave written instructions regarding body disposition. The directions can even be oral, but written directions are, obviously, more secure and less subject to misinterpretation.

If there are no written instructions left by the decedent, legal control over the disposition of the body rests in the next of kin (See F, below, for a definition). This can pose insoluble problems for a friend or lover of the deceased, who knows the deceased wanted a specific type of disposition that the next-of-kin opposes. Without the legal force of written instructions, the friend or lover is powerless to prevent the legal next of kin from determining how the disposition is to be handled. A Power of Attorney from the deceased to the friend or lover is no help, as it is automatically revoked by death of the grantor.

D. The Legal Definition of Death

The legal definition of when death occurs has recently been defined by state law as "total and irreversible cessation of brain function," **or** other "usual and customary"

---

* Health and Safety Code, §7100.

** An example of written instructions is given in the Appendix.

DEATH IN BALI COMES WHEN A PERSON'S SOUL ESCAPES FROM THE MOUTH AND REFUSES TO RETURN. HOWEVER, IT HOVERS NEARBY UNTIL THE BODY IS DESTROYED BY EARTH, FIRE OR WATER. CREMATION IS THE TRADITIONAL WAY OF RELEASING THE SOUL.

procedures for determining death; e.g. failure of all vital signs.* This statutory definition was adopted in response to the fact that medical technology can now keep vital bodily organs functioning, even though the brain has totally and irreversibly stopped. Understandably, a doctor who removes a heart from a body where the brain has totally and irreversibly ceased to function prefers that there be no doubt regarding the fact of the person's death. There is no technical definition in state law of what ''total and irreversible cessation of brain function'' is. Each hospital's doctors make the determination on their understanding of accepted medical standards.** If death is determined by a doctor using the standard of ''total and irreversible cessation of brain function,'' there must be independent confirmation of this by another physician, and **neither** physician can be involved in any removal or transplant procedures from the dead body. There is no legal requirement that a doctor determine death by the ''total and irreversible cessation of brain function'' standard. Any other traditional, medically accepted standard is legally permissible, but the existence of cessation of brain function test in state law probably means that most doctors use it in situations where there is any doubt.

---

* Health and Safety Code, §7100.

** Incidentally, by this standard, a person placed in cryogenic internment — the deep freeze with hopes of being revived later — is legally dead.

E.   The Natural Death Act

California has adopted a statute that allows a person the choice of whether he will use medical machines to prolong life artificially.* This right only comes into play if two doctors have certified that the person is in a terminal condition and that death is imminent. To this extent, and this extent only, Californians have a legal "right to die." To commit suicide, or attempt suicide, is legally a crime. To assist a suicide attempt is a crime. "Mercy killing" remains a crime. No one legally has the right to cause, or assist in, another's death for any reason, even if the person is in horrible pain and wants to die. What the Natural Death Act does is to allow a person to choose that his life will run its natural course, if his condition is terminal. It does not allow a life to be ended sooner than its natural span.

To employ the Act, you must sign a document, called a "Directive." This is given to your doctor and instructs him not to use artificial methods to extend the natural process of dying. The Natural Death Act is cautiously and precisely drafted as regards the limits of the effects of a Directive. A sample Directive is printed below.

Directive to Physicians

Directive made this _____ day of _____ (month, year).

I _____, being of sound mind, willfully, and voluntarily make known my desire that my life shall not be artificially prolonged under the circumstances set forth below, do hereby declare:

1. If at any time I should have an incurable injury, disease, or illness certified to be a terminal condition by two physicians, and where the application of life-sustaining procedures would serve only to artificially prolong the moment of my death and where my physician determines that my death is imminent whether or not life-sustaining procedures are utilized, I direct that such procedures be withheld or withdrawn, and that I be permitted to die naturally.

2. In the absence of my ability to give directions regarding the use of such life-sustaining procedures, it is my intention that this directive shall be honored by my family and physician(s) as the final expression of my legal right to refuse medical or surgical treatment and accept the consequences from such refusal.

3. If I have been diagnosed as pregnant and that diagnosis is known to my physician, this directive shall have no force or effect during the course of my pregnancy.

4. I have been diagnosed and notified at least 14 days ago as having a terminal condition by

_____, M.D., whose address is _____

_____, and whose telephone number is _____.
I understand that if I have not filled in the physician's name and address, it shall be presumed that I did not have a terminal condition when I made out this directive.

5. This directive shall have no force or effect five years from the date filled in above.

6. I understand the full import of this directive and I am emotionally and mentally competent to make this directive.

Signed _____

City, County and State of Residence _____

_____

* The Natural Death Act, §7185, Health and Safety Code.

The declarant has been personally known to me and I believe him or her to be of sound mind.

Witness _____

Witness _____

This Directive complies in form with the "Natural Death Act" California Health and Safety Code, Section 7188, Assembly Bill 3060 (Keene).

The Directive can be agreed to by any adult, and does not have to be notarized. It must be witnessed by two adults who:

1. are not related to you by blood or marriage;
2. are not mentioned in your will;
3. are not your doctor, or anyone employed by him;
4. would have no claim on your estate.

If you're in a hospital when you sign a Directive, neither of the witnesses can be hospital employees.* No one can force you to sign a Directive. Insurance or health services cannot be denied because you have not, or have, signed a Directive. If you do sign a Directive, it cannot affect your insurance, or any other right you have to accept or reject medical treatment. A doctor is bound by the Directive only if:

1. he is satisfied that the Directive is valid;
2. another doctor has also certified your condition as terminal; and
3. at least fourteen days have gone by since you were informed of your condition.

If you signed a Directive while in good health, your doctor may respect your wishes but is not bound by the Directive.

IMPORTANT: Regardless of the binding or nonbinding nature of the Directive, it is not to be given effect until it is determined that death is imminent, whether or not "life-sustaining procedures" are utilized. Such procedures include mechanical or other "artificial means" which sustain vital functions only to postpone the moment of death, but do not include medications deemed necessary to alleviate pain.

The Directive is valid for a period of five years, at which time you may sign a new one. The Directive is not valid during pregnancy. You may revoke the Directive at any time, even in the final stages of a terminal illness, by:

1. destroying it;
2. signing and dating a written statement revoking it; or
3. by informing your doctor.

No matter how you revoke the Directive, be sure your doctor is told of your decision. **If the Directive is implemented, the Act states that the death is not suicide.**

F. Legal Requirements Concerning Body Disposition

By law, a dead body has to be disposed of by those responsible for doing so "within a reasonable time" after death. As stated in Section C of this Chapter, those responsible are legally obligated to carry out the expressed intentions of the decedent regrading his

---

* If you are in a Skilled Nursing Facility when you sign a Directive, one of the witnesses *must* be a "patient advocate" or ombudsman designated by the State Department of Aging.

burial. Unless the decedent has given other directions, the right to decide what happens to the body and the duty to interment and liability for its reasonable cost, is legally held by the following person(s) in descending order:*

    1. the surviving spouse;

    2. children of decedent;

    3. parents of decedent;

    4. the closest kin, as degrees of kinship are defined in the California Intestacy laws.

(See Chapter 5, *Probate*.)

    Ignoring the legal responsibility to dispose of a body is technically a misdemeanor. In addition, the body may be disposed of by someone else, who may then sue those responsible for three times their cost. Neither this author nor anyone else I spoke with while preparing this book has ever heard of a misdemeanor prosecution or civil lawsuit under this section, nor are there any reported California cases. If an entire body (not just certain organs) is donated to medical science, the institution accepting the donated body is responsible for interring it (or at least the parts that they don't use).

    As might be expected, indigents don't do too well when it comes to burials. If none of the relatives responsible by law exist, or can be found (and no directions were left), the county coroner is responsible for disposition of the remains and it will be done in a cheap manner — remember old Boot Hill?

G. Death Certificates

    A death certificate must be completed by the attending physician and filed with the local registrar of health of the district where death occurred, within five (5) days of death **and** prior to the disposition of the remains.**Certified copies of the death certificate are required in numerous aspects of estate distribution. The person responsible for supervising the decedent's estate should obtain certified copies of the death certificate as soon as possible. Morticians normally do this as part of their services. Death certificates can be obtained from the County Health Department, at a cost of roughly $3.00 per certified copy. At some time after death, location of the death certificate is switched and copies can then be obtained from the **County Recorder's Office** (except in San Francisco and San Diego counties, where the certificates remain at the County Health Department). If some of the estate transference will be done without an attorney — such as collecting life insurance, or transferring joint tenancy, you will need certified copies of the death certificate for each transaction. So, get many copies, at least 8 or 10, and get them as soon as possible.

    A funeral director or ''person acting in lieu thereof'' must prepare a burial certificate and file it and the death certificate with the local registrar, who then issues a **permit** for disposition of the remains.

H. Autopsies and Inquests

1. Inquests

    All lovers of murder mysteries are familiar with the Coroner, inquests and autopsies. The Coroner, a county official, is responsible for inquiring into and determining ''the circumstances, manner and cause of all violent, sudden or unusual deaths,'' and all other unusual types of death, whether from drowning, fire, alcoholism, ''criminal means,'' while in prison, caused by occupational disease, and so on.*** The Coroner makes the

---

* Health and Safety Code, §7100.

** Health and Safety Code, §10200.

*** Government Code, §27491.

decision whether a death requires an Inquest; he cannot be compelled to hold one.

The Coroner has many duties under state law, from holding a field investigation into the cause of a death to testing blood or urine samples of persons killed in traffic accidents for blood alcohol. **Inquests** themselves are formal inquiries into the circumstances of a death. The Coroner summons a jury of between 9 to 15 persons. Witnesses, including doctors, eyewitnesses to the death, and police, testify, and then the jury renders its verdict as to the cause of death. This verdict is inadmissible in any later civil or criminal proceeding, but normally determines whether any further actions will be taken by police, district attorney, etc.

2. Autopsies

An autopsy is an examination of the deceased body to determine the cause of death. Inquests normally include an autopsy, but every autopsy does not require an inquest. The Coroner will perform autopsies: (1) in an inquest; **or** (2) if requested to do so, in writing, by the deceased, or the surviving spouse, or by a surviving child or parent (if there is no surviving spouse) or the legal next of kin (if no closer family relations exist).* If a Coroner's autopsy is performed because of such written private request, the person requesting the autopsy (or the decedent's estate) must pay the costs.

The Coroner's authority in performing an autopsy in connection with an inquest is broad. He can order funeral/burial services delayed pending an autopsy, or compel a buried body to be disinterred. He can order an autopsy even if that conflicts with religious views, or expressed instructions of the decedent and/or his family. Also, for purposes of preserving a body for an autopsy, the Coroner can order the body to be embalmed, unless expressly forbidden to do so by the next of kin, or by written instructions of the decedent.

Autopsies can also be performed by private doctors, if proper authorization is given (if not, it's a misdemeanor to perform an unauthorized autopsy).**Authorization for a private autopsy can be given in writing, or by telephone ''and recorded on tape or other recording device,'' by:

1. the decedent, before his death;
2. the surviving spouse;
3. a surviving child or parent;
4. a surviving brother or sister;
5. any other person who has legal control over the disposition of the body of the decedent.***

I.   Public and Private Funeral Benefits

No matter what decisions you make regarding funeral or body donation, there are costs involved for body transportation, burial or disposition, cremation or funeral. These costs can be paid from the decedent's estate, and often are. There are also some other sources of funds specifically for funeral and burial costs, including pension and retirement plans.

---

* Government Code, §27502.

** Health and Safety Code, §7114.

*** Health and Safety Code, §7113.

Veterans receive veterans' funeral benefits of $250, plus free burial in a national cemetery (if space is available); if they are buried in a private cemetery, there is an additional $150 payment.* Social Security provides a lump-sum payment for actual funeral expenses up to a maximum of $255. To be eligible for payment, an insured worker must have been covered for a total of ten years (40 quarters) during his life, **or** for one and a half years (six quarters) during the last three years. Most anyone who has held a job is eligible. The surviving spouse or person who paid for the funeral can receive this money by filing a simple claim, available at any Social Security office, or it can be assigned directly to a funeral parlor.

Other sources of funeral benefits include:

Medicare; unions; Federal Employees Group Life Insurance program;** and California Public Employees Retirement System. Persons eligible to receive the $500 lump-sum allowance under the Public Employees Retirement System should use State Form 241 to name a beneficiary and thus avoid inclusion of the $500 in their probate estate.

J. Choices Regarding Disposition of the Body

There are many choices available to Californians regarding disposition of their body on death. The two major types of choices are:
1. **Some form of funeral or cremation; or**
2. **Donating all or parts of your body for medical uses.**

Planning is particularly important if you're considering the second alternative. **If you don't make arrangements to leave your body for medical uses, it won't happen.** There is great need now for many body organs, used in transplants. The ability of medical science to utilize different body organs in life saving body transplants has increased dramatically in recent years; most people are not aware of how great the current need is. The following material will give you some idea of what is occurring now regarding organ transplants, but the field is progressing so rapidly that this material may be dated by the time you read it.

K. Donation of Body Organs

If you want to leave your body to help humanity, you have two choices:
1. you can leave your entire body to medical science, usually a medical school; or
2. you can donate certain of your body organs, tissues, etc. to transplant facilities.
You cannot do both.

Medical schools will not accept a body from which any part has been removed, except sometimes for eye transplants. Donations of body parts seems the greatest need. Many medical schools are currently not accepting whole body donations. The total number needed in California is around a thousand each year. Thousands of individual body transplants are, or could be performed each year if there were sufficient donations.

1. How To Do It Legally

MENABE TRIBESMEN OF MADEGASCAR LEAVE THE BODIES OF SOCERERS AND CRIMINALS TO BE EATEN BY DOGS.

---

* Other benefits include: the right of the veteran's spouse and minor children to free burial in a national cemetery, if they predecease the veteran, and the veteran intends to be buried in a national cemetery; free headstones, U.S. flag, etc. Any V.A. office has full details and forms needed.

** The Superintendent of Documents, U.S. Printing Office, Washington, D.C. 20402 prints two useful pamphlets: "Railroad Retirement and Survivor Benefits" (60¢) and "Federal Benefits for Veterans and Dependents" (70¢).

We hear most about heart transplants, but many more organs, tissues, and bones can and are being transplanted, including: middle ear, eyes, liver, lungs, pancreas, kidneys, skin tissue, bone and cartilage, pituitary glands, and blood. The need is great. For example, in 1980 many thousands of persons in the United States will be waiting for kidney transplants, most being kept alive by dialysis machines in the meantime.

California has adopted a statute concerning the donation of body parts, the Uniform Anatomical Gift Act.* All California licensed drivers learn of one provision of this Act, when they receive a little pink DMV card which they can sign, authorizing body donations:

```
Pursuant to the Uniform Anatomical Gift Act,
I hereby give, effective upon my death:

A_____Any needed organ or parts

B_____Parts or organs listed    _____

Date    _____

Signature of Donor
_____
Witness
_____
Witness                    DL-290 (NEW 7/76)
```

Any competent adult can make an anatomical gift simply by signing this card, having it witnessed and carrying it. The program is so recent that it's difficult to tell yet how effective it is, but by itself it seems unlikely to result in significant increases in the number of body parts made available for transplants. To be used, body parts must be removed quickly, between a few minutes and a few hours after death, depending on which part is needed. It seems doubtful that the existence of a small pink card in someone's wallet would normally be sufficient notice to allow surgeons to reach the body and operate in time. A recent change in California law may be helpful. Policemen are now authorized to search the body and property of a person who died in a traffic accident to see if there is an anatomical donors card. The most important benefit of including the Anatomical Gift Act card with all DMV license renewals is probably that it exposes millions of people to the existence of the Act, and the possibility of donating parts of their body for transplants upon their death.

Under the Anatomical Gift Act, a gift of body parts can be made either by signing the donor's card, or by will; if made by will, the donation is effective regardless of the validity of the rest of the will. Also, the person who has legal control over the disposition of the body* can decide that a donation shall be made, "in the absence of actual notice of contrary indication" by the decedent, *or* unless at the time of death the decedent was known to be a member of a religion with tenets that would be violated by donating parts of his body. Any type of gift can be made, including the gift of a specific organ to a specific person, or a general donation of any body parts needed by a transplant center.

Legally eligible receivers of a donation are :

---

* Health and Safety Code, §7150.

** If that person is not in fact available at the time of death, the authority to decide if a body donation will be made passes to the closest next of kin (or person named in the will) who is immediately available.

1. any hospital, surgeon, physician for any medical, scientific or transplant use, etc.;
2. any accredited medical or dental school, college or university;
3. any bank or storage facility;
4. any specific individual for therapy or transplant.

A body donation can be revoked in many ways, depending on the type of donation made. If a will or card was delivered to a specific person for a gift to him, that gift may be revoked by:
1. delivering to him a signed statement or revocation;
2. by an oral statement made in the presence of two persons and communicated to him;
3. a statement of revocation to a doctor during a terminal illness and communicated to him;
4. a signed card or statement of revocation found on the (once) donor's body, or in his effects, upon death. If a document of donation has not been delivered to a particular person, the gift also can be revoked (in addition to the above listed ways) by the donor by destruction/cancellation of the document, and all copies. If the donation was made by will, it can be revoked by alteration of the will (See Chapter 12, Wills).

2. If Body Parts Are Donated There Will Still Be A Funeral

Once the body parts needed for transplant are removed, control over the body returns to the person who originally had legal control over its final disposition. The body is normally released by the operating medical facility within 24 hours after death. So, if you plan for donations of body parts, you should also plan for the eventual disposition of your body, by arranging the type of funeral (cremation) service you want, and leaving appropriate written instructions.

3. How A Transplant Donation Works (Procedurally)

There are quite a few California organizations involved in obtaining body parts for transplants; major ones include:

(1) Northern California

The Northern California Transplant Bank
751 South Bascom Avenue
San Jose, CA. 95128

The "Gift of Life" Program
(Kidney Foundation of Northern California)
100 So. Ellsworth Avenue, Suite 301
San Mateo, CA. 94401

The Inland Empire Human Resource Center
2 West Olive Avenue
Redlands, CA. 92373

(2) Southern California

The Gift of Life Program
(Kidney Foundation of Southern California)
1281 Westwood Boulevard, Suite 205
Los Angeles, CA. 90024

The U.S. Naval Tissue Bank
U.S. Navy
San Diego, CA. 92135

Many other organizations are involved in some aspect of body part procurement, including the American Red Cross, the Regional Organ Procurement Agency, the California Society of Transplant Surgeons, the Institute for Burn Medicine. It is not difficult to obtain more detailed information regarding any aspect of donation of body parts.

When a donor of body parts becomes ''available'' (i.e. just died or death is imminent), one of the organ procurement agencies is contacted. (Clearly, it is desirable to have made some arrangements with a particular agency or hospital beforehand). The major procurement agencies will, within their geographical areas, send its own team of surgeons to remove a body part from a donor who dies where there are no local surgeons available to perform the removal, and the body itself cannot be transported to another locale fast enough to allow timely removal of the body parts needed. The major procurement agencies attempt to coordinate the need for all body parts. Each patient needing any kind of transplant is put on a regional, and national (computerized) waiting list. If a donor does not specify that his donation is made to a specific person (which will, of course, be honored), the donated body parts are first used locally, if possible. The donor's organs are matched with the patient list for blood type, tissue match, blood match for antibodies, and urgent need. If there is no local patient with immediate need for the body parts and the body compatibility with those particular parts, the search for a recipient is expanded first to the state-wide California list of patients, and then, if need be, to the nation-wide list.

4. How A Transplant Donation Works (Medically)

Most organs must be removed within 24 hours of death. Following is a list of the criteria generally adhered to for removal of body parts.

	Removal TIME LIMIT (hours)	Age Limit TRANSPLANTS (years)	Age Limit RESEARCH (years)	Exclusions for Transplantation
Bone	24	15–45	15–45	Cancer, bone disease
Cartilage	24	15–45	N/A	Cancer, bone disease
Dura Mater (Spinal Cord protective membrane)	24	15–65	N/A	Cancer, bone disease
Ear (middle)	24	none	14–90	Cancer
Eye	6–8	6–70	none	none
Heart	varies	12–50	N/A	Heart disease
Kidney	varies	1–55	N/A	Intra-abdominal sepsis

(for Heart and Kidney, the time limit is one hour after death if no sustaining machines are used)

Skin	12–24	1–70	N/A	Cancer (exception: brain cancer), Hodgkin's Disease
Pituitary	24–36	none	none	none

General Exclusions: viral hepatitis, tuberculosis, syphilis, generalized sepsis, and many automobile accident victims.

Eye Transplants

The most common use of human eye tissue is for cornea transplants; other parts of a donated eye can be used to repair structurally weakened eyes or for treatment of detached retinas. A person who wears glasses may donate corneas, because the cornea itself is normally not affected by the sight impairment, which is caused by the shape of the eye.

Skin Transplants

For many years, surgeons used skin grafts from other parts of a burned patient's body to cover the wound. Recently it has been found that transplanted skin can be used to cover burns temporarily, to sustain life while natural healing occurs. Also, permanent grafts of donated skin have been successfully made. Often 15 to 20 square feet of skin is needed for a burn patient. The skin recoverable from one donor is about 3 or 4 square feet, taken from the back and taut parts of the legs. Over 100,000 Americans are hospitalized each year with burns that need temporary (or, less often, permanent) skin grafts to aid healing.

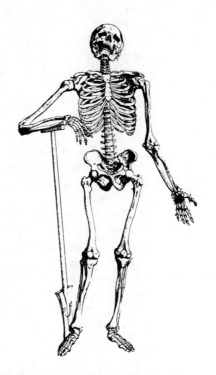

Bone

Orthopedic surgeons can now use live bone matter, rather than a mechanical construction, to replace some knee and hip joints. Cartilage can also be transplanted for plastic surgery and other uses. Other bone tissue can be used for spinal fusions, and for replacement of bone defects caused by cancer or congenital abnormalities.

Ears

Transplants of middle ears were pioneered in California. Now, eardrum and middle ears can be used to restore hearing where loss was caused by disease.

Heart

Stanford University has the largest heart transplant program in the country. The rate of successful heart transplants is increasing. Of transplants performed at Stanford since 1973, one year survival is roughly 70%, and projected five year survival 43%.

Kidney

Dialysis machines (used to filter blood for people whose kidneys have failed) is big business, about one billion a year. About 3,000 kidney transplants per year are performed in the United States. Over 2,000 Southern Californians are awaiting a kidney transplant.

Liver

Like heart transplants, the survival rate for liver transplants has increased markedly in the past few years.

A successful liver transplant, like those of other vital organs, appears to depend on genetic similarity of the donor and recipient, and anti-rejection therapy. The body's immunization-protection system (somehow) either accepts a body part (blood, tissue, organs, etc.) or rejects it as non-self. If a transplanted body part is re-rejected as non-self, the receiving body produces anti-bodies to destroy the foreign matter.

The minimum legal age to donate body parts is 18. No money can be paid for a body part donation. Except in the special case of one member of a family donating a kidney to another member of the family, donations can only be made after death. Whether a donation will actually be used depends, of course, on the condition of the body at death, and the need of transplant patients. But donations are urgently needed, so it is very likely a donation will be used, quite possibly to save another's life.

Removal of body parts does not produce disfigurement. The body is returned to the person legally in charge of it, and whatever funeral service is desired can then be carried out (unlike the donation of a whole body to medical science, in which case the body is **not** returned).

Since time is truly of the essence for the removal of donated body parts, anyone desiring to do so on death should make arrangements beforehand, including discussing his intentions with family and friends. This is surely a matter than can be easily procrastinated. Since I'm sure I'll live until I'm at least 90, why bother with thoughts of body part donations (and death) now? This logic of procrastination applies, of course, to all aspects of estate planning; the matter of donation of body parts upon death is one area where the limits of this logic are most starkly seen. Suppose the question is put: whenever it is that I do die, do I want to donate any of my body parts that can be used to help others? In the author's case, the answer is yes, I definitely do. I (obviously) cannot predict when or how I will in fact die. If my assumption that I'll live until I'm 90 proves (very) wrong, the fact that I haven't made any arrangements may well mean that no donation will be effectuated. So, even if I don't get around (for awhile) to making any other arrangements, I do carry a signed "Gift of Life" card, the one from the DMV, in my wallet.

Donating An Entire Body to Medical Science

The procedure for donating a whole body to medical science varies depending on whether you live in Northern or Southern California. Medical facilities do not pay the cost of transporting a body to the facility. It's up to you to pay the transportation expense and make the arrangements. In Northern California all donations of a body are handled by the State Curator for Northern California, University of California, San Francisco, CA 94143. (Stanford Medical School maintains its own program and should be contacted directly.*) This Curator's office serves about forty medical schools, colleges and junior colleges. It accepts approximately three hundred and fifty bodies a year.

The Curator's office will send the forms required to complete a donation, and a "registration card." Your next of kin (the person with legal control of your body when you die) must sign a "release of claim" form, and cooperate with the Curator's office. No payment of money can be made for a body donation. The Curator will not accept a body after autopsy or embalming, or if the body is not deemed otherwise suitable for scientific

---

* At Stanford School of Medicine, Department of Human Anatomy, Palo Alto, California 94305.

purposes. The institution utilizing the body for study assumes the expense for preparation and final disposition. When studies have been completed, remains are cremated. Ashes are not returned. Reports on examination of findings are not issued to the next of kin. Finally, the Curator's office retains the right not to accept a registered, donated body if by doing so, it will exceed the number needed "for scientific and educational needs."

In Southern California there is not, at present, any central coordinating office for body donation to medical science. If you live there and want to make a body donation, you must make arrangements directly with a medical school. Generally, their policies regarding donations are the same as those of the Curator's office, although at least one, Loma Linda, charges a "processing fee," and some many not accept bodies during certain months. The major medical schools are:

UCLA School of Medicine

USC School of Dentistry

University of California at Irvine

UCSD School of Medicine
(University of California at San Diego)

USC School of Medicine

Loma Linda School of Medicine

California State University at Pomona

L. Funeral and Burials

1. "Traditional" Funerals
The traditional American funeral, as provided by a commercial parlor, normally includes the following:

a) the funeral director takes care of the paper work required for death and burial certificates, and removal of the body from the place of death;

b) the embalming of the deceased's body; and

c) the showing of the deceased's embalmed body at an open-casket ceremony.

Many funeral parlors have their own chapels and encourage all services to be held there, rather than in churches.

The funeral business is a crowded, and generally secretive, business. There are over 20,000 funeral parlors in the United States. Half average 60 funerals or less per year. Until recently, there has been very little price competition. Funeral directors are faced with the ultimate in what economists call an "inelastic market"; they have absolutely no way, short of arsenic in the soup or other anti-social methods to increase the number of persons who need their services. So traditionally funeral parlors adhered to an "all-in-the-same-boat" philosophy, keeping their prices fixed, and high, and revealing as little as possible of their costs and operation. While this has changed slightly, it's still very difficult to obtain accurate, reliable figures on the overall average costs of traditional funerals.

Our funerals are products of our culture. English culture, probably typically, has been ambivalent about funerals. In some ages, expensive funerals and burials have been scorned as ostentatious, wasteful, and the norm has been a simple, dignified and inexpensive service. In other times, as in 17th Century England, expensive funerals and grand tombs have been in vogue, for those with the status and wealth to afford them. Today, in the United States, we seem more familiar with the tradition that exalts the expense and show of the final resting place. We know a lot about the Egyptian tombs and their regal

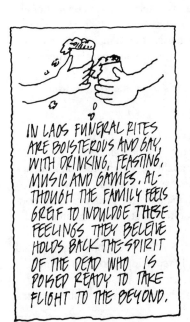

IN LAOS FUNERAL RITES ARE BOISTEROUS AND GAY, WITH DRINKING, FEASTING, MUSIC AND GAMES. ALTHOUGH THE FAMILY FEELS GRIEF TO INDULGE THESE FEELINGS THEY BELIEVE HOLDS BACK THE SPIRIT OF THE DEAD WHO IS POISED READY TO TAKE FLIGHT TO THE BEYOND.

EVEN THE BEES AND THE CATTLE ARE GIVEN NEWS OF A FAMILY DEATH IN RURAL HUNGARY. ALL SLEEPING PERSONS ARE AWAKENED. CANDLES ARE LIT AND THE CLOCKS ARE STOPPED.

splendor; the importance of burial in the *Iliad,* the need for a well-equipped send off for the voyage to the underworld (although cremation was common in ancient Greece) and the elaborate coffins of the Japanese and Chinese aristocrats. We're less familiar with the methods of cultures which don't insist on expensive burials, and handle the matter simply. In Switzerland, for instance, there have been no private commercial undertakers since 1890. Every Swiss citizen has the right to a free, state-paid for funeral, by municipal funeral personnel. The grave, coffin and hearse are also free.

Many Americans hold religious ceremonies when a person dies, but there is no generally accepted American cultural tradition concerning funerals and burials. Particular ethnic traditions survive, such as the Jewish tradition of mourning and burial within 24 hours and the Irish wake, but there is still a significant cultural vacuum, the lack of a traditional ceremony and institutions to handle funerals and burials. As should come as no surprise, this vacuum has long been filled by business people.

Before the Civil War, burials in America were simple affairs — a religious ceremony, a plain pine box, and quick burial. Undertakers were not a separate trade until roughly the 1860s; originally they practiced some other trade, often carpentry. During the Civil War, bodies of dead soldiers were embalmed by undertakers so they could be shipped home for burial. As undertakers evolved into funeral directors and began to proclaim themselves professionals, the dumping of the body into the pine box was definitely a sideline. The cost of their services rose accordingly. In the late 1800s embalming the dead body and showing the embalmed remains became standard funeral parlor practice — a practice which adds substantially to the cost of burial, and a practice that is unknown, and regarded as barbaric, in most other countries. The funeral industry also invented a way to rationalize the cost of embalming. They claimed that viewing the embalmed body is useful for the living, because seeing a lifelike body (somehow) enables the viewers to cope with their grief. The term they invented for this is "grief therapy."

As many people sense, at least vaguely, there is something odd, as well as expensive, about "traditional" American funerals. Much of this awareness stems from *The American Way of Death,* by Jessica Mitford, a fascinating examination of commercial American culture in one of its more rapacious and grotesque areas. Written with wit and grace, Mitford's book raised many questions about American funeral customs. Partially as a result of her book, beneficial changes in funeral parlor practices have been instituted. In California, laws and regulations have been changed to allow alternatives to conventional funeral parlor practices. This has aided the growth of funeral societies which have introduced price competition into the commercial funeral business, at least in large urban areas. Now some commercial parlors have begun to advertise very inexpensive funerals, comparable to those offered by funeral societies.

If you want to patronize a traditional funeral parlor, it's advisable to shop around.

2. Embalming

The greatest expense of a traditional funeral is caused by embalming the body.* California law does not require embalming, unless the body will be transported by common carrier, or if the county health officials order embalming as a protection against the spread of infectious or contagious disease (a **very** rare event). There are those who claim that embalming is a necessary health measure, but there is little evidence to support this. If a body must be preserved for a short time, refrigeration is at least as reliable, and cheaper.

In embalming, preservative and disinfectant fluid (formaldehyde solution) is injected into the body arterial system and body cavities, essentially replacing blood. Embalmed bodies are not preserved for eternities, though medical science can preserve a body (e.g. Lenin's) for exceptional reasons. Generally, American embalmers do not use the strongest

---

* For a full account of development of burials into a costly ritual of embalming, open-casket viewing, and "grief therapy," read *The American Way of Death,* by Jessica Mitford, or Ruth Harmer's fine book, *The High Cost of Dying.*

chemicals that would preserve the body the longest. An embalmed body normally begins to decompose rapidly within a few weeks.

By embalming the body, a funeral parlor can preserve it sufficiently to allow "open casket" viewing of the body at a funeral service. The author believes open-casket viewing is ghoulish, but it does seem to be a popular practice with many Americans. How one feels about embalming is a private matter. The important point is to realize that it is not the inevitable practice, and survivors, or anyone who decides to make plans for his own burial, should consider whether it is desirable for them. Commercial undertakers normally embalm a body, unless they are explicitly instructed not to. Many people probably don't consciously choose to have a body embalmed, but by the time they realize that they had a choice, the funeral service with the embalmed body is long over.

3. Costs

By industry custom, the price of the funeral used to be totally determined by the price of the casket. Not surprisingly, funeral directors urged as expensive a casket as possible. Legally, in California, the costs of the funeral can no longer be determined solely by the cost of the casket, but the casket cost remains the single most significant factor in determining overall cost.* The cost of a traditional funeral can easily be many thousands of dollars. There's normally a charge for each extra, and there are a lot of possible extras, including: flowers; flower vehicle; burial clothing; additional limousines; clergyman's honorarium; music; card; etc., etc., etc. Transporting a body from a distant place of death can be particularly expensive, often costing several thousand dollars.

NOTE: If you must arrange for the return of a body from a distant place of death, have a local funeral parlor (or funeral society) arrange it, rather than having one at the place of death do it. It will usually be much cheaper.

4. Flowers

Flowers have become traditional at American funerals. Roughly 65 to 70% of all flowers sold by commercial florists in America are sold for funerals. Not surprisingly, this big business (with an annual gross from flower sales of somewhere near 1 billion dollars) resists any attempt to reduce the sending of flowers to a funeral. Some people do not desire flowers at a funeral, but prefer that money which would have been spent on flowers be given to a particular charity. Sometimes funeral notices, or announcements, are printed that state "Please Omit Flowers." The American Florist Association has fought this whenever possible. Many major newspapers have been pressured by threatened loss of advertising revenue into declining to print "Please Omit Flowers" provisions in funeral notices. Whether flowers are a beautiful and moving statement or an unnecessary expense is a choice each person can make; again, the point is to realize that there is a choice.

5. Prepaid Funeral Plans

Prepaid arrangements (usually called "preneed plans") may be made with funeral parlors. By state law, the funeral parlor or plan must hold the money in trust and pay interest.** Limited administration expenses may be paid from the income of the trust but

---

* Some funeral parlors are now renting the use of a fancy casket complete with hermetic seals, etc., for the funeral. When the service is over, the casket (which has no bottom) is simply lifted off the body, and returned to storage. The body is buried in a cheaper box.

** Business and Professional Code, §7735.

none of the trust itself may be used for payments of commissions. Prepaid plans, sometimes called ''burial policies,'' have, at times, been little more than a swindle. On the other hand, some people deeply want the security of knowing they have provided the financial means to insure they will be buried as they desire. If you desire a prepaid plan (and are not interested in joining a funeral society), the problem is to distinguish between a legitimate business and a fly-by-night outfit. Here are some factors to evaluate:

Were high pressure tactics used? How do the prices compare with other plans? How long has the plan been in existence? Does it have any tie-in or contract with reputable groups such as churches or consumer groups? What services are included? How reliable and financially solvent does the firm seem to be? Will it be around for a while? (Hopefully, you will.) What happens if you move? What happens if you want to cancel the contract or switch to a lower price funeral and/or grave? What is the penalty for late payment of any installments due? What happens if you die before all payments are made?

6. Your Legal Rights When Dealing With Funeral Parlors

One of the significant results of the exposes of funeral parlor practices has been legal reform. Recent changes in California law are designed to protect people from the worst excesses of the free enterprise funeral industry. California law requires each casket to be priced separately and individually, regardless of the type, or cost, of funeral selected.* The law provides several other rights or duties, all of which are attempts to eliminate, or at least reduce, funeral parlor pressure tactics. Like car repair shops and others in the service trades, morticians have to provide potential customers with a written or printed list containing the complete price of the services they offer, including the price of the caskets. The price of each casket must be ''conspicuously displayed'' on the casket. And, each ''potential purchaser'' of a funeral director's services is entitled to a specific written memorandum of the costs of those services before being legally bound. The memorandum must include the total charges, the cost of the casket, the cost of all other merchandise selected, as well as all charges for transportation, flowers, etc. The law provides that the cost of these items must be listed ''provided such information is available at the time of the execution of the contract,'' whatever that means. If some of these charges aren't known then (say, the cost of flowers, or long distance phone calls), they must be provided ''within a reasonable time.''**

It is a criminal offense (and grounds for disciplinary action as well) for a funeral director, or his agents, to make any false or misleading statement about any law or regulation pertaining to burial of the dead ''made willfully to obtain business.'' Thus, if done intentionally to get business, it is a misdemeanor for a funeral director to falsely state that the law requires embalming, or any particular type of funeral. There is (and has been since 1976) a state agency regulating funeral parlors. If you have any complaints, file them with the State Board of Funeral Directors, 1021 ''O'' Street, Sacramento, California, 95814. I have no first-hand experience with the Board, but it does have a majority of members who are not associated with the industry.

Critics of the funeral industry are pressing for further regulations, both from the state and the Federal Trade Commission, and have urged such measures as requiring that funeral parlor quote prices over the telephone (a practice many funeral parlors discourage, or prohibit, now); explain in detail the limits of embalming; and abolish ''grief therapy.'' If you are interested, you may want to contact your state legislators.

THE AZANDE OF THE CONGO COMMEMORATE THE DEAD WITH A BEER DANCE ON THE ANNIVERSARY OF THE DEATH. IT IS THEN THAT STONES ARE PLACED TO MARK THE GRAVE. MILLET BEER IS PREPARED IN ADVANCE TO THE TUNE OF WOMEN SINGING SPECIAL SONGS WITH OBSCENE LYRICS.

---

* Business and Professions Code, §7685.1.

** Business and Professions Code, §7685.2.

7. Funeral Societies

Funeral societies are private, non-profit organizations, open to any who wish to join. They are devoted to the concept of simple, dignified burial services provided for a reasonable cost. Funeral societies are, essentially, cooperatives, run (at least theoretically) by their members. There is usually a small membership fee for joining. Members are entitled to the burial programs offered through the society. California funeral societies do not employ their own morticians, or own their own cemeteries; rather, they have contracts of varying types with cooperating local mortuaries, crematoriums, and cemeteries to provide simple, economical services for their members.

At first, funeral societies were bitterly opposed by segments of the commercial funeral industry, and a new society often had considerable difficulty finding any funeral director who would work with them.* This has changed. Although the relationship between funeral societies and the commercial funeral industry could not be described as amicable, the two groups have generally learned to co-exist. Partially, this is due to the growth (and resulting economic clout) of funeral societies. From modest beginnings, they have grown substantially in recent years. A number of new societies have been formed in areas that never had them, and overall membership has significantly increased to the point where around 100,000 Californians are members. For reasons unclear to this writer, funeral societies have not attracted minorities, and minority membership is, proportionately to population, low. Competition from funeral societies, and the morticians working with them, has helped to force funeral parlors to offer more economical burial services.

Funeral societies in California are each separate legal entities, run by their own Board of Directors or governing officials. Specific policies, funeral costs and options, vary somewhat, but the basics are common to all. Dignified, simple funerals can be arranged for hundreds of dollars, not thousands. Members are concerned not only with reducing the excessive costs, but at least equally with what they believe are the gross excesses and lack of spiritual values inherent in many commercial funerals. As the literature of the funeral societies notes, in the ''traditional'' funeral the emphasis is on the dead body—lying in an open casket, the body embalmed, often painted, rouged, or otherwise cosmeticized in the belief that the embalmer's skills will make a more ''lifelike'' body, and that viewing a ''lifelike'' dead body is a sign of respect or affection. Funeral societies are opposed to the cost of embalming, and equally so to the emphasis on the corpse. Funeral societies normally prefer a memorial service for the dead person—a service where the body is not viewed, and the emphasis is on remembering the person.

California funeral societies want new members, and readily provide information on their programs. You can easily check out a funeral society's membership rules, the type of services they offer (and what's not included), what it will cost, and the names of all cooperating mortuaries. The morticians conduct the services, themselves or in cooperation with any religious or spiritual ceremony that is planned. Funeral societies do not, generally, have contracts with cemeteries. You must select the cemetery, if you want one, yourself (or through the cooperating mortician). The cost of the burial plot can be far more than a funeral society funeral; one society estimates that the average cost of funeral plots in San Francisco Bay Area cemeteries as $500 and going up. Finally, if you move, there's a good chance you can transfer your membership to another society. There are over 170 cities in the United States and Canada with funeral societies and the fee for transfer is normally only a few dollars.

Here is a list of the California funeral/memorial societies. It's up to you to check them out. I can't guarantee the reliability of every one, although they are all reputable from everything I've heard:

THE SOCIETY OF NEGLECTED BODIES VISITS GRAVEYARDS IN CHINA. THEY RECOMMEND REPAIRS TO FAMILIES WHOS GRAVES HAVE FALLEN INTO DISREPAIR. THEY ALSO PROVIDE BURIALS FOR THE POOR IN THIS LAND WHERE CARE OF ONES ANCESTORS IS A SOLEMN RESPONSIBILITY.

---

* The first funeral society in the United States was founded in Seattle, Washington in 1939.

Humboldt Funeral Society
666 11th Street
Arcata, California 95521

Kern Memorial Society
Post Office Box 2122
Ridgecrest, California 93555

Bay Area Funeral Society
Post Office Box 264
Berkeley, California 94701

Sacramento Valley Memorial Society
Post Office Box 502
Sacramento, California 95803

Valley Memorial Society
Post Office Box 101
Fresno, California 93717

San Diego Memorial Society
Post Office Box 16336
San Diego, California 92116

Los Angeles Funeral Society
Post Office Box 9456
North Hollywood, California 91609

Central Coast Memorial Society
Post Office Box 679
San Luis Obispo, California 93401

Tri-County Memorial Funeral Society
Post Office Box 114
Midway City, California 92655

Channel Cities Memorial Society
Post Office Box 424
Santa Barbara, California 93102

Stanislaus Memorial Society
900 Brady Avenue
Modesto, California 95350

Funeral and Memorial Society of Monterey Bay
Post Office Box 2147
Santa Cruz, California 95063

Peninsula Funeral Society
168 California Avenue
Palo Alto, California 94306

San Joaquin Memorial Society
Post Office Box 4832
Stockton, California 95204

If you are interested, contact the one nearest you. Or you can obtain general information from the California Federation of Funeral and Memorial Societies, 417 South Ancalpa Street, Ventura, California 90003; or the Continental Association of Funeral and Memorial Societies, 1828 L Street, Washington, D.C. 20036.

8. Cremation

Cremation means the burning of the body. Cremation is common in many parts of the world. For example, over half of those dying in England are cremated. It is opposed by certain religions, such as the Muslims, Greek and Jewish Orthodox creeds. Catholics are supposed to request and receive the permission of their local bishop to be cremated, but the Catholic Church no longer bans cremation outright.

The number of cremations has increased greatly in California. Recent estimates are that 30 to 40% of all California's dead are now cremated, with the national average running less than 10%. Both funeral parlors and funeral societies are now normally prepared to handle cremation at low cost. In addition, there are several profit-making, state-wide organizations established exclusively for cremations, such as The Neptune Society, Teleophase, or Memorial Cremation Society.* Except for their commercial nature, they function similarly to funeral societies. For a small membership fee, you join the organization, and then select the type of cremation service desired. This is available at a comparatively low cost—usually between two and three hundred dollars.

By California law, a crematorium cannot require that a casket (rather than a bag) be used in cremation. This makes sense as it seems particularly needless to pay for an expensive wood casket that is almost immediately burned. Cheaper wood caskets are often used, by custom, if no contrary directions are given. Any crematorium must have a columbarium, burial park, or mausoleum ''amply equipped'' for the inurnment of cremated remains.

THE KORYAK PEOPLE OF SIBERIA GENERALLY CRE-MATE THEIR DEAD, BUT WHEN THEY LIVE WHERE WOOD IS SCARCE. THEY THROW THEIR DEPARTED FROM A HIGH CLIFF IN-TO THE SEA.

---

* Addresses available in major metropolitan phone book. Any of these organizations will readily send you literature explaining their services and costs.

Until recent legal changes, ashes could not be scattered, except at sea. Now they may be scattered at sea or over private land. Scatterings were rare a few years ago, but there has been a marked increase in the number of scatterings as the number of cremations has grown. Cremated remains can be removed from the place of cremation or inurnment and disposed of by scattering by the person with the legal right to control the remains. A permit from the County Registrar (in the County Clerk's Office) is required for scattering, whether at sea or over private land.* Once these permits are obtained, there is no other legal impediment to scattering ashes on private land. The crematorium, funeral parlor, or funeral society involved should handle the paperwork. Once again, the giving of specific instructions regarding disposition can save considerable troubles.

Cremated remains cannot legally be inurned in a private residence, or any place except a licensed columbarium, burial park, or similar establishment. So, if remains are not scattered, the cost of inurnment must be paid. Crematoriums make good profits from the sale of urns, niches, "perpetual care," etc., so they may discourage scattering ashes. Some are more inventive. Jessica Mitford recently reported that some ingenious crematoriums now offer plush extras, such as the rental of an elegant bar-equipped yacht to carry family and friends to a sea scattering.

9. Burials

Unless a body is cremated and the ashes scattered, it must be interred somewhere. If there is a funeral, "traditional" or not, the remains must be buried in a graveyard.

Most American graveyards are private businesses. To be buried in one you have to buy your way in. Cemeteries are normally separate businesses from funeral parlors, although they often have working relationships with each other. Sometimes they compete and some cemeteries do sell caskets. Usually, though, the fact that cemeteries are separate means only that there's one more transaction to arrange—the buying of a funeral plot. This purchase can often be arranged through a funeral society or a funeral parlor. If there's a specific cemetery you desire, you should be sure the funeral parlor or society can arrange for that particular purchase. Also, you might save money if you select your own cemetery as prices can vary significantly.

Probably the best known graveyard in the world is Forest Lawn Cemetery in Los Angeles. Evelyn Waugh's justly famous satire of Forest Lawn, *The Loved One,* hasn't diminished the success of the place and many people still choose (or their relatives choose) to be buried in its gaudy splendor. Depending on how much splendor is desired, this can be quite expensive indeed.

Cemeteries as a private enterprise, operated for personal gain, are a rather unusual concept. In most other countries, cemeteries are usually maintained by the family, tribe, community, state, or religious institution. In this country, there is a wide variety of cemetery types, including profit-making ones, large mutually-owned ones, church burial grounds, small co-ops, municipal ones, and national cemeteries, in which most veterans, and their wives, are entitled to free burial.

Cemetery costs, like everything else, are going up. The minimum cost includes:
1. the plot;
2. the coffin enclosure which normally consists of a vault or grave liner of concrete and steel. Cemetery owners state that vaults are required to prevent the land aside the grave from eventually collapsing. Yearly vault sales have recently been estimated to amount to nearly one-half billion dollars. Many vaults are bought through a funeral director, although they are usually cheaper if bought from a cemetery;
3. opening and closing the grave; and
4. upkeep expenses.
Many cemeteries sell "perpetual care" which they claim means that the grave will be

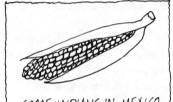

SOME INDIANS IN MEXICO CONTINUE A CUSTOM WHICH DATES FROM AZTEC TIMES OF PLACING CORN ON A CASKET SO THE DEAD WILL HAVE NOURISHMENT FOR THE JOURNEY TO THE LAND OF THE SPIRITS.

---

* In addition to the permit required from the County Registrar for cremation in the first place.

attended "for eternity." This sounds pretty grandiose until you realize that this really means that the grass will be cut, as graves, themselves, don't require much other care. Cutting the grass is now made as simple as possible, since most urban cemeteries no longer use headstones. Instead they use plaques that are planted flush to the ground, so as not to interfere with the power mower.

You can purchase a "prepaid" (or "preneed") plan from most cemeteries. This means you pay now and the cemetery reserves a space for your eventual burial. In *The American Way of Death,* Jessica Mitford depicts fast-buck hustlers in the "preneed" cemetery business selling plots that might not even exist, or selling them in places not likely to remain a cemetery by the time they are to be used. So, if you are interested in a "preneed" burial plot, be sure to check out the reliability of the cemetery involved. And try to figure out just how much additional money the security of this "preneed" plot is costing, or saving, you. Ask the same type of questions that I have suggested above for prepaid funeral plans. If you have any complaints regarding a preneed plan, or salesman, you can try your luck with the Cemetery Board of the Department of Consumer Affairs of the State of California, 1434 Howe Avenue, Suite 88, Sacramento, California 95814. For years the State Cemetery Board was headed by the President of Forest Lawn, so consumer sympathy was not rampant. Recently, the composition of the Board has been changed to a majority of ordinary folks, not cemetery owners/employees, and the Board is reportedly more impartial.

If you haven't got enough to worry about, you could worry about what will happen when we run out of cemetery land. It'll take awhile, surely, although one expert suggests that in only 500 years, at the present rate of graveyard growth, all the land in the United States would be graveyards. One cemetery, the National Veterans' Cemetery in Los Angeles, has no cemetery space left, only room for cremated remains. A new veterans' cemetery at 22495 Van Buren Avenue, Riverside, California 92508, opened in 1978, and has space for ground interment. Space can be obtained there and the veterans' paperwork handled by the funeral parlor or society selected.

3

Estate Taxes

A. Introduction

The ancient maxim goes that the only two things certain in life are death and taxes. Well, bombs have replaced armies, cars have cut into the chariot business and Jane Fonda holds the attention the world once reserved for Cleopatra and the peerless Helen, but death and taxes, like old man river, just keep rolling along.

You can't take it with you, and they'll tax what's left behind. Taxes on the property a person owns at death are the result of decisions society as a whole has made regarding inherited wealth. In the days of "survival of the fittest" capitalism in 19th Century America, there were no federal inheritance taxes. In England today, death taxes take the major portion of substantial estates. In the United States of the 1980s, we're somewhere in between. Californians are subject to federal death taxes, which, though not confiscatory, can take large bites from your estate. The amount of the tax imposed is determined by the size of the taxable estate, with the general rule being that, if you have more, you pay more.

PLEASE REMEMBER: Taxes are completely separate from the probate procedure. It makes no difference for tax purposes whether property is transferred by will or intestate successions which result in probate, or by other means outside of probate.

* Federal estate tax law allows exemptions of certain amounts of money which can be transferred free of estate tax. **For anyone who dies in 1983, $275,000 can be transferred free of tax. * The exemption will increase yearly through 1987, up to a maximum of $600,000 which can be transferred estate tax free.**

* **Any amount of money left to a surviving spouse is exempt from estate tax.**

---

* Assuming none of the federal ''tax credit'' has been previously used for taxable gifts; see Chapter 4, *Gifts and Gift Taxes*.

California's death taxes (called "inheritances taxes") were repealed by Propositions 5 and 6 in the June 1982 elections. The practical effects of their repeal are discussed in detail in section C of this Chapter, and where appropriate, throughout the book.

The process of planning to avoid taxation at death has been criticized by many. In truth, estate planning has often been a rich man's game, and the question arises, why do we allow inherited wealth at all, or inherited millions? I have no answer to this, except to point out that even most socialists seem to prefer to have whatever wealth they've acquired be given to family friends, or worthy causes rather than consumed by governments. Certainly I believe that it makes good sense to try and preserve as much of your estate as possible for your inheritors.

Tax planning is sometimes thought of as a form of lawyer's magic, by which death taxes can be avoided completely. There is some gimmickry in many schemes of the very rich to avoid death taxes, although not as much as there used to be. But, and this is important, there is no magic way to avoid death taxes completely. The best estate planning can do is use all lawful means to reduce death taxes as low as legally possible.

Estate tax planning involves a careful assessment of your desires regarding your estate. If there are death taxes to be paid, how do you want them paid? Distributed pro-rata among your inheritors? Or paid from one specified source? Are there any adverse estate tax consequences from leaving your estate the way you want to? Is there any reason for those additional taxes to lead you to change your estate plan? Obviously, the first step here is understanding how estate taxes work, and calculating the likely federal and state taxes on your estate.

Fortunately, the basic aspects of estate taxation are not difficult to understand. It can be a little dull — law often is — but there can be large amounts of money saved, and substantial security achieved, by understanding the legal estate tax game, and playing it yourself.

B.   Federal Estate Taxes

Federal estate taxes, like federal income taxes, are relatively new; the current estate taxes are derived from those first implemented in 1916. Like income taxes, federal estate taxes are "graduated" — the bigger the taxable estate, the higher the tax percentage rate. Federal estate taxes usually take the largest bite from large estates. In the 1981 tax bill, Congress significantly increased the size of an estate that can be transferred free of federal estate taxes. First, all property/money left to a surviving spouse is totally exempt from estate tax. Secondly, the worth of an estate which can be transferred to anyone other than a surviving spouse free of estate taxes increases yearly from the 1981 limit of $176,625 to a maximum of $600,000 in 1987. Following are the year-by-year amounts that can be transferred free of estate taxes.

Death during 1982	$225,000
1983	$275,000
1984	$325,000
1985	$400,000
1986	$500,000
1987 and thereafter	$600,000

1.   How To Determine the Net Value of An Estate for Federal Estate Tax Purposes

It is obviously important to determine the net taxable value of the estate. As described in Chapter 1, the "taxable estate" is different from the "probate estate." **All property owned by the decedent is included in the taxable estate, however it is owned**

and whether it is transferred to inheritors through probate or by other means. But how do you figure out how much property is worth for tax purposes? This is not difficult in theory. **The worth of property in the taxable estate is determined by its fair market value.** * But the actual determination of the dollar amount of the net estate, for federal tax purposes, can be very tricky. This may be a good reason to have the valuation done as part of the probate procedure,** even though much of the property has been passed to inheritors outside of probate (this concept will become clearer as we proceed). **All** the assets of the estate must be valued at the same time, either as of the date of death, or six months after the date of death (or when the assets were actually sold, distributed to inheritors, etc. **if** within six months after death). There are often technical problems of figuring out exactly how much a piece of property is worth. Here are some simple general rules:

◐ The worth of a house is the owner's equity in it, not the full market value. To figure out the equity, simply subtract any mortgages, liens, etc. from the market value.

◐ **All** the worth of property held in joint tenancy (explained further in Chapter 10) will be included in the decedent's taxable estate, less any portion that the surviving joint tenant(s) can prove they contributed. *** The government's position is to presume the decedent contributed all the cost of any joint property, and the survivors nothing, until they demonstrate otherwise. This is usually not the case and, if the survivor can prove that

---

* Except there are optional extended valuation dates for certain small businesses and family farms.

** Preparation of a federal estate tax return may be considered "extraordinary" services and not included in the standard probate fee.

*** Except for marital joint property, for which equal contributions are presumed.

he (not the decedent) contributed all the money to purchase the joint property, none of its value will be included in the decedent's taxable estate.

Example: Rachael and Sean bought a house together in joint tenancy putting $30,000 down. Rachael dies (just like in Victorian novels). The government will "presume" she paid all the $30,000. However, Sean has a cancelled check for the $20,000 he contributed. So, only the amount Rachael actually contributed—one-third of the purchase price (or ⅓ value of the house if it has increased in value) is included in Rachael's taxable estate.

Establishing proof of a contribution to joint tenancy property, especially if it has been owned for a long while, may not be easy.* Indeed, it may often be difficult for the survivor (or probate attorney) to establish the market value of many items—works of art, closely held businesses, stock in small corporations, etc. Saving cost receipts, book-keeping records and other documents containing the actual cost of items of property can be very useful and can save time and money later.

The way certain types of property, such as life insurance, are owned can have federal estate tax consequences, so you should not make your final calculation of your potential federal estate tax liability until you've read the entire book. Your job now is simply to make a rough calculation of your tax liability which can be adjusted as you read on.

Family Farms and Small Businesses
NOTE: There are special options and valuations rules for determining the worth of family farms and family or closely held businesses which allow them to be valued as presently used, not at their market value if sold for other uses. If your estate includes one of these, talk to a lawyer about it. (See Chapter 11, Special Estate Problems).

2. How Federal Estate Taxes Work
Federal estate taxes are imposed on, and payable by, the estate of any decedent if it is large enough. The tax is due nine months after the date of death. Unless the decedent's will directs otherwise, or sets up a special fund to handle the taxes, they are, in effect, pro-rated between persons (and institutions) benefiting from the estate. This means of course that those receiving a larger proportion of the estate pay a larger proportion of the taxes.

The filing of a federal estate tax return is not required unless the taxable estate exceeds the exempt amount. If a return must be filed, it is normally prepared, and the actual taxes paid, as part of the probate process. The federal estate tax return is a complicated sixteen page document. The fine print instructions for completing it take another sixteen pages. This complexity is one good reason to avoid doing it **all** yourself unless you have special knowledge in the area.

a. The Mathematics
Once the net worth of the estate has been calculated, and any allowable deduction (discussed just below) taken, you can determine if the estate is subject to federal estate taxes. The tax rate is:

---

* Not everyone retains cancelled checks for 25 years or so.

Unified Federal Estate Tax Rate Schedule			
Column A	Column B	Column C	Column D
net taxable estate over	net taxable estate not over	Tax on amount in column A	Rate of tax on excess over amount in column A
			(Percent)
0	$10,000	0	18
$10,000	20,000	$1,800	20
20,000	40,000	3,800	22
40,000	60,000	8,200	24
60,000	80,000	13,000	26
80,000	100,000	18,200	28
100,000	150,000	23,800	30
150,000	250,000	38,800	32
250,000	500,000	70,800	34
500,000	750,000	155,800	37
750,000	1,000,000	248,300	39
1,000,000	1,250,000	345,800	41
1,250,000	1,500,000	448,300	43
1,500,000	2,000,000	555,800	45
2,000,000	2,500,000	780,800	49
2,500,000	3,000,000	1,025,800	53
3,000,000	3,500,000	1,290,800	57
3,500,000	4,000,000	1,575,800	61
4,000,000 *	infinity	1,880,800	65

Technically, federal tax law does not exempt estates (except those transferred to a surviving spouse) from estate taxes. Instead, the tax law provides for a "tax credit," relieving all estate tax liability up to a specified limit.** Here are the tax credit figures along with a repeat of the sizes of estate each credit allows to be transferred free of estate taxes:

Year of Death	Tax Credit	Amount Exempt from Federal Estate Tax
1982	$ 62,800	$225,000
1983	79,300	275,000
1984	96,300	325,000
1985	121,800	400,000
1986	155,800	500,000
1987 and thereafter	192,800	600,000

* The maximum tax rate will be reduced by 5% a year to 1985. Thus in 1983 the maximum rate is 60%, in 1984 55% and in 1985 and thereafter 50%. This reduction only benefits estates in excess of $2.5 million.

** Again, assuming none of this "tax credit" has been used to relieve liability for gift taxes. See Chapter 4.

What's the practical significance of these "tax credits"? None whatsoever, **if** your estate is exempt from tax. However, if your estate is subject to tax, the technique of using "tax credits" becomes very significant, because the tax rate will be based on the worth of the total estate, not just the amount over the exempt amount. For example, Jones dies in 1983 with an estate worth $350,000. Practically, $75,000 of this is subject to estate tax. The tax rate applied, however, is **not** the rate for a $75,000 estate—a 26% tax rate, or a tax of $16,900. Rather, the tax rate is the rate applied to a $300,000 estate, or a 34% tax rate, or a gross tax of $87,000; the "tax credit" forgives $62,800 of this tax, so the net tax assessed is $25,000.

In other words, the effective estate tax rate, in 1982, runs from 32% to 65%. By 1987, the rates will start at 37% (for an estate $1.00 over the $600,000 limit) to a maximum of 50% (for estates over $2,500,000).

3. How Exemptions From Federal Estate Taxes Work

After you compute the net worth of your taxable estate and before you actually compute your estate taxes by looking the tax rate up in the tax table, you deduct from your estate all allowed "exemptions." These exemptions are in addition to the exemption provided by the federal estate tax credit which I just discussed and which you should now understand.

a. The Marital Exemption

By far the most important exemption from federal estate taxes applies to property left to a surviving spouse. The rule is clear and simple: **All property left to a surviving spouse is exempt from federal estate taxes.** Before the 1981 Tax Act there were complex estate tax exemptions for property left to spouses called the "marital deduction." These have been repealed. Now it makes no difference how much money or property is left to the surviving spouse; whether it's $10,000 or $10,000,000, all that money or property is exempt from estate tax and from inclusion in calculations of the value of the taxable estate. Likewise, it makes no difference what (legal) type of property is left to the surviving spouse—i.e., whether it's community property, joint property, "quasi-community" property or separate property.*

Caution: For larger estates, the fact that no federal estate tax is assessed when property is transferred to the surviving spouse may lead to a substantial estate tax liability when the second spouse dies. See section 5 of this chapter for an explanation, and examples, of how estate planning can be used to reduce the eventual estate taxes paid when the second spouse dies.

UNMARRIED COUPLES NOTE: There are no exemptions similar to the marital exemption for lovers, or "significant others." The United States Government can't stop any one from living as they choose, but the estate tax laws do encourage and reward traditional relationships. If either spouse is divorced (from a prior marriage), the divorce must be valid or no marital exemption is allowed. If the divorce is granted in California, be sure that the final decree was properly entered. Whatever your intentions or emotional reality, the marital exemption is not applicable to those who aren't legally married.** However, you can marry right up to the day of death to qualify for the "marital exemption."

IN MELANESIA A WIDOWER OF THE TUBETUBE PEOPLE WILL GO LIVE WITH A BROTHER, MARRIED SISTER, OR HIS CHILDREN. HIS OLD HOUSE IS SOON AFTER DESTROYED

---

* For an explanation of these terms see Chapter 7, Families and Community Property.

** Perhaps there is a certain fairness in this as unmarried couples normally receive significant income tax benefits if both have income. For a thorough discussion of the legal rights and responsibilities of unmarried couples, see *The Living Together Kit*, Warner & Ihara, Nolo Press.

b. Other Exemptions

The other main exemptions from federal estate taxes are:

1) **the expenses of last illness, burial costs, probate fees and expenses;**

2) **certain debts,** including a credit for state death taxes (and death taxes imposed by foreign countries on property the decedent owned there).

3) **all valid (tax-deductible) charitable bequests made by the decedent in his will.**

4. The "Basis" Tax Rules and Estate Planning

Simply put, "basis" is a word used to describe the value put on property you acquire, to determine your profit, or loss, when you later sell that property. Normally, the "basis" of property is the price you paid for it, plus the cost of any improvements. The 1976 Tax Reform Act introduced some very complicated, confusing rules for valuing the "basis" of property received by inheritors; fortunately, Congress repealed these basis rules in the Excess Profits Tax bill of 1980, before they ever went into effect. So, except for the one situation I discuss below, you don't have to worry about what "basis" means for your estate planning.

If you're married and own community property (see Chapter 7 for a full discussion of community property in California) there's a tax "basis" rule that can be of significance for your estate planning. This tax rule provides that on the death of one spouse, the "basis" of the community property interests of *both* spouses is "stepped up" to the property's market value at time of death, rather than retaining the "basis" of its original cost.

Example: Alicia and Rex, an elderly couple, own a house they bought for $50,000. When Alicia dies in 1981, the market value of the house is $200,000. Because of the "stepped-up basis" applicable to their property when Alicia dies, the tax basis of each spouse's one-half interest in the house becomes $100,000. Before Alicia died, the basis of each spouse's interest was $25,000, one-half the purchase price. If the house is sold for $200,000 shortly after Alicia's death, neither Rex nor Alicia's inheritors have made any taxable gain, because the sale price equals the "stepped-up basis" of the house. In contrast, if the house had been sold before Alicia died, the total taxable gain to Alicia and Rex would be $150,000.

What all this means is that there's a considerable tax advantage if an elderly couple retains community property that has substantially increased in value since they purchased it until one of them dies, rather than selling that property late in their lives.

5. Estate Taxes and Estate Planning: An Example

One aspect of estate planning surely leads to others. Or to put it another way—it's hard to put a jig-saw puzzle together without all the pieces. For example, spouses who plan to leave their surviving spouse significant amounts of money, should plan further. Quite often both spouses in such circumstances are old, and they desire their children, and grandchildren, to share their estate after they both die. So the question arises—what are the tax consequences upon the death of the second spouse, the one who received a large estate from the first spouse? Is there any way to lessen those "second death" taxes? The answer is yes. Use of a testamentary* trust is a common method. (Trusts are explained in more detail in Chapter 9. A trust is used here as an example of the interweaving and interacting of one facet of estate planning with another).

---

* A testamentary trust is one established by a will. See Chapter 12, *Wills.*

Example: An elderly married couple, with two grown children and several grandchildren, want to leave all their assets, community property with a net value of $1,060,000, first to the surviving spouse, and then equally to their children. The husband dies first, in 1983. He leaves an estate of $530,000. His wife receives directly her (equal) share of their community property, $530,000. The cost of the husband's last illness, burial and probate of will are (roughly) $30,000. His wife receives the balance of his estate, $500,000, free of estate taxes. The value of her total estate is $1,030,000.

Now assume the wife dies in 1984 with her estate intact, leaving it to her children. What are the estate tax consequences upon her death?

Wife's Death (1984)

	Total Estate	$1,030,000
[less]	Burial, probate costs, etc.	<30,000>
	Taxable Estate	$1,000,000
	Tentative Tax	345,800
[less]	Tax Credit	<96,000>
	Federal Tax Payable	249,500
Net	Amount Received by Children	$750,500

Now let's do a little tax planning, using trusts. Both the husband's and wife's wills state that if he or she predeceases the other, their estate is to be put into trusts for their children. Thus, in this instance, the husband's estate would be put into trusts. The trusts can take various forms. A commonly used one would provide that the income from the trusts go to the wife for her life, with the entire trusts going to the children on her death. If this is done, the assets in the trust completely escape taxation in the wife's estate. This tax advantage won't be lost even if the wife is given a right to invade the principal of the trust up to 5%, or $5,000, whichever is greater.

Now let's examine the estate tax consequences of the deaths of the husband and wife.

Husband's Death (1983), Estate Left in Trusts for Children

Total Estate		$530,000
[less]		
Burial, probate costs, etc.		<30,000>
Taxable Estate		500,000
Tentative Tax		155,800
[less]		
Tax Credit		<79,300>
Federal Tax Payable		76,500
Net amount transferred to trusts		$423,500

Wife's Death (1984), Estate Left to Children

Total Estate		$530,000
[less]		
Burial, probate costs, etc.		<30,000>
Taxable Estate		500,000
Tentative Tax		155,800
[less]		
Tax Credit		<96,300>
Federal Tax Payable		59,500
Net amount transferred to children		$440,500

Total amount transferred to children using trusts = $864,000

Total amount transferred to children without trusts = $750,500

Net (tax) savings by using trusts (excluding the costs of establishing and maintaining the trusts, which are relatively insignificant) = $113,500 *

---

* Whether it is socially desirable to allow such a variance in estate taxes, depending mainly on the forms of transfer, is debatable, surely. The author would undoubtedly be more favorable to it if he were likely to inherit large amounts of money.

C.   California Inheritance Taxes

As I imagine most all readers know, California's inheritance taxes were repealed by state (constitutional) referendum in the June, 1982 election. Two propositions, 5 and 6, passed; both repealed the inheritance taxes. Proposition 6 received the higher number of votes; under California law its provisions therefore control the details and mechanics of the repeal. The following are some notes on how the repeal will work.

1) Proposition 6 is prospective only. It is effective as of June 9, 1982. California's previous inheritance tax laws continue to apply to the estate of any who died on or before June 8, 1982.

2) One small portion of California's inheritance tax scheme was **not** repealed. Federal estate tax law allows a credit for state death taxes paid (analogous to the deduction for state sales or income taxes allowed in federal income taxes).

In any case where: 1) federal estate taxes are due, and 2) this tax credit would have been applicable under the **prior** California inheritance tax law, Proposition 6 directs that a "pick-up tax" be imposed on the estate, up to the amount of the allowable credit. In other words, Proposition 6 directs that money which would otherwise be payable to the federal government be paid instead to California. There is no net cost to the estate itself.

This "pick-up tax," by definition, applies **only** to estates which are liable for federal estate taxes. If the estate is not liable for federal estate taxes (because it is less than the amount that can be transferred tax-free under the estate tax credit), there will be no "pick-up tax" assessed. In any case, the amount of the "pick-up tax" will be relatively small.

3) The mechanics of how this "pick-up tax" will be assessed, and collected from estates liable for it were not determined by the time this edition of this book went to press. Probably California will require that a copy of any federal estate tax form filed with the U.S. Government be filed with state tax authorities along with a short California (pick-up) estate tax form. If you need to learn how the "pick-up tax" will actually operate, contact the California State Controller, Division of Inheritance and Gift Tax at 800 12th Street, Sacramento, CA 95802 (P.O. Box 247), (916) 445-6321.

4) There are numerous questions and problems raised by the repeal of the California Inheritance Tax that will take time to work out. For example, before the repeal, the taxable value of an estate was determined by an inventory filed with, and an "appraisal" made by, a state inheritance tax referee. This "appraisal" was used as the value of the estate for many purposes including federal estate tax evaluations and for probate. But now inheritance tax appraisals are no longer necessary. Thus, some other method of determining the value of the estate for federal estate tax and probate purposes will be needed. One possibility is that private appraisers, acceptable to the I.R.S., will be required to appraise and evaluate estates.

Another uncertainty caused by the repeal of the California Inheritance Tax involves the releasing and transferring of property partially owned by a decedent, such as joint bank accounts, stocks co-owned with another, etc. As part of the "Inventory-Appraisal" process under the former California Inheritance Tax, "Consent to Transfer" forms were generally required to be issued by the Controller's office before such property could be transferred to the surviving owner. In other words, the California Inheritance Tax procedures contained the governmental control mechanism used to insure property was only released to those entitled to it. With the repeal of the inheritance tax, those control mechanisms were eliminated. As of the publication of this edition, the problems raised by eliminating that control mechanism hadn't been resolved. Is any control mechanism needed? If so, will it be done by private not governmental procedures? Once again, if you need information on this type of question, contact the Controller's office in Sacramento.

D. How to Get Tax Forms and Information

1. Federal Tax Forms

Federal estate tax forms are available at any local I.R.S. office, and the I.R.S. claims that assistance will be given in completing the forms if you need it. Practically speaking, I can't imagine your wanting this assistance. It would be a little like asking your cocker spaniel to keep an eye on your steak dinner. Any estate large enough to require a federal estate tax return can afford to pay competent personnel to complete tax forms. Federal estate tax forms are mailed to I.R.S. Service Center, 5045 East Butler Avenue, Fresno, California 93888.

More information about federal estate (and gift) taxes can be found in A Guide to Federal and Estate Gift Taxation, I.R.S. publication no. 448, available at many local I.R.S. offices or by mailing a request for it with $.75 to Superintendent of Documents, U.S. Government Printing Office, Washington, D.C. 20402.

2. State Inheritance Tax Assistance

The California State Controller, Division of Inheritance and Gift Tax, will provide assistance (and forms if you need them) for persons with questions about state inheritance taxes. The Division of Inheritance and Gift Tax has a reputation for being cooperative and helpful. As I've indicated before, the Inheritance and Gift Tax Office is located at 800 12th Street, Sacramento, CA 95802 (P.O. Box 247), (916) 445-6321.

3. Income Taxes

Aside from death taxes, a decedent's estate remains liable for income taxes on money earned by the decedent during the year of death. Also the estate of the decedent is liable for income taxes for any earnings received from assets in the estate, if the earnings are over $600 a year. A beneficiary, i.e. one who receives any property of the decedent, does not have to pay any income tax on bequests received (except for executor's fees or receipt of wages due the decedent without withholding taxes taken out). Clearly, it would be double taxation to tax beneficiaries on bequests received after the estate has already been subject to estate taxes on the same property.

The tax year of the decedent ends on the date of his death. Income payable to him received after the date of death is **not** included in his final tax return, but is included in returns filed by the decedent's estate. The surviving spouse can file a joint return for the tax year when the decedent died. In any case, a 1040 form must be filed for the decedent; if a refund is due, an extra form, #1310, must also be filed.

The decedent's income tax return generally computes income and deductions as they were handled in previous years. Deductions may be itemized if they had been in the past. Medical expenses, including those for last illness, may be deducted from the decedent's individual income tax return, rather than from the estate income tax return, if those expenses are paid by the estate within one year of death. As an alternative, these medical expenses can be deducted, if that is more desirable, from the worth of the gross estate. If the estate is small or moderate, and clearly not liable for federal taxes, it is obviously desirable to deduct last medical expenses from the individual's income tax return.

Deductions do not have to be itemized. The standard deduction can be taken if desired. For the purpose of computing income tax exemption, deductions, or credits, the decedent is treated as having lived a full year, i.e., the full yearly exemptions can be taken no matter when the decedent died in the year; no probation is required. The decedent's individual return is normally filed by the executor of the estate. However this, like the filing of a federal estate tax return, is considered an "extraordinary service." If there is no executor—if all property is transferred outside of probate—the decedent's beneficiaries are responsible for getting the return filed.

IMPORTANT: Suppose the return can't be filed on time? If someone dies near the date yearly taxes are due (for most taxpayers, near April 15), the survivors will normally have plenty of problems without preparing a sudden income tax form,* and it'll be weeks until an executor and probate lawyer can handle matters efficiently. You can get an automatic two month extension from the I.R.S. by filing I.R.S. form 4868 at the I.R.S. center where the decedent's income tax return is to be filed. The I.R.S. will contact you after the 4868 form is filed only if for some reason it is not complete and the extension cannot be granted without more information. It's also possible to get further extensions, but they're no longer automatic. You must individually apply for any other extension, giving the circumstances justifying it in I.R.S. form 2688. An explanatory cover letter should help.

Interest will be charged for any late tax payment, but if, when the return is finally filed, it is demonstrated that there was a reasonable cause for the delay, no late payment penalties will be imposed. The income taxes payable by an estate can be assessed against it in various ways, depending on the choice of the decedent. See Wills, Chapter 12. If no provision for paying the taxes is made in the will, they will be assessed pro rata against the beneficiaries' respective shares.

a. Income Taxes and the Surviving Spouse

The Joint Return. Normally, the executor prepares the decedent's half of the final joint return. The surviving spouse may file the joint return for both parties if there is no executor appointed by the date the tax return of the survivor is due, and the return is filed.

In subsequent years, the surviving spouse may still be entitled to some income tax advantages as a result of her marriage. For two years after the year of the spouse's death, the surviving spouse is entitled to the joint tax return rates if: the surviving spouse (1) could have filed a joint return with the decedent in the year of death (even if they in fact chose to file separate returns); (2) hasn't remarried; (3) has a dependent child or stepchild; (4) furnishes more than half the cost of a home which is the principal residence of the child.

After the two year period as a "surviving spouse" is over, the survivor can still get a small tax advantage by qualifying as a "head of household." This tax rate is also available for the first two year period if there is no dependent child in the home. To qualify, the surviving spouse must: (1) remain unmarried; (2) supply over half the cost of maintaining a household; (3) reside with the child or a relative for whom the surviving spouse can claim a dependency deduction.

b. The Death of a Child

If a decedent child earned sufficient income, his parents are liable for the filing of his last income tax return. No return is required unless the child earned more than $2,950, or if any refund is claimed, no matter how much was earned.

c. Death Benefits

Many employees are covered by benefit plans that provide for death payments to certain survivors or perhaps to the decedent employee's estate. Any person (for the estate) receiving such benefits can exclude such amounts up to $5,000 from his gross (i.e., taxable) income. Above that $5,000, any amounts must be included as regular income. However, once an employee retires and starts to receive a pension annuity, any payments to survivors upon his death do not qualify for this $5,000 death benefit exemption and taxes must be paid.**

---

* Assuming the decedent didn't file a return himself.

** There are many more rules under the Employment Retirement Income Security Act of 1974, as well as many other rights of pensions, individual retirement plans and other benefits that are beyond the scope of this book. Some matters involving social security and other benefits are covered in Chapter 11, *Business and Benefit Programs.*

4

Gifts and Estate Planning

A. Gifts and Taxes

Commonly, gifts are personal matters. The giving of normal birthday, Christmas or anniversary presents doesn't have any tax consequences. However, if the gift involves an asset or cash worth more than $10,000, the rules change. Suppose rich, ill, old Uncle Harry tried to reduce his eventual estate by "giving" each of his ten grandchildren $200,000 rather than having the money pass by his will? Or suppose Uncle Harry is not ill, just generous, and decides he wants to give his grandchildren his money? Obviously, if a person could give away any sum he desires without tax consequences, all estate taxes could be evaded by the simple means of giving away one's estate before death. To prevent this, federal law has elaborate provisions governing the tax consequences of substantial gift giving.

The most important rule is that any gift (or series of gifts) over $10,000 given to any one person (or non-charitable institution) within one year is subject to federal gift tax. Thus, Uncle Harry could give each of his grandchildren $10,000 each year without any tax consequences. **With a married couple, each spouse has a separate $10,000 tax exemption, so the maximum the two of them can give, tax-free, to any person is $20,000 per year.** Any gift over the $10,000 (or for couples, $20,000) yearly exemption is subject to Federal gift tax. Thus in theory, gift tax returns must be filed if you give a friend a $14,000 fur coat.

Gifts of a "future interest" do not qualify for the $10,000 exemption. A "future interest" is some right in property that a person will (or may) have only at some future date, not now. A future interest has an appraisable present worth (what the market value is now for that future interest) and that's the value of the gift.

Gifts for medical bills, or for school tuition are **not** subject to the $10,000 limit, i.e., any amount of money can be given free of tax for medical or tuition costs.

Gift tax rates are the same as estate tax rates.

The second most important rule to learn is that federal gift and estate tax rates are the same. Gift taxes are imposed on the giver, not the receiver, of a gift. For years, federal gift taxes were lower than estate taxes on the transfer of the same amount of money. So anyone elderly or seriously ill had a distinct tax incentive to make large gifts. The 1976 federal tax amendments eliminated this incentive, by taxing gifts and death transfers at the same rate. That's why the federal rate is called "the **unified** estate and gift tax." Here's how gift taxes work.

B. Federal Gift Tax Rate

A donor (gift-giver) is subject to tax on all gifts in excess of $10,000 per year per person. If $15,000 is given to one person, the donor is subject to gift tax on the $5,000 above the exempt limit. The tax rate is the same as that for estate taxes. **The unified federal tax credit, discussed in Chapter 3, is (as its name implies) applicable to gifts. The I.R.S. takes the position that use of the credit is** *mandatory*. A gift-giver cannot choose to "save" all his estate/gift tax credit for use with later gifts or his estate. Thus, let's suppose that Uncle Harry gives his nephew $20,000 in a year. We have just learned that $10,000 of this amount is exempt from tax under the yearly gift tax exemption, so $10,000 of the gift is subject to federal gift taxes. The tax would be $1,800. Under present I.R.S. rules, Uncle Harry *must* use $1,800 of his gift/estate tax credit to satisfy this tax liability: he cannot actually pay the tax and "save" all his credit for later gifts or his final estate. If Harry dies in 1983 (assuming he has made no other taxable gift), his estate tax credit will be reduced from $79,300 to $77,500.

Federal gift tax returns now have to be filed only once a year (before 1982, quarterly returns could be required) when the taxpayer files his regular return (normally April 15) no gift taxes are assessed for gifts made to any tax-exempt organization. However, if charitable gift(s) exceed(s) $10,000 a year, gift tax returns must be filed even though no tax payment is due.

The gift tax is cumulative. In determining the gift tax rate, the value of all gifts given in previous years since January 1, 1977 (above $10,000 exemption) must be included. As the donor gives away more, the gift tax rate increases. The reason for this is that otherwise large estates could be transferred at a lower tax rate by piecemeal giving. Thus, to continue the previous example, suppose Harry gives his nephew $10,000 two years in a row. Each year, $10,000 of the gift is exempt. The second year, the total amount Harry has given that is subject to tax is $20,000, so that gift tax rate is based on this $20,000 amount. The total taxes assessed on this amount are $3,800; Harry gets to deduct any portion of those taxes previously paid, or $1,800, so the taxes actually assessed on the second $10,000 gift are $2,000, or $200 more than on the first $10,000.

There Are Special Rules for Gifts Made Within Three Years of Death

The value of some gifts, made within three years of death, will be included in the decedent's gross estate for federal estate tax purposes.* In other words, for estate tax purposes only, the gift is disallowed. The most significant type of gift which is disallowed if given within three years of death is a gift of life insurance. Other types of gifts which are disallowed are, for average folks, more esoteric—e.g., "reversionary interests", "powers of appointment", etc. If you're considering such gifts or want to understand their meaning and uses, see a lawyer.

At first glance, it wouldn't seem to make any tax difference whether a gift is allowed or not—after all, the tax rate is the same for gifts as for estate taxes. However, a gift of life insurance removes the proceeds of that policy from inclusion in the value of the taxable estate. If the gift is given more than 3 years before death, the "value" of the gift, for gift tax purposes, is far less than the value of the proceeds if included in the taxable estate.

Example: Clementine gave away a life insurance policy to her daughter in 1982. Its value was then $4,000. When Clementine dies in 1984, the policy pays $50,000. There were no gift taxes when the gift was made, as the gift was exempt because it was worth less than $10,000. However, **all** the $50,000 must be included in the decedent's taxable estate because Clementine died within the three year period.

---

* If gift taxes have already been paid, that amount will be credited towards any estate taxes due or, if none are due, refunded.

C. California Gift Tax Rules

California's gift taxes were also repealed by Proposition 6. As I mentioned in the discussion of this proposition's repeal of California's State Inheritance Taxes (see Chapter 3, Estate Taxes, Section C), it applies to the estate of anyone who dies on or after June 9, 1982. The previous gift tax rules apply to the estate of anyone who died before June 9, 1982. If you have any problems concerning California gift taxes, contact the California State Controller, Division of Inheritance and Gift Tax, 800 12th Street, Sacramento, CA 95802, (P.O. Box 247), (916) 445-6321.

D. The Strategy of Gift Giving to Reduce Estate Taxes

1. What is a gift?

A "gift" is any transfer of property that is not, basically, commercial in spirit. The crucial element in determining whether a "gift" was made, legally, is "intent," which can become murky. You obtain a valuable painting from Frank. Did Frank intend to give you that painting, loan it to you, or was he hoping to sell it? As we'll see, it can be helpful to accompany a gift with some written statement stating it is a gift so that the status of the transaction is clear.

Gifts are normally created in the following circumstances:

◑ The creation of an irrevocable trust for another person.

◑ Permitting others to withdraw funds from money you've deposited in a joint (not community property) bank account.

◑ Irrevocably assigning a life insurance policy to another.

◑ Forgiving a debt.

◑ Assigning a mortgage or judgment to someone without receiving fair compensation in return.

Any item that has any (cash) value can be given. A gift is defined in California and federal law as a transfer of property made voluntarily and without "consideration."* Intent plays the key part in evaluating whether a gift has been made. When property is transferred for "less than adequate and full" consideration in money or property having ascertainable worth, the amount by which the value of the property exceeds the value of the consideration is a gift. However, this rule applies only to transfers made with a donative (gift-giving) intent.

---

* "Consideration" is a legal term meaning anything of value given in exchange. Consideration does not require that you exchange items of equivalent dollar worth — that would eliminate bargaining and the *caveat emptor* philosophy dear to capitalism, plus creating endless lawsuits to determine if each side in a transaction got (roughly) the same dollar value.

Example: Suppose Linda exchanged $15,000 for some worthless item, such as an ordinary rock. If the tax authorities question this transaction, and Linda didn't want it to be treated as a gift, she must convince them it was a bona fide commercial transaction (i.e., that she thought the rock was a diamond), as opposed to being a disguised gift. If Linda's diamond story was somehow believed, and the taxman said there was no gift tax liability, the receiver of the $15,000 would have to report the $15,000 as ordinary income. If Linda was not believed (a rock is a rock is a rock, saith the taxman), she must pay gift tax (plus whatever penalties are assessed for trying to dupe the tax authorities—a practice they frown upon).

Gifts can either be **"inter vivos"** (between the living) or **"causa mortis"** (made in contemplation or fear of death, to take effect on the death of the giver). A gift causa mortis can be revoked by the donor, if she survives, whereas a gift inter vivos, once made, is irrevocable. A gift made during a last illness "which would naturally impress" the ill person "with an expectation of speedy death" is presumed to be a gift causa mortis. Such a gift is automatically revoked if the ill person recovers (unless the receiver of the gift has, in the meantime, sold it to a bona fide purchaser).* However, a gift in view of death is not affected by a previous will, and takes precedence over conflicting provisions in such a will.

a. Legal Elements of a Gift

It would seem that giving a gift couldn't be simpler (we all do it often enough, certainly). Legally, however, there are several requirements for a valid gift. If the gift is of a substantial asset, it should be given properly. This means that the following elements are present:

(1) The donor is competent;

(2) There is a voluntary intent on the part of the donor to make a gift;

(3) The gift is delivered (either actually or symbolically);

(4) The donee accepts the gift;

(5) The donor is divested of all dominion and control over the gift; and

(6) There is no consideration (money or property given in return) for the gift.

Oral Gift Note: Oral gifts can be made of anything, except for real property. A valid oral gift must comply with the above rules. If anyone legally contests the fact that an oral gift was really made, the proof that a gift was made must be established by "full, clear and convincing" evidence (as opposed to the usual standard for civil cases, a "preponderance" of evidence). Also—and this is important—for an oral gift to be valid, the means of obtaining possession and control of the thing given must also be given. If the gift is capable of delivery, there must be "actual or symbolic" delivery to the person who was given it (the donee). Actual delivery is safer. Symbolic delivery is for rarer instances where actual delivery is somehow unfeasible. Suppose Harry, living in Los Angeles, orally gives you his tool chest, located in his summer home in the Sierras. He can't give you the actual tool chest at the time of the gift, so he gives you the keys, or some other "symbol" that you've acquired ownership. Clearly, oral gifts have potential for later conflict. It's best to follow the famous advice of grandmothers "better safe than sorry," and make all major gifts in writing, or by a clear and unequivocable transfer, such as depositing money in the receiver's bank account. (Even then, some **could** claim that was a loan.)

b. Completing a Gift

To complete a gift, and be liable for gift taxes, the donor must have given up all control over the property, and no longer have the power to affect its disposition. If Harry

---

* A bona fide purchaser is one who buys the property in good faith, believing the seller to be the legal owner. In this case, the buyer must be unaware that the seller had received the property as a gift "causa mortis" from a person who subsequently recovered.

puts $10,000 into a joint bank account with Desiree, there's no gift until she withdraws the money. When a tangible item is given (cash, an heirloom, a picture) relinquishment of control is usually easy to ascertain, or prove, if the receiver gets possession of the property. In many other situations, relinquishment of control may be a more difficult matter. If a gift is contingent on a future event, that event must be determinable by some ascertainable standard. ''To Desiree, when she becomes 21,'' or ''when she travels to Paris'' is ascertainable; ''when she's happily married'' is not.

If the giver retains any power to alter the gift, then it is not completed. Suppose Harry puts (gives) money in a trust for baby Jane. If the trustee can alter or revoke this gift, **and** Harry has retained the right to substitute a new trustee, there has not been the full loss of control as he can get what he wants by firing the trustee. Likewise, if the donor, an establisher of a trust, retains the power to change who will benefit from it, even if he himself is specifically excluded as a possible benefactor, there is no valid gift.

c. Complexities of Gift Giving

Like anything involving money and taxes in America, gifts can get quite complicated. Some examples:

❖ Suppose an elderly husband and wife own a summer home worth $160,000 (all equity). They know they will leave their house to their only son and the $160,000 value will be included in the taxable estate. They could give the house to their son outright, but then they would be subject to gift taxes on $140,000 ($160,000 less the $20,000 married couple exemption). But, suppose they transfer the house to the son for a ''loan'' of $160,000, and even record a mortgage of $160,000 in their names with the son to make payments of $16,000 a year due for ten (10) years. As each year's payment comes due, they forgive it, i.e. make a gift of that amount. In ten years, the house and its worth has been fully transferred to their son and is excluded from their taxable estate, without any tax payment or tax liability at all.

❖ Now suppose you make an interest free loan of $12,000 to a close friend. Is there a gift of the interest you didn't charge? The I.R.S. has contended (and still does) that there is a gift. At least a couple of courts have disagreed stating that there is no legal duty to charge interest (one cannot be penalized for failing to act like Scrooge).

❖ If you're wealthy, there are many other options available that can involve gifts. These include ''pooled income'' funds, transfers to charitable pools, and charitable remainder annuity trusts. These types of abstruse devices aren't capable of being used by people with average incomes or estates and so aren't covered here. We advise anyone making, or contemplating making, a gift of a substantial amount of property to check it out with a tax attorney or accountant. A consultation to go over your plan should not be expensive.

2. What Is the Best Property to Give?

Some gifts, such as a life insurance policy, can, as explained below, substantially reduce your taxable estate. Even if your estate will not be subject to federal estate taxes, gift giving may still be desirable. First, giving gifts will always reduce the size of the estate for probate purposes which lowers probate fees. Also, the giver can feel pleasure and satisfaction in making a gift while living and seeing the help it brings.
living and seeing the help it brings.

And here is another important benefit of gifts. The income produced from a gift is taxed to the person who receives it. This is usually a lower rate than the giver's. Thus, if rich Uncle Harry gives a struggling student $10,000 he's been keeping in the bank, the interest payments received by the student are taxed at a much lower rate (or perhaps not at all) than they would be if received by Harry.

It also makes much sense to give an asset that is likely to appreciate greatly in value in the future. Suppose Harry has a valuable piece of real property. If he waits to transfer it until his death (by will), then the market value of that property at the time of death will be included in the value of his gross estate. But, if he gives it away, then any appreciation in value will not be taxed to the estate. The gift tax will be on the value of the house when transferred. Likewise, if you own a work of art that you expect will rise greatly in value, it can be wise to give it away before that increase.

Giving gifts can be a means of reducing the (eventual) tax and probate costs on an estate. If a person knows her estate will be subject to federal estate taxes, she can possibly avoid those taxes altogether by giving her beneficiaries-to-be gifts of $10,000 per year while she lives. As you should now realize from reading this Chapter, these gifts are not subject to any taxes. Over a period of years, they can substantially reduce the amount in an estate.

Example: A prosperous married couple with four grown children give the maximum exempt amount, $20,000, to each of their children each year. In ten years, they have transferred $800,000, free of all taxes.

Of course, the loss of money by gift giving is precisely why many people don't make them. They want to hang on to every nickel they've got while they're alive. The security they feel they obtain outweighs the fact that taxes or probate costs on their estate will be greater than if they had given some of their money away while living.

Certainly I wouldn't encourage a person to give away money when the consequences could be that they become impoverished, or suffer money fears and anxieties. However, those with more than adequate wealth for their foreseeable needs should seriously consider the giving of tax-exempt gifts while alive. To begin to decide whether gifts make sense, determine if your estate would be subject to federal death tax. If so, determine the amount of tax that would be eliminated by various tax-exempt gifts. Simply multiply the total years of gifts by $10,000 (or $20,000, or whatever lesser amount under that you're considering giving) and deduct that amount from the estate, and figure what taxes, if any, would be due on the balance.

Gifts of property where value is difficult to ascertain may be wise, as the tax authorities are prone to accept any reasonable statement of their value. Thus, closely held stock, with no readily ascertainable market value, can be a good gift item if you can argue plausibly that it's not worth too much because there is no market for it. Charitable gifts can also be sensible for extremely valuable items that probably can't be readily sold for their appraised worth, thus removing their full value from the estate.

Timing Note: Non-charitable gifts (above the $10,000 exemption) are often given near the close of the taxable year. The gift taxes are the same, and you can retain the asset longer. Charitable gifts are often given near the beginning of the tax year to remove the asset (and the income it produces) from as much personal income tax liability as possible.

3. How Do You Determine the Value of Property Used for a Gift?

If you give property instead of cash, the value of the gift, for your (the donor's) gift tax purposes is the fair market **value on the date the gift was made.** Likewise, the value ('basis') of the gift, to the receiver is also the fair market value of the gift, when given.

4. Life Insurance Can Be an Excellent Gift
a. Advantages of Gifts of Life Insurance

Gifts of life insurance are one of the more commonly used forms of estate planning. Under I.R.S. rules, the value of a gift of a new life insurance policy is its cost. If it's a paid-up policy, its value is its replacement cost (what it would cost to buy a similar policy), at the time of the gift, not its cash surrender value. In the case of a premium paying policy, the value of the gift is the "interpolated terminated reserve as of the date of the gift, plus any prepaid premiums".* Other special types of insurance policies also have

---

* Yes, these words seem crazy. All you have to know is the right words though; then the insurance company, knowing what you want, can give you the dollar worth of a gift of a premium paying policy.

a gift tax value based on their present worth. Most insurance companies will provide, on request, an informal approximation of the gift tax value of a policy (in advance of making the actual gift) and will also provide the appropriate forms (usually Treasury Department Form 938) for submission with the gift tax (if any). Gifts of premiums due on a policy after the policy itself has been given are separate gifts.

Important: Simply naming a beneficiary of a life insurance policy is not a gift. The actual policy itself must be given to a new "owner" for there to be a gift.

However the value of the gift of an insurance policy is calculated, it will be much lower than the amount paid in the event of the insured's death, which is usually referred to as the face value of the policy. If the policy was owned by the person who died, the full amount of the face value payment is included in his taxable estate. Insurance thus makes an excellent gift because a policy that will pay off large sums at the time of death isn't taxed heavily when the transfer (gift) is made. Also, the lump sum payable to the beneficiary as a result of an insured's death is exempt from federal taxation. (See Chapter 8, *Insurance*.)

CAUTION! Remember that, for federal estate tax purposes, any gift of life insurance made within three years of death is disallowed and the full face value of the policy is included in the decedent's taxable estate. Also, any gifts of life insurance policies, within three years of death, are not entitled to the $10,000 annual gift exemption.* In other words, if a life insurance policy is worth $2500 at the time of the gift, **but** the giver dies within three years after making the gift, the gift is disallowed and the full amount of the policy will be included in the decedent's taxable estate. So, when giving life insurance, it is particularly wise to make the gift long before there appears to be any possibility of death.

Life insurance gifts have another extremely important benefit. At the insured's death, the proceeds do not get held up in probate. This means that the people to whom the giver gave the policy will get cash quickly. This is called "liquidity". While it is true that needy families can obtain permission from a probate court to take money for necessary expenses from an estate while it is being probated, the existence of insurance proceeds makes this sort of request unnecessary. Also, insurance proceeds can be made available to more than the immediate family and collection doesn't involve much red tape. Reputable insurance companies normally pay off policies promptly upon notification (with a death certificate) of death.

Annuity insurance policies can also be given. An annuity is a form of private pension plan in which the insurance company agrees to pay you a set amount in periodic intervals for every year you live (beyond a set age) in return for your purchase price. For example, you could buy an annuity for your son, who isn't good at managing money, that would pay him $1,000 on the first of every month commencing when he turns 65, and lasting until his death. The gift tax value of an annuity is determined by reference to the sale by insurance companies of similar benefit programs to persons the same age as the gift recipient.**

b. How to Make a Gift of Life Insurance

To make a valid gift, a giver of life insurance must surrender all "incidents of ownership" of the policy. If he does not, the I.R.S. will claim he still owns the policy at his death. The "incidents of ownership" are the power to:

---

* But, if an insurance policy is transferred, by gift, more than three years before the death of the giver, he can make tax-exempt gifts (up to $3,000 per year) to be used to pay the premiums on the policy, and these gifts will not be disallowed under the federal three-years-before-death rule. Thus, the tax laws encourage estate planning and gifts of life insurance and penalize those who wait until the last minutes (or years).

** If you want to determine the actual value, for gift tax purposes, of an annuity, the simplest way is to ask an insurance company.

- change the beneficiary;
- surrender or cancel the policy;
- assign the policy, or revoke an assignment;
- pledge the policy for a loan or borrow the cash value from the insurer;
- make payments on the policy.

The "incidents of ownership" are strictly construed by the I.R.S. and to make a valid gift of life insurance care must be taken to insure that all these "incidents of ownership" are given away by the gift giver. For instance, if a policy is given to two beneficiaries, the I.R.S. has claimed that since no one person had all the incidents of control, there was no completed gift. To be safe, if you want to give policies to two or more persons, transfer separate policies to each person.

As is discussed in more detail in Chapter 8 on insurance, valid transfers of insurance can be tricky. One of the real problems can be proving the donor surrendered the "incidents of ownership". Suppose, for example, that a man gives his policy to his wife. If subsequent payments on the policy are made from community property funds, hasn't he retained some control over the policy? To be safe, the wife should pay the remaining premiums on the policy from her separate funds, and it should be clearly provable that they were her separate funds.*

A written form for the giving of life insurance, specifically relinquishing all "incidents of ownership" is provided in Chapter 8, *Insurance*. If you give an insurance policy, I recommend that you complete this form. Also, any gift of insurance should probably be checked, or at least noted by your insurance agent. Many insurance companies provide preprinted gift/transfer forms for the making of gifts of insurance policies.

E. Gifts to Minors

---

* Or the husband could expressly "give" his wife his one-half interest in any community property funds used to pay the premiums.

The "Uniform Gifts to Minors Act" has been adopted in California. This reduces the problems a giver faces when planning to make a gift to a minor (in California, any child under age 18). By reference to the title of the act, or by using certain phrasing the act specifies, in the making of the gift, all the provisions of the act are automatically incorporated in that gift. To avoid confusion, some writing should be used that refers to the act, or uses the correct phrasing.

The Uniform Gift to Minors Act is not the only law applicable to the making of a gift to a minor. Any gift to a minor that complies with the general legal requirements for making a gift is valid. However, if a gift of any significant amount is to be given to a minor, it is wiser to refer to the act and use it. If you don't, complicated legal issues regarding guardianship, custodial duties, control and the like can arise when the minor (or his guardian) try to use the gift.*

I.R.S. regulations provide that in order to make a valid gift to a minor, the property of, and income from the gift:

1. must be used for the minor's benefit until he reaches majority;
2. the remainder (if any) will be legally his once he reaches majority; and
3. if the minor dies **before** reaching majority, the remainder is payable into his estate.

If there are "substantial restrictions" on a gift established for a minor, there is no completed gift. "Substantial restrictions" are any significant limitation on the use of the money/asset transferred, such as restricting use of a trust fund for school tuitions, or only for illness. Gifts to minors are eligible for the state and federal $3,000 annual gift tax exemptions and the other California relation exemptions. The income from gifts to children (bank account, stocks, etc.) is taxable to the child, thus getting the money out of the giver's tax liability.

The Uniform Gifts to Minors Act provides that a custodian responsible for administering or maintaining the gift be appointed. Essentially that is the only requirement of the act, aside from using the right words in making the gift. Any competent adult or financial institution, such as a bank, can be named custodian. It is also wise to nominate a successor custodian as well; otherwise, if the original custodian dies, or resigns, there might have to be court proceedings to select a new custodian.

The form of the wording of a gift under the act depends upon what is given. If the subject of the gift is a security in registered form, such as stock in a company listed on a stock exchange, the gift is made by registering the security in the name of the donor, another adult person, or trust company, followed in substance by the words: "as custodian for _____ (name of minor) under the California Uniform Gifts to Minors Act."

Example:

Harry wants to give his stock in the Trueglue Racetrack to cousin Freddie, age 12; Harry makes himself the custodian. The stock certificate is completed:

Trueglue Racing Association
5000 shares **Owner :** Harry Tones, as custodian for Frederick (Freddie) Tones under the California Uniform Gifts to Minors Act.

* Since minors cannot have estates in excess of $2500 in California, any large gift to a minor requires some form of adult supervision.

❷ If the subject of the gift is a security not in registered form (such as stock in a family corporation), the gift is made by delivering the stock certificate to an adult person, or to a trust company, accompanied by a statement of gift in the following form, signed by the donor* and the person designated as custodian*:

GIFT UNDER THE CALIFORNIA UNIFORM GIFTS TO MINORS ACT

I, _____ (name of donor) hereby deliver to _____ (name of custodian) as custodian for _____ (name of minor) under California Uniform Gifts to Minors Act, the following security(ies): [insert an appropriate description of the security or securities delivered sufficient to identify it or them].

Dated: _____   _____ (signature of donor)

_____ (name of custodian) hereby acknowledges receipt of the above-described security(ies) as custodian for the above minor under the California Uniform Gifts to Minors Act.

Dated: _____   _____ (signature of custodian)

---

❷ If the subject of the gift is money, the gift is made by paying or delivering it to a broker or a financial institution for credit to an account in the name of the donor, another adult person or a bank with trust powers, followed by placing the words on the account such as this: ''as custodian for _____ (name of minor) under the California Uniform Gifts to Minors Act.''

❷ If the subject of the gift is a life insurance policy or an annuity contract, such policy or contract is assigned** to the donor, another adult person, or a bank with trust powers, followed by words such as these: ''as custodian for _____ (name of minor) under the California Uniform Gifts to Minors Act.''

IMPORTANT: Any gift made under the provisions of the Uniform Gifts to Minors Act can be made to only one minor, with only one person named as custodian (excluding successor custodians which are permissible to name in case the original custodian dies, resigns, etc.).

The act specifies, in considerable detail, the rights and duties of custodians, and alternate procedures for appointing successor custodians. The custodian ''shall collect, manage, invest, and reinvest the custodial property'' and the custodian must act ''in highest good faith'', and ''as a prudent man''. However, this has been interpreted by courts to mean that he has broad discretion to act in what he believes are the minor's best interests. Thus, the most important decision in making a gift under the act is the selection of a wise and prudent custodian who, clearly, should be someone you trust both for honesty and good judgment. The minor, if over age 14, or his or her guardian (no matter the age of the minor) may petition the local Superior Court for funds from the gift if necessary for the minor's support, maintenance, or education.*** Once the minor reaches age 18, the custodian pays out to him the remaining balance left of the gift with an accounting of all funds previously distributed.

---

* They can be the same person.

**The assignment itself should also be in writing; the forms provided in Chapter 8, *Life Insurance,* for life insurance assignments should be used.

*** Even if the minor is over 14, and has no general guardian, a ''guardian ad litem'' must still be appointed to handle the legal petition.

The custodian is entitled to reasonable compensation from the gift property for his services. No bond is required. If the custodian is not compensated (because he and the donor so agree which is common among friends and family), the technical legal standards the custodian must meet are lowered, and mere negligence does not render the custodian liable. Of course, this is (or should be) academic as you will want to name a very careful person as custodian whether or not compensation is paid.

The great advantages of the Uniform Gifts to Minors Act are its ease and inexpensiveness. A large gift can be made to a minor without any court proceedings, legal fees, necessities to establish a trust, appointment of a guardian, or other complexities. There are really no drawbacks to using the act, except that if the minor dies before reaching 18, you cannot specify who then receives the gift. It goes to the minor's estate and you have no control over it. So, if you plan a substantial gift to a minor, choose an honest and wise custodian, and use the appropriate magic words with the gift, being sure that you deliver the document of gift (containing the magic words) to the person named as custodian.

5
Probate

A.   What's Probate?

"Probate" is the word given to the legal process which includes filing the will of the decedent with the local Superior Court, locating and gathering the decedent's assets, paying off his legal debts, including death taxes, and (eventually) distributing what's left as the will directs. If the decedent did not leave a will, or his will is not valid, the estate will undergo probate through similar legal proceedings called "intestacy" proceedings, with the only difference being that the property will be left as California "intestate succession" law dictates (see Section G of this chapter). Probate is allegedly designed to prevent frauds in the transferring of a decedent's assets. More realistically, probate establishes a paper record of order, so that if there is a fraud, none of the lawyers, accountants, tax people, or others involved or responsible for any aspect of the transfer can be (legally) blamed. Probate does take a while—at least months, and often years. It takes one and a half years until the actual distribution of assets in the "average" California probate case. If there is a will contest, a challenge by the taxing authorities, or other legal dispute, probate will take longer, often much longer. I once worked in a law office that was profitably entering its seventh year of handling a probate estate—and a very wealthy estate it was. By comparison, transfers of a decedent's assets by legal means not involving probate can usually be completed in a matter of a few days.

Probate proceedings seem murky and confusing, evoking images of greedy lawyers consuming most of an estate in fees, while churning out reams of gobbledygook-filled paper as slowly as possible. There is some truth in these images. Probate usually takes a long time and requires mounds of tedious forms, most of which are completely routine. While the fees charged will not actually devour the whole estate, they are substantial. In the normal uneventful probate proceeding, the attorney's secretary fills in the mountain of forms, keeps track of various deadlines and technicalities, while the attorney makes a couple of routine court appearances and signs a few documents. Probate also requires an "executor" of the estate, normally appointed in the will.* The executor is theoretically

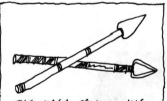

THE WOGAL FOLK OF AUS-
TRALIA TAKE CARE TO
BURY ALL THE POSSESSIONS
OF A DEAD MAN WITH HIM.
EVEN SUCH VALUABLE ITEMS
SUCH AS NETS, SPEARS AND
HIS CANOE.

---

* If the person died without a will, the court appoints an "administrator" to serve the same function.

responsible for supervising the estate, which means making sure that the will is followed. In practice, he's usually a friend or spouse of the decedent's and does no more than sign where the lawyer tells him to, while wondering why the whole business is taking so long. For these services the lawyer and the executor each collect, by law, a fixed percentage of the worth of the probate estate. (The secretary, of course, gets her normal regular salary.) Probate work is lucrative. For handling a routine estate with a gross value of $100,000 (these days little more than a house and car), the attorney and the executor receive a fee of $3,150. If there are any "extraordinary" services performed for the estate, the attorney or the executor can petition the court for additional fees. If the executor and the attorney are the same person, he can collect both fees.

Marilyn Monroe's estate provides a good example of how outrageous probate fees can be. Since she died (in debt) in 1962, Monroe's estate received income, mostly from movie royalties, in excess of $1,600,000. In 1980, her executor announced that debts of $372,136 had been paid, and $101,229 was left as the final assets of the estate, for distribution to inheritors. This means that well over a million dollars of Monroe's estate was consumed by probate fees!

The "normal" probate fees are based on a percentage of the gross probate estate by Probate Code Section 901, as follows:

4% of the first $15,000;

3% of the next $85,000;

2% of the next $900,000;

1% of all over $1,000,000.

TO REPEAT: The executor and probate attorney **each** receive a fee based on the above schedule.

B.   A Smidgen of History (and a Little Perspective)

Why is probate so complicated and expensive? Why is court approval required for so many routine actions when there is no conflict whatsoever?

Aside from the mystique of professionalism and greed, probate's history supplies most of the answer. In medieval England wealth and power were almost exclusively in the ownership of land. It passed, by feudal law of primogeniture, to the eldest son. Inheritance of land was a political matter of direct concern to the king, and land probate was done in the king's courts, inappropriately called "common law" courts.

The proceedings were technical, formal and costly. On the other hand, transfers of personal property, which in those days was of little political concern and commonly had small value, were handled through the church ecclesiastical courts and required little formality. As newer forms of property evolved (stocks, bank accounts), they were handled by the "equity" courts (derived in part from the ecclesiastical courts), which also were much less formal than the common law courts. When the United States became independent, it accepted and followed the traditional British legal system for land inheritance. But instead of calling our courts "common law," we called them "probate courts." And more important, instead of distinguishing between land and personal property, we tossed everything into the new "probate" court. This meant that the efficiencies of the "ecclesiastical" and "equity" courts were eliminated; in post-revolutionary America, all property could be transferred at death only through complicated formal proceedings. Our current probate system then evolved (or rather, like Topsy, it "just grow'd"). Because a complicated, formal probate system means mounds of paperwork and substantial fees for lawyers, naturally the legal profession has invented a suitably complicated rationale for why we need it. They draw themselves up like Charles Laughton in "Witness For The Prosecution" and tell us portentously that "We're doing it for your own good."

Recently the assurances of the legal profession have begun to sound hollow. Even the British no longer require tedious, expensive probate proceedings. In 1926 probate in England was greatly simplified. After a death there, the person named in the will as the executor simply files an accounting of the decedent's assets and liabilities with the tax authorities who appraise the inventory and assess any death tax due. This is the only inventory required. Next, the executor applies at a court administrative office for a general grant of probate. If the executor is not an attorney, he can apply in person and the administrative personnel are supposed to assist him in technical matters. If the papers are in order (as they should be in all routine probates), a "grant of probate" is issued in as little as seven days. The executor then handles all the estate's problems without any further court proceedings. He pays the decedent's bills, collects assets, distributes bequests. Lawyers play little or no role in uncontested probate proceedings, unless the will happens to name a lawyer as executor. Only if there is a problem with the papers such as a will contest or some other uncertainty, is the matter referred to the Principal Registry, the functional equivalent of the Probate Court.

In civil law countries* probate is even simpler. Wills are presented to a notary when signed. The notary, under civil law, is a quasi-judicial official (not just anyone with a rubber stamp), who is responsible for insuring the validity of papers presented to him. As a result, notarized wills there are largely free from attack. Upon death, the decedent's successor (as named in the will) performs the probate functions without any judicial supervision. If there are disputes such as contests of the will or disputed creditors' claims, these are handled like any other legal conflict.

In sum, other countries do not have the expensive and form-filled probate proceedings we do and seem to accomplish the same basic task considerably faster and considerably cheaper. Why is it that even the English can simplify their legal proceedings while we, who merely inherited their ancient methods, follow them still? Why is it that we refuse to come to grips with the fact that the legal profession usually puts its interests before our interests?

C. Avoiding Probate

Because probate has come to be viewed by many as an unnecessary device designed to fill lawyers' coffers, some have concluded that probate must be avoided at all costs. In

---

* States or countries whose legal system is derived from the French Code Napoleon, including most of Western Europe, Latin America (and Lousiana).

order to avoid probate, they transfer all their property by other means than a will—such as joint tenancy, trusts or gifts (I discuss these alternatives in Chapters 10, 9 and 4). There is a great deal to be said for avoiding most probate fees, but rather than establishing probate avoidance as a strict goal, it makes more sense to be flexible. Although it may surprise you after the discussion on the previous pages, there are several reasons why it can be wise to let some property (usually a small amount) go through probate, including:

1. A will, which normally requires probate, can have many estate planning advantages (see Chapter 12) that are not easily available with other types of transfers. For example, a will easily allows you to be specific in making bequests of personal items such as jewelry, heirlooms, etc.;

2. California Inheritance Tax and other transfer forms that are required in any event will be prepared as part of probate (I know I've said this before, but it's an important point);*

3. A will can allow you to avoid certain drawbacks of other transfer methods. For example, trusts can be cumbersome, joint tenancy a risk, etc. You want to avoid the "avoid probate at all costs on every piece of property" syndrome in which probate avoidance becomes the only goal and decisions are made to achieve it which defy common sense.

IMPORTANT: Because some (even a small part) of your estate goes through probate does not mean that all of it must. People can and should avoid probate with a large portion (in many situations this will be almost all) of their estate. If there are one or two items, such as a house, business, or savings, that constitute the bulk of the estate, it's almost always advisable to transfer them outside of probate, to keep the fees down.

Time Out for a Word About "How to Avoid Probate"

Norman Dacy in his pioneering work entitled *How To Avoid Probate* emphasizes the use of one type of legal device to pass all (or most) of the property a person has. This device is the revocable "inter-vivos" trust (see Chapter 9) and serves to avoid probate entirely. This type of trust does not take effect until your death, at which time the property in the trust is transferred to the trust beneficiary outside of probate. Dacy recommends that you put **all** your property in revocable inter-vivos trusts—your house, car, jewelry, business, the whole lot.

Because the Dacy book is so widely read, I want to comment briefly on its recommendations. It is my belief that inter-vivos trusts, though legally permissible, should not be over-emphasized as an estate planning device. As is discussed in more detail in Chapter 9, inter-vivos trusts *are* formal trusts, requiring written trust documents, transfers to the trust, tax returns for the trust and other expenses, which can create as many problems as they solve. Sometimes just the use of inter-vivos trusts is the best estate plan, and unquestionably they are one valuable method of estate planning. They are not, however, in my opinion the "legal wonder drug" Dacy claims them to be, and I do not recommend putting everything into standard form inter-vivos trusts in all situations.

D.   Special Types of Estates That Can Avoid Probate

In California there are two types of estates where normal probate proceedings can be easily avoided altogether, by special "summary probate" proceedings.

1. Estates under $20,000. Summary probate methods for such estates, which can be done by a non-lawyer, are described in Chapter 6.

---

* Technically, an attorney could apply to a court for an additional fee for the "extraordinary" service of preparing a State Inheritance Tax Return, but in practice this is and should be included in the normal fee.

2. Community Property Estates where property is left to the surviving spouse. The summary probate-avoidance method of transfer, a "community property petition" is described in Chapter 7.

E. Avoiding or Reducing Probate Attorney and Executor Fees

As with other legal proceedings, probate can, legally, be handled without an attorney. This means that the executor can appear "in pro per" as the representative of the estate, and results in the probate attorney's fee being saved. However, although this is legally possible, I do not advise pro per representation for probate proceedings. Probate is a tedious and form-filled process. Learning to complete the forms, understanding all the intricacies of court petitions, estate inventories, proof-of-service declarations, and so on (and on and on) can be done by a non-lawyer, but it is not easy. As there is no simple published material on the subject, a large amount of time, research and energy will be required. The courts and clerks will not usually be sympathetic (to put it mildly), so any mistake is liable to cause long delay, as well as embarrassment. I do not defend such judicial and administrative attitudes (there is no defense), I simply note that they exist. There is not even one set of probate rules for all of California—most counties have local probate rules, in addition to the state-wide rules which are found in the California Probate Code, the probate forms and reported case law.

Rather than try to have your estate probated without an attorney, it makes more sense to reach an agreement with the future executor, and attorney, that they will do your probate for less than the statutory fee, as well as reducing the size of your estate subject to probate. You cannot require, by your will, that the executor or attorney handle the probate of your estate for a reduced fee. In fact, legally you do not have the power to select the attorney at all. The law gives this decision to the executor. In addition, the executor can legally revoke any waiver of fees she made while you were alive, and claim her full statutory fees. But, obviously, there's no reason for you to pick an executor you don't completely trust; usually, for moderate estates, an executor is a spouse or a close friend. So, if she agrees to serve at a reduced fee, she likely will. Likewise, if you make an arrangement with an attorney to handle the estate at a reduced fee, you should be able to rely on the person you name as executor to designate that person as the probate attorney. If the probate of your estate is routine, it will be sufficiently profitable even at a fee lower than the statutory rate. There's nothing illegal or unethical about bargaining with an attorney to reduce her fees. It's probably a good idea to be definite on the terms of the fee, and put something in writing, even if it's only a letter confirming this arrangement. Still, the lawyer must be someone whose word you can trust because that's finally all you can rely on.

TO REPEAT: There are some advantages to having an experienced person prepare tax forms and handle other technical matters. But it is silly to pay large probate fees for this service. So the best a person with a moderate estate can do is to allow only a small amount of property to go through probate and to try to keep the fees low. In Chapters 6 through 12 I discuss a number of ways that property can be passed easily and safely outside of probate.

F. How Probate Works in California

It is useful for an executor, a beneficiary under a will, a person leaving property, and anyone who wants to give his inheritors an idea when they will actually receive their inheritance, to understand how probate actually works in California. There's no way I can tell you everything there is to know about the intricacies of probate, short of writing another book which could be lots longer than this one. But even if you don't know every detail, you can learn enough to distinguish between the inevitable delays of any probate, and law office procrastination. In the probate of a routine estate, it's fair to say that the lawyer's most important job is to keep the paperwork flowing efficiently.

Here's what the lawyer and his staff normally do in a probate proceeding where there is a will:

1. The executor named in the will files (via the lawyer) a petition in the county superior (probate) court for probate of the will. The petition establishes that the decedent is dead, left property and a will, and was a resident of the county. Petitions for family allowances or homesteads can be presented at this time (see Chapter 7, *Families and Community Property*).

2. Legal notices of hearing on the petition are published. This is usually done in the local legal newspaper and theoretically provides notice to anyone who may want to challenge the will. Notice of the hearing is mailed to all direct heirs, and all persons named as beneficiaries under the will.

3. The hearing on the will is held by the probate court, where:

a) at least one witness to the will establishes the valid execution of the will by the decedent. This can be done by affidavit or live testimony;

b) the executor is officially appointed;

c) any persons contesting the will are heard; any matters raised such as a claim that the will was fraudulent, or was executed under duress or insanity, or that the executor does not have a ''moral character'' suitable to his position, etc., will be decided by the court, or more likely, scheduled for a further hearing;

d) the will is ordered admitted to probate (or, very rarely, ruled invalid, or submitted to a further will contest proceeding).

4. A ''Notice to Creditors'' is published in the local legal newspaper. Creditors have four months from the date of first publication to present their claims (with certain exceptions). Incidentally, there is even a provision in the Probate Code for what is to be done if

the probate judge is one of the estate's creditors, and the judge's claim is contested by the executor.

5. a) The assets and debts of the decedent are traced, itemized, and valued for the "inventory" of the estate;

b) the inventory may be prepared by a (former) inheritance tax appraiser. The appraisers who in theory should be out of their jobs because Proposition 6 abolished the inheritance tax, will probably survive as part of the probate process, adding to probate costs. This is one more substantial reason to try to avoid probate;

c) any federal estate taxes due are also calculated (extra fees can be charged for this);

d) the inventory is then filed with the court. This must be done within three months of the executor's confirmation, although extensions are readily granted.

6. Creditors file claims against the estate. If approved by the executor, and then ratified by the court, they are paid; if they are contested by the executor, the dispute is resolved by the court.

7. Any federal estate taxes due are paid. They are due within nine months of death. Any audit questions must be resolved, especially those by the IRS through the Federal Estate Tax Examiner.

8. The executor files a petition with the court accounting for the expenses of administration (publication costs, court fees, taxes paid, etc.), the assets remaining for distribution, and how they are to be distributed. If the petition is in order (i.e., complies with the will and law), distribution to the inheritors is ordered.

The minimum amount of time that this can take is five months. The average time for a simple, uncontested probate is at least a year. Why? Because each one of these steps involves preparing forms and, even though in the larger view many of them are silly, they do have to be done right. Do we need probate reform? Need you ask?

G. Notes on Specific Aspects of Probate

1. Executor's Responsibility

Although the lawyer's office in reality does the paperwork, it is the executor who is legally regarded as a "high fiduciary" and responsible for completion of probate. The executor cannot profit personally at the expense of the estate and is legally responsible for preserving the estate. However, the executor is not required to search for missing heirs — or missing assets.

2. Family Matters

Families of the decedent have rights that can be enforced in the probate proceeding. These are described in more detail in Chapter 7, *Families and Community Property,* but include:

The Family Allowance: The surviving spouse, minor children, or incapacitated adult are entitled to a "reasonable allowance" from the estate "necessary for their maintenance according to their circumstances." In any well-planned estate, this shouldn't be needed because life insurance, a savings bank trust or other estate planning devices have been used to provide enough carry-over cash until the final distribution of the probate estate.

Furniture and Clothing: The surviving spouse and minor children are also entitled to possession of the wearing apparel, household furnishings and other property of the decedent until the inventory is filed. During the administration, the court has the power to order that such property remain set aside for the spouse and/or children even if, under the decedent's will, that property will eventually wind up elsewhere.

The Family House: The court **may** set aside to the spouse the recorded homestead* on the family house, or, if there was none, the court may select and set aside a "homestead" (the family house), for the use of the surviving spouse and/or minor children.

In sum, even the Probate Code tries to protect against families of a decedent being suddenly thrown out into the street.

3. Creditors' Claims Against the Estate

Generally, claims not presented within four months of the first published notice to creditors are forever barred. However, if you have one of the following claims, there is a different time limit;

A claim for personal injuries (against the decedent, and therefore against his estate) may be filed within one year from the date of the accident (the normal statute of limitations period) upon order by the probate court;

If you were out-of-state, and submit an affidavit that you did not receive any notice of either the death or probate proceeding, the probate court can extend the time for you to file a creditor's claim. However, it is risky to file a delayed claim because the probate might have been a speedy one and, if the assets are all disbursed by the time the claim is filed, there is no estate to collect from;

If you claim ownership of any property that is involved in the probate proceeding, you must file your claim with the probate court. This sort of dispute normally means that you'll have to hire a lawyer. This could happen, for example, if you claimed you bought a painting from the decedent, but the executor disputed your claim and included the painting as part of the probate estate.

4. The Order in Which Debts Are Paid

The priority of payments from an estate is set by law. This is mostly important when there isn't enough money to go around. Surprise! The lawyers get theirs first—even before the family. Here is how payments are made with the debts set out in order of priority:

a) Fees and costs of administration (attorney's and executor's fees);

b) Funeral expenses;

c) Expenses of last illness;

d) Family allowance;

e) Debts having preference by the laws of the United States (e.g., federal taxes);

f) Wages up to $900 of each employee for work done or personal services rendered within 90 days of the death;

g) Mortgages, judgments that are liens against property, and other liens if they can be paid out of the proceeds of the sale of that specific property. If these proceeds are insufficient, the balance is included as part of the general claims against the estate;**

h) Judgments that are not liens rendered against the decedent in his lifetime and all other demands against the estate.

5. Will Contests

Contesting a will can be done in various ways. Before probate, any person can file a petition challenging the will. The petition is served on all "parties" (i.e., the executor, heirs, beneficiaries under the will). If the petition is not withdrawn or no compromise is

---

* A "homestead" is a document recorded with the County Recorder protecting the homeowners from attachment by creditors up to $45,000. See *Protect Your Home With A Declaration of Homestead,* Warner, Sherman and Ihara, Nolo Press, $5.95.

** For example, the decedent owes $10,000 to a friendly loan company, who took a lien against his household furnishings. However, the furnishings turn out to be worth only $6,000. The loan company must try to collect the remaining $4,000 like any other creditor, against whatever assets remain in the estate.

arrived at, a trial must be held. This will be a jury trial if requested. As it takes at least a couple of years, in urban California counties, to bring a case to trial in Superior Court, a will contest will greatly delay probate.

After probate has been commenced, the same four month period that applies to creditors applies to challenges of the will, which must then be done in the probate proceeding. If the person making the challenge was out-of-state and had no actual knowledge of the proceedings, the four months can be extended.* Minors (i.e., those under 18) and persons of unsound mind may contest a will within four months of becoming adults, or becoming legally competent.

6. Getting Property Before Probate Is Complete

If there is a particular item left to a person by will that the inheritor wants to get as fast as possible (before probate is completed), he can petition the court for transfer of that item two months after the first publication of notice to creditors. If the court accepts that there will surely be enough money in the estate to pay all creditors and fees, even if that item is transferred to the beneficiary, the court can order that item transferred at once.

7. The Independent Administration of Estates Act in California

Unless the decedent's will prohibits this type of administration (which it rarely does), California law allows the executor to obtain an order from the probate court (after notice and a hearing) authorizing him to perform many estate functions without direct judicial supervision or reporting. He must, however, give written ''advice of intended action'' to the inheritors under the will for a number of specific acts. These include the sale or exchange of personal property; leases of real property for more than one year; payment of family allowances, and the investment of the funds of the estate. If any of the beneficiaries object to the executor's action, they can obtain an automatic restraining order from the probate court, forbidding the executor from so acting until he obtains judicial approval. Finally, the executor is still required to obtain court approval for sale or exchange of real property; allowance of executor's and attorney's fees; preliminary or final distribution of the estate assets; paying family allowance beyond twelve months; borrowing money or pledging security for a loan, and similar matters, mostly involving real property.

This recent amendment to the Probate Code (adopted in 1975) unfortunately does not alter probate fees for either the executor or attorney, even though both will do less paperwork under these provisions. But at least they should speed up the final distribution to those inheriting under the will, even if the fees aren't lowered.

H.   What Happens When There's No Will — ''Intestate Proceedings''

If you die intestate (either because you did not prepare a will, or for some reason your will is declared invalid), the distribution of your property is controlled by California probate law. Also, the property of persons who cannot make a valid will, such as minors or incompetents, is distributed under these intestacy laws. Lawyers thus say that everyone has a will — if a person doesn't write a valid one, the state of California ''has written one for him.''

---

* The courts are reluctant to extend the time for any person to challenge a will beyond the four month period; anyone who tries for such an extension needs a good excuse.

An intestate estate must be "probated" (called "administration"), just like one where there's a will. The supervisor of an intestate estate, the "administrator," is appointed by the probate court. This is one of many possible examples of the loss of powers, without any offsetting benefits, that occurs when one dies intestate. Another is the fact that the administrator must post a bond, adding to the costs of administration. In a will, the requirement of a bond is normally waived.

The inheritors in intestacy proceedings are always exclusively limited to a spouse, children or "lineal descendants"* and other blood or adopted relations and "next of kin." If you want to leave any property or bequest to anyone who isn't such an heir (for example, an unrelated person you are living with or another friend), you must do it by will or other specific property transferring device such as insurance or a trust. It is particularly important that unmarried couples realize that intestate succession rules leave them out in the cold. In intestacy proceedings, your property is distributed by mathematical formula, as follows:

1. Community Property

If the decedent was married and died intestate, all of his one-half share of community property passes to his surviving spouse. The other one-half share is already owned by the surviving spouse (see Chapter 7, *Families and Community Property,* for a discussion of these types of property).

2. Separate Property

If the decedent also left some separate property, its distribution depends on his family situation. If there is:

a) a surviving spouse and one child (or grandchildren** of a deceased child) the separate property of the estate is divided one-half to spouse, one-half to child;

b) a surviving spouse and more than one child (including one child living and grandchildren of one or more deceased children), the separate property estate is divided one-third to the spouse, and the remainder (two-thirds in all) in equal shares to children (and lawful issue of deceased children) by "right of representation."***

---

* A "lineal descendant" is one in a direct line of descent. A child, grandchild, and great grandchild are lineal descendants of a father or mother, while a brother or cousin is not. Sorry to have to use this term, but it's one of those words of art for which there is no substitute.

** The legalese term for the children of a deceased person is "lawful issue," which includes children, grand-children, great-grandchildren, etc., whether legitimate or illegitimate.

*** "Right of representation" means that the "lineal" descendants of a deceased person succeed to that person's share of an estate. There is one exception to the rule that the pie is first divided into equal shares between living children and deceased children with living lineal descendants. The exception applies in the situation where a person dies and all his or her children are dead, but there are lineal descendants. Probate Code Section 221 says simply that, if all the children are dead, the pie is no longer initially divided at this generation, but now at the grandchild generation with all the grandchildren sharing equally.

EXAMPLE: Decedent, surviving spouse, three deceased children, #1 and #2 have two surviving children, #3 has four surviving children.

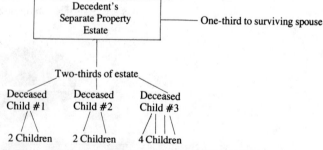

If two-thirds of the estate were divided by "right of representation" which would be the case if even one of the children survived, the two-thirds of the estate would be divided into three equal portions, one for each deceased child, and the children of Child #1 and Child #2 would each receive one-half of their parent's share; the children of Child #3 would each receive one-fourth of their parent's share. Instead, under Section 221 all eight children share equally in the two-thirds of the estate — each receives one-eighth of the total two-thirds.

Thus, if there is a surviving spouse, one surviving child, and two grandchildren of a deceased child, the surviving spouse receives one-third of the estate, the child one-third, and the grandchildren each get one-sixth of the estate (totalling the one-third their deceased parent would have received).

c) If there is no surviving spouse, the entire estate goes to the decedent's children, or the "issue" of dead children if one or more children has died, leaving children of their own. If all descendants (say children) are of the same degree of kindred to the decedent, they share equally; otherwise the people in the first generation share equally and those in the next generation take by right of representation.

In other words, if a decedent (whose spouse died) leaves five children, all share equally. If all her children are dead but four grandchildren are alive, they all share equally. But if four children are alive and also four grandchildren, all of whom are the children of the fifth child who died before the decedent, the pie is divided into five equal shares. Each child gets one-fifth of pie, and the remaining one-fifth is divided by the four grandchildren. This means that each grandchild gets one-twentieth of the estate.*

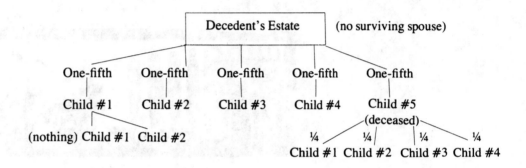

d) If there is a surviving spouse and no children or "issue," the separate property estate goes one-half to spouse, and one-half to decedent's parents in equal shares, or to the surviving parent if one parent is dead, or, if both are dead, to their issue (brothers and sisters of decedent), and the issue of either of them (nieces and nephews) by right of representation.

e) If there are no surviving spouse, children, grandchildren, etc. or immediate family such as parents, sisters, brothers, nieces or nephews, the estate goes to the next of kin.

Numerous intricate family situations are covered by the specific intestacy provisions of the probate code. If there is no next-of-kin, no living relation at all, the property "escheats" (one of my favorite legal words) to the State of California. In the old days, property "escheated" to the king (after he'd first beheaded you for treason).

Intestate inheritance can get complicated, especially if there is no immediate family. If such an unusual question does arise in your life, you can probably figure out who gets what by puzzling your way through the probate code sections, commencing with 3200, and determining which section applies to your situation. Or you can pay a lawyer to do this for you. As most people will never have to deal with these problems, either because the decedent left a will, or the family inheritance situation is quite simple, I won't spend more time on it here.

---

* If some of the living children also have children, these grandchildren get nothing. Only the "issue" of deceased children participate by right of representation.

I. The Case of the Missing Millionaire, or . . .

What happens if someone who owns property in California disappears? What can the family, or friends, do, legally, to control and manage the property of a person who cannot be found? The answers are found in the California Probate Code. Essentially, after a person who is (was) a resident of California is missing for 90 days, a trustee can be appointed to manage his affairs, until the person is found. If a person owns property in California (whether or not he was a resident) and has been missing for at least seven years, the Probate Court can be petitioned to distribute his estate as if he were dead. In most cases, there is a three year waiting period before final distribution, so before the estate of a missing person can be distributed to his inheritors, at least ten years from the date of disappearance must have passed. Once these ten years have passed, and a person has been declared legally dead and his property distributed, he cannot later regain it, even if he can prove who he is, and that in truth he's very much alive.

There are special provisions applicable to persons missing while serving in the Armed Forces; hopefully those provisions were last and finally used for Vietnam P.O.W.'s.

J. Probate Reform

Probate ''reform'' is something almost everyone claims to be in favor of, like reducing gasoline consumption, preventing drought, or keeping snails out of the garden. Yet there appears to be no serious pressure on the California legislature to adopt real probate reform on the order of the simplified estate distribution system used in England or civil law countries. Probate reform is certainly not a hot, glamorous issue, so without public pressure, politicians (many of whom are lawyers) are unlikely to become seriously interested in it. Some of the forces deterring reform are obvious: inertia, public confusion about what probate is, and lawyers' greed. After all, what did lawyers go to law school for, if not to be able to live like aristocrats?

There's more at work here, though. Ours is a society professing devotion to equality, but also to freedom, and that leaves us a little confused about money, especially inherited wealth. We don't have any blood aristocracy, but the grandchildren of capitalists like Rockefeller, Vanderbilt or Kennedy can inherit money taxed at a much lower rate than any English lord or French duke can. Lawyers are the priests of money. So corporate lawyers dress in priest-like garb (dark, dull clothes), have grave demeanors and somber offices. Part of the law's function (quite a large part indeed) is to legitimize wealth. Those millions may have been ill-gotten gains when some robber baron acquired them by crushing his competitors and exploiting labor, natural resources and consumers, and often bribing several politicians as well. But after three generations of lawyers get through with that money, it becomes respectable, clean and almost holy. Probate is one essential part of the sanctification process. If you make the legal process surrounding the transfer of money on death complex and formal, it seems to help keep attention off more basic matters, like who decides what the rules are about money anyway, and who gets benefits from them.

As I have said, probate is obviously not designed for the efficient handling of the average moderate estate where there are almost never any contests, frauds or conflicts. The only real incentive to probate reform is the fact that no one with any sense uses the system any longer except for small amounts of property. Americans are as good at avoiding rules as they are at inventing them. It may start to occur to lawyers that something is wrong when absolutely no one uses their overpriced, over-complicated, time-consuming dinosaur.

6

Simple Probate Methods
for Estates Under $30,000

A. Introduction

If the probate estate is worth less than $30,000 and does not include real property in California,* very simple probate methods are available which avoid the cost and delay of normal probate. These methods can work well when combined with other probate-avoidance or estate reduction methods such as joint tenancy or inter vivos trusts. As you will see by reading section B below, significant amounts of property are exempt from being counted as part of the $30,000 maximum, so, in fact, the maximum (depending on the circumstances of the particular estate) is often considerably more than $30,000.

When these simplified procedures are used, there is no "administration" of the estate. This means that the usual (tedious) steps of a probate proceeding which I outlined in Chapter 5 are not required. Instead, through quick, summary methods, the estate can be claimed by the heirs or inheritors. Unfortunately, because of dollar and other limitations, these procedures are of limited use.** But, because of the potential savings of time and expense involved, it is worthwhile to plan beforehand to see if an estate can qualify to use these methods.

EXAMPLE: Suppose Harry, knowing he is ill, wants to transfer what (relatively little) he has to his wife, or to his minor child, if his wife predeceased him. Harry has an estate consisting of a house, with a market value of $100,000 and an equity of $25,000. His personal property (mostly savings accounts) is worth $17,000. If Harry leaves all his estate by will, the probate estate fees will be based on an estate of $117,000; and probate will take months. **But,** if Harry transfers the house outside of probate (via joint tenancy, say), his probate estate will be only $17,000 (the personal property), which can be easily transferred to his heirs as discussed in this chapter.

---

* Real property transferred by joint tenancy or inter vivos trust is not an "interest" in real property for this purpose. See Chapter 9, *Trusts,* and Chapter 10, *Joint Tenancy.*

**There are other (truly specialized) summary methods. For instance, under the Military Veterans Code, if the decedent was residing in a California Veterans' Home, all the decedent's property must be summarily delivered to the decedent's spouse, next-of-kin, heirs, etc., upon their presentation of proof of their relationship to the decedent, without any probate.

B.   How to Transfer the Property — the "Affidavit of Right"

If the decedent leaves an estate of less than $30,000 (net) and leaves no real property or interest in real property in California, certain lawful heirs or inheritors can obtain that estate simply by filing an "Affidavit of Right" with the person or institution holding the decedent's asset(s).* An affidavit of right can be filed independent of any probate proceeding and, if properly filed, is fully sufficient to enable the inheritors to obtain legal title and actual possession of the decedent's property.

The affidavit must specifically swear that the total value of the decedent's estate in California is less than $30,000, but there are certain important items of property that may be excluded from the $30,000 total. Assets which may be owned in addition to $30,000 include (1) any motor vehicle the decedent owned; (2) any amounts due the decedent for services in the U.S. Armed Forces; (3) any salary due the decedent below $5,000, "including compensation for unused vacation;" (4) real property held in "joint tenancy" or an "intervivos trust," or any real property outside of California.

The affidavit of right can be prepared and filed by any of the following person or persons, if they are entitled to all of the decedent's estate, either by will, or, if there is no will, by the laws if intestate inheritance as discussed in Chapter 5.

Surviving spouse	Parents(s)
Children	Brothers or sisters
Lawful issue of a deceased	Conservator, guardian or trustee
brother or sister	of such person(s)

---

* Under Section 630 and following sections of the Probate Code.

If there is more than one beneficiary under a will (or the intestacy laws if there is no will), all the beneficiaries must be in the classes set out above, and all must agree to sign the affidavit of right. If they do not, it cannot be used. So affidavits of right cannot be used to leave property to friends, lovers, or other non-blood relations.

The person(s) entitled to the decedent's estate either by will or intestate succession can obtain those assets by giving the person or organization who actually holds the assets proof that they belonged to the decedent, as well as the affidavit of right. If a will was left by the decedent, this must also be presented. The person or organization receiving that proof must promptly release the assets to the person(s) who filed the affidavit. The release of the assets "shall fully discharge the person, representative, corporation officer or body (holding it) from any further liability" regarding it. Moreover, the Probate Code specifically states that the person shall release the asset "without the necessity of inquiring into the truth of any of the facts stated in the affidavit."

There is no procedure established by which the affiant's declaration that the decedent's (net) estate in California is worth less than $30,000 is to be verified. In this one instance, the Probate Code appears to go by the honor system. Any deliberate, knowing falsification of the worth of the decedent's estate is, of course, fraud, and can be punished (if detected) by the civil or criminal penalties imposed on persons guilty of fraud.

The basic purpose of the "Affidavit of Right" is to enable families of a decedent who left a small estate to obtain the cash and other assets they need immediately without a lot of red tape.

EXAMPLE: Suppose Harry dies and by his will his sole beneficiary is his adult daughter, Myra. Harry owned no real estate, and his estate totals $17,000. Let's say he lost his house in his divorce, which is why Myra and not his ex-wife is his beneficiary. Of the $17,000, $5,000 is owed to him by his friend, Charley, $7,000 is in a savings account, and $5,000 is personal property. Myra simply completes the affidavits such as the one shown below and attaches a copy of the will. She then gives one set of documents to Charley, another to Harry's bank, and the third to the holder(s) of the personal property. Charley then owes the $5,000 to Myra, on the same terms as he owed it to Harry. The bank and the holder(s) of Harry's personal property must release it to her promptly. If they don't, she should show them a copy of the Probate Code, Section 630. If this doesn't work, she should see a lawyer, who can probably straighten things out with a phone call.

Here is a sample "Affidavit of Right."

━━━

_____ hereby declare(s):

1. (I/We) make this Declaration in order to induce _____
to transfer to (me/us) the property described in paragraph(s) 2a, b, and/or c below under the provisions of Section 630 of the California Probate Code, and to that end represent that the following statements are true.

2. (The Decedent) died in the City of _____,
County of _____,
State of _____,
on or about _____ 19_____,
leaving

(either)

a will, and leaving no real property in the State of California, nor interest therein, nor lien thereon.

(or)

no will, and leaving no real property in the State of California nor interest therein, nor lien thereon.

(continue)

The total value of Decedent's property in California **(excluding any motor vehicle of which Decedent is the owner or the legal owner)** over and above any amounts due to Decedent for services in the armed forces of the United States, and over and above the amount of salary not exceeding five thousand dollars ($5,000), including compensation for unused vacation, owing to Decedent for services from any employment, does not exceed thirty thousand dollars ($30,000), and includes the following:

    a. The sum of $_____ on deposit with _____ at its _____ Office which (was/was not) community property of Decedent and (his/her) surviving spouse;

    b. The contents of safe deposit box No. _____ at the Office of _____, which (was/was not) community property of Decedent and (his/her) surviving spouse; and

    c. Personal property valued at $_____, consisting of

_____

_____

which (was/was not) community property of Decedent and (his/her) surviving spouse.

    3. (I am/Each of us is) the surviving spouse, a child, the lawful issue of a deceased child, a parent, a brother or sister, the lawful issue of a deceased brother or sister, of the Decedent, or the conservator of the property or guardian of the estate of any such person.

(either)

(I/We) have a right to succeed to the property of Decedent;

(or)

(I am/We are) the sole beneficiary(ies) under the last will and testament of Decedent;

(continue)

and (my/our) name(s), address(es), relationship(s) to Decedent, and age(s) are as follows:

Name	Address	Relationship to Decedent	Age

    4. No probate proceeding is now being or has been conducted for Decedent's estate.

(optional)

    5. (I/We jointly and severally) agree to hold _____ harmless and indemnify it against all liability, claims, demands, loss, damages, costs, and expense whatsoever, which it may incur or suffer by reason of the transfer, payment, or delivery to me (us) of any property pursuant hereto.

(continue)

    (I/We) declare under penalty of perjury that the foregoing is true and correct, and that this Declaration is executed on _____, 19_____, in the City of _____, County of _____, State of _____.*

_____   _____

_____   _____

_____   _____

Affidavits of Right are not used as commonly as you might think. Many estates either contain some interest in California real property, or exceed the $30,000 limitation. There are at least two instances though, where planning for the use of an Affidavit of Right is advisable:

---

* A notary can be used, but is not required. The declaration under penalty of perjury is sufficient.

1. Where most of the decedent's estate is in another state and will be probated there. Instead of ancillary probate administration in California, assets here may be able to be claimed by filing Affidavits of Right;

2. If the bulk of an estate is transferred, or can be transferred, by probate-avoidance means, the estate could be reduced below the $30,000 limit, and probate then avoided altogether. In this case, however, there might be federal estate taxes to be calculated and paid.

EXAMPLE: Aunt Myra has an estate consisting of a house in San Francisco, a summer cottage at Stinson Beach, the inexpensive furnishings of her two houses, a bank account of $60,000, lots of life insurance, and various heirlooms worth a total of $18,000. She wants to distribute this estate to her deceased sister's children. Myra thinks she doesn't have much property; she acquired her houses years ago, when "a dollar was a dollar" and prices low. But, in fact, her estate is worth at least a couple of hundred thousand dollars. Rather than have all this property subject to regular probate, she transfers it as follows:

1. She transfers the houses and furnishings into revocable inter-vivos trusts;

2. She creates a "totten trust" bank account for her savings (see Chapter 9);

3. She assigns her life insurance policy and relinquishes all incidents of ownership. (There may be gift taxes due. See Chapter 4.)

The only asset remaining in her probate estate is thus the heirlooms, worth less than the $30,000 limit for affidavits of right. She can distribute these by will, and her sister's children can claim them simply and speedily by using an affidavit of right. Federal taxes may be assessed against the entire estate though, so some means of arranging payment of them must be arranged.

C.   Problems When Using "Affidavits of Right"

There will normally not be federal estate taxes due on any estate eligible for summary transfer by affidavit of right, because the amounts involved are well under the limits that can be transferred federal tax-free.

There are no longer any California inheritance taxes so none can be owed. Since California no longer issues "Consent to Transfer" forms, there may be problems with the person or institution who receives the "Affidavit of Right." What proof can they require that you are legally who you claim to be—the person entitled to the decedent's property? At present, this isn't clear. The affidavit of right should suffice by itself. If you encounter resistance, try a little patience: explain the affidavit of right procedure and produce valid I.D. (as if you were cashing a check).

D. Obtaining Legal Title to Cars, Boats or Other Specific Types of Property

If an estate that qualifies for transfer by affidavit of right contains items like a car or a boat, there are specific procedures available to get legal title to those items transferred to the new owner.

❖**A Car.** A person entitled to a car by affidavit of right can have ownership transferred to him by submitting to the Department of Motor Vehicles:

a) the original certificate of ownership (pink slip);

b) the registration card;

c) the completed affidavit of right, with an assertion that there are no (remaining) creditors of the decedent (DMV Form 5 can be used for this purpose);

d) (In most cases) a smog-control compliance certificate.

The DMV does not require a certified copy of the death certificate.

❖**A Boat.** A Person entitled to a boat by affidavit of right can have ownership tranferred by submitting to the DMV:

a) the affidavit of right, with an assertion that there are no unpaid creditors of the decedent;

b) the certificate of ownership, and the vessel number certificate.

Again, a death certificate is not normally required.*

❖ **Miscellaneous Personal Property.** A person entitled to the decedent's personal property, by affidavit of right, can simply take possession of it, if there is no other person who had possession of it when the decedent died. This would include property stored in a garage or in the decedent's apartment, etc. If someone else has possession of property (had borrowed the decedent's tractor or living room set), the affidavit of right should be presented to them unless they are willing to release the property informally.

❖**Property the Decedent Was Entitled to from the Probate of Another's Estate.** In the rare instance where an affidavit of right can be used for property the decedent was entitled to from another estate, the affidavit must be filed by the executor of that second estate in.that probate proceeding, and the probate judge will then order the property released.

---

* Section 9916, Vehicle Code.

E. Probate Code Section 630.5 — Collection of Bank Accounts by Surviving Spouse

Section 630.5 of the Probate Code allows a summary means for a surviving spouse to collect a bank account not exceeding $500.00 if the decedent's total estate is under $5,000. The section is so restrictive that it appears to have almost no practical use, expecially since the adoption of community property petitions allows a spouse to avoid probate for all community assets left to her. In any case, here's how this bank account provision works.

If the value of an estate is less than $5,000* whether or not it contains an interest in real property, the surviving spouse (if entitled to inherit by will or intestate law) can obtain money up to $500 the decedent had in a bank account(s) by filing an affidavit of right with the bank. The only time this type of affidavit would even possibly be useful is where the decedent has a very small estate, but some interest in real property, so the normal affidavit of right procedure could not be used. It's have to imagine any estate that has any interest in real property (at today's market prices) that would be worth less than $5,000.

F. A Decedent's Immediate Family Has Right to Estates Under $20,000

There are special Probate Code sections authorizing the Probate Court to "set aside" an estate under $20,000 to the surviving spouse or minor children of the decedent. This summary transfer can be ordered whether or not the decedent left his estate to his family. This is one rare instance in California law of a legal limitation on the right of any person to dispose of his property by will however he chooses. If the total estate is worth $18,000, and the surviving spouse is left only $10,000 of it by will, she can claim, and obtain, all $18,000 under Section 640.**

It isn't clear to this observer why a spouse with an estate under $20,000 cannot fully disinherit the surviving spouse and/or minor child, while a spouse with a larger estate can. Perhaps the legislature determined that in larger estates there will be enough community property to assist the surviving family. Or maybe they didn't think about it. Or perhaps the provision of a "family allowance" was deemed sufficient family protection for larger estates (see Chapter 7). In any case, the Probate Code is quite clear. If the (net) estate is under $20,000, this section applies. There does not appear to be any "discretion" for the judge to refuse to award the spouse this money, no matter what the judge thinks of the situation. If the estate is over $20,000, normal probate procedures (including the possibility of a family allowance) are followed.

For purposes of "setting aside" an estate under Probate Code Section 640, the value of the estate is determined by appraising all of the assets in it, and then deducting: (1) the amount of all liens and encumbrances; (2) the value of any homestead interest available to the spouse or minor children.*** Property held in joint tenancy is not included as part of the probate estate. Thus, non-joint tenancy real property can be included as part of an estate that is "set aside" for the surviving spouse, as long as the net value of the estate is less than $20,000. Unlike the affidavits of right discussed above, there must be some sort of court petition filed to have an estate "set aside" under Probate Code Section 640. In addition, the value of the estate must be appraised; the mere declaration of the surviving spouse that the estate (less liens and homestead value) is under $20,000 is not sufficient here.

A SMALL GOLD COIN IS PLACED IN THE MOUTH OF A LAOTIAN WHO IS BEING PREPARED FOR BURIAL. IT SYMBOLIZES THAT EARTHLY GOODS OF ARE OF SO LITTLE VALUE THAT A SINGLE COIN IS ALL THE DECEASED WILL TAKE WITH HIM TO THE GRAVE.

---

* The Probate Court does not state how the $5,000 figure is calculated, but since this section is in the same article as are affidavits of right, presumably the exclusions previously listed are applicable here too.

** The fact that the decedent provided for his spouse or children in other ways outside of his probate estate (say by joint tenancy, insurance or trusts) does not reduce their right to claim a set aside under this section.

*** A "homestead interest" is a family house, protected by a declaration of homestead, either filed before the decedent died, or set aside as a "probate homestead" after his death.

If a petition to "set aside" is filed, it can be done either with a probate proceeding or separately. In either case, the court will order the "executor or administrator" of the estate to "cause an inventory and appraisal" of the estate to be made. It isn't clear what happens if there is a speedy petition filed before the probate proceedings begin, in which case there wouldn't yet be a confirmed administrator or executor. Presumably, the court would have to appoint an appraiser somehow. The executor's or administrator's appraisal is then filed with the court. The court must then determine that: (1) the estate, over and above all liens and encumbrances at date of death and the value of a homestead set apart, does not exceed $30,000, and (2) the following expenses have been paid: last illness, funeral charges, and the expenses of administration, which would include the costs to prepare the appraisal. Then the estate is ordered transferred to the spouse or surviving children.

IMPORTANT: The spouse cannot have remarried at the time of the court order. If so, she loses all her right to have the estate "set aside." Also those obtaining the decedent's property by this method (i.e., either the surviving spouse or the minor children) are personally liable for the unsecured debts of the decedent, up to the value of the estate, for one year after they get title to its property.

Given the existence of the community property petition (see Chapter 7), there appears little advantage to plan to use the "set aside" process described here (the "set aside" was adopted long before the community property petition). I include information on the "set aside" mostly because it exists, not because it is particularly useful, except in the rare situation where a decedent with an estate of less than $20,000 left some of it to someone other than his spouse or minor children.

7

Families and Community Property

A. Introduction

If you're married, there are many special rights conferred on you by California and federal law that are useful in estate planning. These rights are available only to married couples and their families. Single persons can skip this chapter, although if you're really fascinated by estate planning, maybe you too should consider getting married, at least in your autumnal years.* Most of the rights discussed here derive from the legal concept called "community property," an ancient gothic marriage law which passed to Spain sometime in the 7th century, and through the Spanish explorers and settlers to California. Unlike English common law, where in feudal times the husband owned all marital property and a wife had no legal rights and could not even will property, cultures adhering to community property recognized that in a marriage both persons work, so any property acquired by either of them during the marriage should be co-owned by both.

Today, in California, we still follow community property rules. This means that, during the marriage of persons residing in this state, all real property acquired in California and all personal property (acquired anywhere) from either's earnings is community property and both the husband and wife own an undivided half interest in this property. The law also says that both spouses have an equal right to manage the community property—except that a spouse operating a community property business has the right to manage it exclusively. On the death of one spouse, one-half of all community property is always legally owned by the surviving spouse. The other half becomes part (or all, if there is no separate property) of the estate of the deceased spouse.

---

* I can't seriously imagine people signing up with the local computer dating service to save on estate taxes, but unmarried couples may wish to think about marriage, especially in a situation where illness or age makes death imminent. Why? Because, while it is commonly cheaper for a couple to live together unmarried as far as income tax liability is concerned (see *The Living Together Kit*, Ihara and Warner, Nolo Press), it is almost always cheaper as far as death taxes are concerned to die married.

Death tax and probate laws encourage the transfer of the deceased spouse's interest in community and separate property to the surviving spouse. Federal tax law, as discussed in Chapter 3, allows a tax-free transfer of all property left to a surviving spouse. Equally important, recent amendments to the California Probate Code have created a procedure for transferring community property to a surviving spouse **outside of probate** by using a "Community Property Petition." There is no dollar limit to the amount that can be transferred by this method, and it does not require any probate avoidance devices, such as joint tenancy or inter vivos trusts.

The surviving spouse and minor children are also protected by probate law from sudden poverty that might be caused by the death of the family provider. To this end, the law provides the surviving spouse and children with an immediate family allowance from the estate (before probate is completed) if they are needy and have no other source of funds. The surviving spouse and children also have the right to have a "probate" homestead created if there is no existing homestead protecting the family home from creditors (see Section F(5) of this chapter), and to the exemption of certain personal community property (including the decedent's share of that property) from attachment by creditors.

B.   What Is Community and Separate Property?

Determining which assets of a married couple are community property and which are separate property can be crucial for marital estate planning. All separate property can be willed to whomever the testator (will writer) desires, whereas, as you should know by now, she has authority over only her one-half share of the community property. Litigation by bitter ex-spouses has created a large number of judges' decisions regarding fine points of community property law. This chapter does not pretend to cover many of the esoteric problems that can arise.* I do cover the basic rules, which are all you will need for most estate planning situations. Fortunately, these are relatively simple.

There is a presumption that any property acquired during the marriage by either spouse is community property;

All wages earned during the marriage by either person are community property;

Property owned by a person before marriage is that person's separate property, as is income received from that property. To keep this clear, people can draft pre-marriage agreements specifying what is their separate property at time of marriage. See *The People's Guide to California Marriage and Divorce Law* for more details. For example, if Betty owned an apartment complex before she married John, the apartments would remain her separate property as would all rents she received after marriage;

A gift or inheritance made to one person in the marriage is that person's separate property. Often, gifts are made so they are not clearly given to just one spouse and, if there is any uncertainty, the gift will be considered to be community property, because of the presumption that property acquired during the course of the marriage is community property;

Separate property should be kept separate. If separate property is "commingled" with community property so that the two are functionally merged, all that property becomes community property.

EXAMPLE: Brenda and Andy are married, and have a joint (community) checking account. Brenda receives a gift of $2,000 which she puts into that account. Sometime later, after many other deposits of community property wages and withdrawals to pay bills, Brenda and Andy use $5,000 from the checking account to buy a car. The car is fully community property. This is because it can't be proved that the specific $2,000 that was Brenda's separate property was used as part of the car purchase price. The $2,000 was so thoroughly "commingled" with community property that it lost its original character of separate property.

After the date of a permanent marital separation, all earnings and acquisitions (not made by using existing community assets) are separate property. Thus, if John and Betty separate on December 31, 1981 but don't get a divorce until January 1, 1983, the earnings of both during 1982 are separate property;

Neither spouse can make a gift of community property to a third person without the other's consent. Written consent is required for any gift of home furnishings;

Neither spouse can sell community **real** property without the other's written consent. However, community **personal** property can be sold by either party.

There are many specific examples that could be given to illustrate the principles set out above. Here are three. Before going on, be sure that you understand each:

EXAMPLE: Brenda and Andy purchase a life insurance policy on Andy's life with community property funds. Proceeds of a life insurance policy purchased with community property funds are community property—so the surviving spouse has a one-half interest in the proceeds, even if the policy names someone else as the sole beneficiary;

EXAMPLE: Brenda is injured when Albert rear ends her at a traffic signal. Andy owns half of any money she obtains because of the accident. Personal injury recoveries (except for accidents after the parties have separated) are community property;

EXAMPLE: Brenda starts a successful restaurant and earns $50,000 which she deposits in a certificate of deposit. This is obviously community property, but, in addition

---

* See *The People's Guide to California Marriage and Divorce Law*, Warner and Ihara, Nolo Press (see order information at the end of this book for more details).

to a one-half interest in this money, Andy's community property interest in the business includes one-half of all assets, such as "good will," accounts receivable, etc. — not just the cash in the bank.

NOTE: Let me repeat — there are many types of complex questions that can arise as to what is community and what is separate property. If you are faced with a confusing situation regarding your estate, you should probably first check *The People's Guide to California Marriage and Divorce Law* and then double check your conclusions with a knowledgeable attorney. Here are two common problem areas:

One spouse owned a business before the marriage and continues to operate it during the marriage. When either spouse dies, how much of this business is separate property, how much is community property? This can depend on how much of any increase in the value of the business was due to the efforts of the spouses after marriage and how much was the result of the natural increase of the business assets as they existed prior to the marriage, as well as a number of other factors.

Improvements are made to the separate (real) property of one spouse, using community funds. When one spouse dies, how much of that property is separate property and how much is community property? This often depends on the intentions of the parties at the time the improvements were made.

C.   What Is "Quasi-Community" Property?

"Quasi-community" property may sound like legal gibberish, but it is an important concept, particularly for married couples who have recently moved to California. It is property that California law treats as community property, although it was acquired in a non-community property state. Specifically, if during the marriage, while the parties were domiciled (resided) in another state, either or both of them acquire personal property located anywhere or real property in California which would have been community property if they were domiciled here, that property is treated as community property once they move here.

EXAMPLE: A husband, while married and living in New York (not a community property state) buys some stocks, paying for them from his salary and registering them in his name as sole owner. Five years later, the couple moves to California to live. The stocks are now treated as community property (they become "quasi-community" property) and, upon her husband's death, the wife owns one-half of them.*

IMPORTANT: Real property purchased outside of California with community property funds is also quasi-community property, even if owned in only one spouse's name.

For probate purposes, quasi-community property is treated the same as community property. This means that the surviving spouse has an automatic one-half ownership of quasi-community property after the other spouse's death. However, for federal estate tax purposes, quasi-community property is treated as separate property — i.e., here the full value of all the stock would be included in husband's estate, for federal tax purposes.

---

* But the wife cannot dispose of her half interest, or prevent the transfer of this quasi-community property while the husband is alive. If the "non-acquiring" spouse survives the "acquiring" spouse, she is entitled to one-half the quasi-community property.

D. Determining the Value of Your Community and Separate Property

If you are married, you should determine the nature of your property in order to properly plan your estate. As I've discussed, there can be different estate tax, testamentary or probate consequences depending on whether property is community property, quasi-community property or separate property. If you have a simple estate with all your property bought by community funds during the marriage, you have no problem. However, if you have a more complicated estate, with different types of property in it, it's advisable to determine just what the worth of each form of property is. Use the following form to calculate these values:

	I Community Property	II Quasi- Community Property	III Your Separate Property
A. Personal Property			
cash (dividends, etc.)			
savings accounts			
checking accounts			
government bonds			
listed (private corporation) stocks and bonds			
unlisted stocks and bonds			
money owed you including promissory notes and accounts receivable (including mortgages owed, leases, etc.)			
vested interest in profit sharing plan or pension rights			
automobile and other vehicles (include boats and recreation vehicles)			
art works and jewelry			
miscellaneous			

	I Community Property	II Quasi- Community Property	III Your Separate Property
B. Real Estate (do separately for each piece owned)			
current market value			
mortgages and other liens that you owe on the property			
equity (current market value less money owed)			
your share of that equity if you have less than sole ownership			
C. Business/Property Interests (including patents & copyrights)			
1) name & type of business			
2) percentage you own			
3) when acquired			
4) estimate of present (market) value of your interest			
D. Life Insurance (for each policy list) (If you are **neither** the owner nor beneficiary of a policy, exclude it. See, for more precision, Chapter 8 on insurance.)			
1) company and type (or number) of policy			
2) name of insured			
3) owner of policy			
4) beneficiary of policy			
5) amount collectable			
6) cash surrender value, if any			
Total Value of Assets			

	I Community Property	II Quasi- Community Property	III Your Separate Property
Deduct All Liabilities			
Debts			
Taxes (excluding estate taxes)			
Other liabilities			
Total Liabilities			
Total Net Worth			

E. The Community Property Petition

By filing a summary community property petition, a surviving spouse can readily obtain the portion of the decedent's community property left to him. There is no dollar limit either on the total amount of the estate or the amount of the community property that can be transferred to the surviving spouse by this method. Even if some of the decedent's share of the community property is left to others, the spouse can still obtain his portion without probate.

The method followed to prepare a community property petition is simple. A petition is filed, containing the allegations that the surviving spouse is entitled to listed community property. The reasons for his entitlement must be included (e.g., by right of succession if the decedent died intestate, or under a will leaving the spouse part, or all, of the community property of the decedent). Notice is then given to various interested persons that the community property petition has been filed. After state inheritance taxes are settled, a brief court hearing on the petition is held, and the court, if it finds the petition to be accurate, issues an order confirming that the listed (ex-community) property is now legally owned entirely by the surviving spouse and does not have to pass through probate.*

NOTE: The surviving spouse can also have the court confirm that certain property is in fact his half of the community property, thus avoiding any question of probate of that property, or claims by any other person that the property belongs in the decedent's estate. There seems to be no reason not to have this done, and it could be helpful.

Special Rules for Business

There is a special statutory section providing for protection of the interests of creditors of the deceased spouse's business. If the community property passing to the surviving

---

* As an alternative, if there is a probate proceeding, the community property petition can be filed in that case, although it does not actually become part of it, and is still handled in the same summary way.

spouse under this procedure "consists of business or an interest in a business which the deceased spouse was operating or managing at the time of death," the surviving spouse is required to list all known creditors of the business, and the amounts owed them. The court will then issue orders "necessary to protect the interests of the creditors." Otherwise, business creditors of the decedent have no way to learn whether they should file claims against the community property transferred to the surviving spouse.

1. How to Fill Out the Community Property Petition

Even though the community property petition is summary and does avoid probate, it still involves a fair amount of bureaucratic red tape. It is considerably less complicated and time-consuming than probate, but there still must be a court hearing.

If you are, or might be, a surviving spouse, you should consider filing a community property petition yourself, or you can hire an attorney to do it for you. If you hire a lawyer, you may only need forms filled out or you may want an attorney to handle the whole process. I believe that people can do the community property transfer themselves, but it will, obviously, take some study and effort. There is no set attorney's fee for handling a community property transfer proceeding. The usual attorney's charge is about 50% of what a probate fee for a similar size estate would be. However, as these fees are not fixed, it can pay to compare prices. If you are reluctant to go to court yourself but are comfortable with paperwork, you can complete all or some of the forms before you see an attorney and your fee should be much less since all the attorney has to do is send out a few form notices and make a routine court appearance.

Step 1. Prepare the Petition

Here is the petition that must be filed in a community property transfer proceeding, along with explanations as to how the sections are to be completed. You need an original form for filing with the court, and at least one copy for yourself. The petition is filed in the Probate Department of the Superior Court for your county. The forms used, the Petition, Notice of Hearing, and Community Property Order, can be obtained from the local Superior Court Clerk's office (Civil). Once the Petition is prepared, it is filed with the Clerk of the Probate Department of the County Superior Court. The filing fee varies by county but is roughly $75.00. The Clerk files the original and returns an "endorsed filed" copy to you.

202-105

NAME AND ADDRESS OF ATTORNEY:	TELEPHONE NO.:	FOR COURT USE ONLY
Your Name & Address	Your Telephone Number	

XXXXXXXXX IN PRO PER

Insert name of court, branch court if any, and Post Office and Street Address:

Superior Court, _____ County
Addres

ESTATE OF:		Case Number:
Decedent Spouse's Name	DECEDENT	HEARING DATE:
COMMUNITY PROPERTY PETITION AND PETITION FOR APPROVAL OF FEES		DEPT.: TIME:

Check This If You Want Your Half Of The Community Property Confirmed As Yours

If A Petition For Probate Of The Will Has Been Filed, Check This

1. PETITIONER (Name):   Your Name

   requests

   a. [X] Determination of community property passing to the surviving spouse pursuant to Prob C 650 et seq.
   b. [ ] Confirmation of community property pursuant to Prob C 201.
   c. [ ] Approval of fees.
   d. [ ] This petition be joined with the petition for probate or administration of the decedent's estate.
   e. Immediate appointment of an inheritance tax referee.

2. PETITIONER is

   a. [X] Surviving spouse of the decedent.
   b. [ ] Personal representative of surviving spouse.
   c. [ ] Guardian of the estate or conservator of the property of decedent's surviving spouse.

3. FACTS CONCERNING JURISDICTION

   a. Decedent died on (Date):   Complete
   b. [X] a resident of the above named county of the State of California.
   c. [ ] a nonresident of California and left an estate in the above named county.

4. FACTS CONCERNING HEIRS, DEVISEES AND LEGATEES

   a. The names, addresses, relationships and ages of heirs, devisees and legatees so far as known to petitioner are:

   Name and Address   Relationship   Age

      List All Inheritors Named In The Will. If there's No Will
      You Must List Every Person Entitled To Inheritance By Intestate
      Succession (See Chapter 5, Probate, Section H)

(Continued on Reverse Side)

No attachment permitted less than on a full page (California Rule of Court 201(b)).

Form Approved by the
Judicial Council of California
Effective July 1, 1975

**COMMUNITY PROPERTY PETITION AND
PETITION FOR APPROVAL OF FEES**

Prob C 201-205,
650 et seq.

105

b. The decedent is survived by

(1) ☐ child.   ☐ no child.   **Check Whatever Is True**

(2) ☐ issue of predeceased child. ☐ no issue of predeceased child.

(3) ☐ parent.   ☐ no parent.

c. No surviving child or issue of predeceased child has been omitted from the list of heirs.

d. *(Complete only if neither parent nor issue survived the decedent.)*   **Complete If Appropriate**
The decedent is survived by

(1) ☐ a brother or sister or issue of a predeceased brother or sister and none has been omitted from the list of heirs.

(2) ☐ no brother or sister or issue of a predeceased brother or sister.

5. FACTS CONCERNING COMMUNITY PROPERTY (See Notes Following This Form)

a. Administration of all or part of the estate is not necessary for the reason that all or a part of the estate is community property passing or belonging to the surviving spouse.

b. ☐ The legal description of the deceased spouse's property which is community property passing to the surviving spouse, including the trade or business name of any community property business which the deceased spouse was operating or managing at the time of death, is set forth in attachment 5b.[1]

c. ☐ The legal description of the interest in the community property which petitioner requests the court to confirm to the surviving spouse as belonging to the surviving spouse under Prob C 201, is set forth in attachment 5c.

d. The facts upon which the petitioner bases the allegation that the property described in attachments 5b and 5c is community property are stated in attachment 5d.[2]

e. Names and addresses of all persons named as executors in decedent's will, or appointed as executors or administrators:

    Give Name And Address Of Executor

f. Names and addresses of all persons named in decedent's will (in addition to those previously listed herein):[3]

    List Any Such Persons (Usually There Aren't Any)

6. ATTORNEY'S FEES
The information regarding attorney's fees will be presented to the court at the hearing.

7. FACTS CONCERNING JOINDER
A petition for probate or administration of the decedent's estate

a. ☐ is being filed with this petition.

b. ☐ was filed on (Date):   **Complete If A Petition For Probate Of The Will Was, Or Is, Filed**

Dated: **Complete**

. . . .   **Sign** _____
(Type or print name)   (Petitioner)

I certify (or declare) under penalty of perjury that the foregoing, including facts set forth in all attachments, is true and correct and that this declaration is executed on (Date): . . **Complete**. . . . .
at (Place): . **Complete**. . . . ., California.

. . . . **Complete**. . . . .   **Sign** _____
(Type or Print Name)   (Signature of Petitioner)

8. Total number of pages attached: .   **Complete**

[1] See Prob C Section 656 for required filing of list of known creditors of a business and other information in certain instances.
[2] See Prob C Section 650 for requirement that a copy of will be attached in certain instances.
[3] Required only as specified in Prob C 653(6).

Attachments to the Community Property Petition

These should be typed on 11″ legal paper, although regular typing paper may suffice; but if you don't want to buy legal paper, you'd better check with the Clerk of the Probate Court to see if the court will accept non-legal paper.

Attachment 5b: Describe and identify all community property of decedent transferred to the surviving spouse. (This normally is not difficult. However, if any of this community property is a business, you must also list all creditors of the business and the amounts owing them.)

Attachment 5c: Describe and identify all community property of the **surviving** spouse (i.e., you) which you want confirmed as your own property.

Attachment 5d: Present the facts which prove the property described in 5b and 5c was community property, and attach a copy of the will. Proof that the property is community property can simply be the will, and a statement by the surviving spouse to that effect, e.g.,

"I was married to the decedent, Lance Gawain, on September 4, 1965, was married to him at his death, and all of the property listed in Attachment 5b is community property acquired with community property funds during the course of our marriage."

Step 2. Prepare the Notice of Hearing

Once the petition is filed, the Probate Court Clerk will set the date for a hearing to confirm the petition. Once you have received the court date, you must notify certain persons of the hearing. On the following page is a "Notice of Hearing" in which you type in, as specified, the date, time and place of the hearing.

Step 3. Serve the Notice of Hearing

A copy of the "Notice of Hearing" must be "personally served" by mail* by the petitioner **at least 20 days before the hearing date,** on:

1. the executor named in the will (unless the petitioner is the executor);

2. all heirs of the deceased spouse (i.e., all persons named in the will as inheritors);

3. all persons or their attorneys who requested that special notice be sent them (which rarely happens, but might be done by a creditor of the decedent; if so, you should see an attorney);

4. all persons or their attorneys who have given "notice of appearance" (i.e., are somehow involved in the case, usually in a contested probate proceeding; again, if this occurs in your case, see an attorney);

5. in cases where there is any charitable trust or bequest in the will, the Attorney General's office.

> This notice is required by law. You are not required
> to appear in court unless you desire.

1. NOTICE is hereby given that (name):

   Your Name

   has filed a petition for:

   a. ☐ Probate of will and for letters testamentary.
   b. ☐ Probate of will and for letters of administration with will annexed.
   c. ☐ Letters of administration.
   d. ☐ Authorization to administer under Independent Administration of Estates Act.
   e. ☒ Community property determination pursuant to Prob C 650 et seq.
   f. ☐ Community property confirmation pursuant to Prob C 201 et seq. **(check box f, if applicable)**
   g. ☐ Setting aside estate under Prob C 640.
   h. ☐ Petition to compromise action for wrongful death Prob C 578a.
   i. ☐ Petition for resignation of trustee Prob C 1125.1.
   j. ☐ Other (specify):

   reference to which is hereby made for further particulars.

2. A hearing on the petition is set for

   (date): Complete   at (time): Complete

   Name of court:
   (address):

   Complete

                                                        (Have Clerk Complete This)

3. Dated: Complete . . . . Clerk, By _____ , Deputy

4. This notice mailed on (date): Complete . . . at (place): Complete . . . . , California.

   (Continued on reverse)

NOTE: 1. The Petition refers only to those matters checked above.
2. If this notice is published, print only those items of 1 which are checked and do not print those items which are unchecked.
3. For petitions other than those listed, set forth the nature of the petition.

CLERK'S CERTIFICATE OF ☐ POSTING ☐ MAILING

Have Clerk Complete This If Possible

I certify that I am not a party to this cause and that a copy of the foregoing Notice of Hearing of Petition (Probate)

1. ☐ was posted at

   on _____

2. ☐ was mailed, first class, postage prepaid, in a sealed envelope at the place and on the date shown above to each of the persons whose names and addresses are given below

   and that this certification is executed on the date and at the place shown above.

Clerk, By _____ , Deputy

PROOF OF SERVICE BY MAIL

If Clerk Will Not Complete This, You Must Have Someone Else Do It.
My residence or business address is: ## Not Yourself. Have A Friend Do It.

I am a resident of or employed in the county where the mailing has occurred. I am over 18 years of age and am not a party to this cause. On (date): , at (place): , California, I mailed a true copy of the Notice of Hearing of Petition (Probate) in a sealed envelope deposited in the United States mail with the postage prepaid, addressed to each person named below at the address shown.

☐ A copy of the Petition, with all its designated attachments, was included with the Notice.

I certify (declare) under penalty of perjury that the foregoing declaration is true and correct and that this declaration is executed on (date): , at (place): , California.*

_____   _____
(type or print name)   (Signature of declarant)

NAME AND ADDRESS OF EACH PERSON TO WHOM NOTICE WAS MAILED:

List Each Name And Address Required

_____
*The declaration under penalty of perjury must be signed in California, or in a state that authorizes use of a declaration in place of an affidavit; otherwise an affidavit is required.

Step 4. Prepare the Court Order

Following is the form of Order used for a Community Property Petition. Normally, the Order is prepared (by you or your attorney) before the hearing, and presented to the probate judge at the hearing; check with the judge's clerk to make sure you know how the Order will be handled in his courtroom.

202-105A

NAME AND ADDRESS OF ATTORNEY:	TELEPHONE NO :	FOR COURT USE ONLY
Your Name & Address	Your Phone Number	

XXXXXXXXX IN PRO PER

Insert name of court, branch court if any, and Post Office and Street Address:

Superior Court, _____ County
Address

ESTATE OF:

Decedent Spouse's Name

DECEDENT

COMMUNITY PROPERTY ORDER AND ORDER APPROVING FEES	Case Number: Complete

1. Date of Hearing Complete ☐ Dept. ☐ Div. ☐ Rm. No.: Judge:
   THE COURT FINDS

2. a. All notices required by law have been given.
   b. Decedent died on (Date): Complete
   c. ☐ a resident of the above-named county of the State of California.
   d. ☐ a nonresident of California and left an estate in the above-named county. **Check Appropriate Boxes**
   e. ☐ All inheritance taxes due by reason of the transfer of property described in the petition filed pursuant to Section 650 have been paid; ☐ the Inheritance Tax Referee has filed a certification that no inheritance tax is due; or ☐ the State Controller has, in writing, consented to the granting of this order without the prior fixing or payment of any inheritance tax.
   THE COURT FURTHER FINDS AND ORDERS

3. a. ☐ The property described in Attachment 3a is community property and passes to (Name):
   Complete (See Attachment #3 a & b) . . . ., the surviving spouse and no administration thereon is necessary.
   b. ☐ See Attachment 3b for further order respecting transfer of the property to the surviving spouse.

4. ☐ To protect the interests of the creditors of (Business name): . . . .
   . . . ., a community property business, a list of all of the known creditors of which and the amount owing to each is on file;
   a. ☐ Within . . days from the date hereof, the surviving spouse shall file an undertaking in the amount of $ . . . ., conditioned that the surviving spouse shall pay the known creditors of the community property business the amount owing to each.
   b. ☐ See Attachment 4b for order protecting interest of creditors of the business.

5. a. ☐ The property described in Attachment 5a is community property that belongs to (Name):
   . . . Complete . . . ., the surviving spouse, under Section 201 of the Probate Code, and the surviving spouse's ownership thereof is hereby confirmed.
   b. ☐ See Attachment 5b for further order respecting transfer of the property to surviving spouse.

6. ☐ Attorney's fees are approved in the sum of: $

7. ☐ All property described in the community property petition which is not community property passing to the surviving spouse, or belonging to the surviving spouse under Section 201, shall be subject to administration in the above estate under Division 3 of the Probate Code.

Dated: _____

_____
JUDGE OF THE SUPERIOR COURT
☐ Signature follows last attachment

No attachment permitted less than on a full page (California Rule of Court 201(b)).

Form Approved by the
Judicial Council of California
Effective July 1, 1975

COMMUNITY PROPERTY ORDER AND ORDER APPROVING FEES

Prob C 201, 203, 205,

> Judge Will Decide What's Appropriate

Attachments to the Community Property Order
(Typed on legal paper, preferably; see explanation to Step 1)

■ **Attachments 3a & 3b:** This can be the same list as attachment 5b to the Petition. Usually no further order is required for #3b.

■ **Attachments 5a & 5b:** This can be the list of the surviving spouse's half interest in the community property provided in attachment 5c to the Petition.

THE JUDGE:
IDENTIFIES THE PEOPLE INVOLVED. HEARS TESTIMONY. LOOKS AT DOCUMENTS AND DECIDES THE CASE.

THE ROBE:
HIGH FASHION IN THE MIDDLE AGES. PERHAPS A BIT SILLY TODAY, BUT SEEMS TO MAKE THE JUDGE FEEL IMPORTANT.

THE CLERK:
ANNOUNCES THE CASE. COLLECTS AND MARKS THE DOCUMENTARY EVIDENCE.

THE BAILIFF
GENERALLY DOES NOTHING, BUT IS PRESENT TO PRESERVE ORDER.

Step 5. The Court Hearing

On the day and time of the court hearing, you go to the Probate Court. The court will probably have several matters on the calendar. Notify the clerk that you have arrived, and find out when the court will call your case, and hand the clerk the Order you have prepared, if he wants it then. When your case is heard, the court may ask you a few questions. This will be routine, unless someone challenges the Petition (or the judge is in a particularly grumpy mood). The court will then determine that the listed property is community property to be passed to the surviving spouse (if there are no problems, as there shouldn't be). You then hand the clerk the Order, if you haven't given it to him earlier. The court order:

1. confirms that the surviving spouse's one-half interest in the community property is valid;

2. orders that any of the decedent's community property passing to the spouse is passed to him or her.

In both cases, the order will preclude any further probate proceedings regarding the property. If there is other property also involved, the court can, in its order, declare that the property which is **not** community property passing to the surviving spouse is subject to probate.

F. Community Property and Survivors' Rights

1. Bills

"You can't take it with you" but, even after you're gone, your debts linger and must be paid. All the community property, including the one-half belonging to the surviving spouse, is liable for all debts of the deceased spouse which are chargeable against the community property. The surviving spouse's separate property is not liable for the community property debts of the deceased. Also, the funeral expenses and last illness bills of a person who died are chargeable solely to the decedent's portion of the community assets; the surviving spouse's one-half of the community property is not liable for these debts.

2. The Family Allowance

The decedent's community (or separate) property can be used to provide for a "family allowance" for his or her surviving family. This family allowance is a right that exists independent of the deceased's will or other property transfer devices. Even if he or she cut off the surviving spouse and kids without a dime, the surviving spouse and minor children* are temporarily entitled to a "reasonable allowance" from the estate "as shall be necessary for their maintenance according to their circumstances." This allowance is obtained by filing a simple petition with the probate court, and can be, and usually is, made retroactive to the date of death. The family allowance gets priority over all matters except the costs of last "illness" and "costs of administration" (as always, lawyer's and executor's fees come first, even before starving families). The family allowance can last the length of the probate proceeding.**

Some states have a widow's or widower's "right of election" commonly called "taking against the will." A widow or widower could claim a certain portion of the deceased spouse's estate, even if left less, or nothing, in the decedent's will. California law does not have this "right of election."*** As Chapter 12, *Wills* explains, you can completely disinherit a spouse and/or your children. However, if you marry after the will was made, it is "presumed" you revoked the will as to your wife, even if you never changed the will, and she will receive her intestate share of the estate.**** The disinheriting of children must be clearly and explicitly done. If they are simply omitted, the law will assume that the will writer simply forgot them, and they will receive the share of the decedent's estate they would have been entitled to if he had died without leaving a will. But let me repeat: if it is clearly done, one spouse can deny the other and/or his children any rights at all in his estate.* However, as we have learned, this power does not extend to surviving spouse's right to her own one-half interest in the community property. One-half of the community property already belongs to each spouse and can't be given or willed away by the other.

---

* And any **adult** children who are physically or mentally incapacitated from earning a living and were at least partially dependent on the decedent for support.

** Unless the estate is insolvent (has more debts than assets), in which case the family allowance can only last one year.

*** California lawyers do refer to a "widow's election" which means a will that requires a spouse to allow **her** half of the community property to be disposed of by the decedent's will, or she loses rights to inheritance of the decedent's property. If you are involved in this type of will, see a lawyer.

**** Unless she has been previously provided for by agreement or there is a clear statement in the will that you intend to exclude any future wife (wives).

* Unless the estate is under $20,000, in which case the estate can be ordered "set aside" for the wife or children no matter what the will directs. See Chapter 6.

In practice, the granting (and size) of a family allowance will be entirely up to the probate judge. It is not clear, under the specific wording of the statute, what requirements of actual "need" of the family must be shown. The practice seems to be that, if just one person (i.e., the surviving spouse on behalf of the whole family) applies for a family allowance, "need" is not scrutinized, although the court still must be presented with figures of expenses so it can make a specific dollar figure allowance. However, if there's more than one application (e.g., one from a spouse and another from dependent adult children), the court then examines more closely the parties' actual "needs."

In most cases (certainly in any well-planned estate), there will be no need for any family allowance, since there will be sufficient cash provided (from insurance policies or other assets that don't go through probate) to meet a family's immediate needs. If it's not actually needed, there's normally no reason to apply for a family allowance.

Under the "Independent Administration of Estates Act" (see Chapter 5, *Probate*, Section G(7)), the executor, without court approval, can pay a "reasonable" family allowance to the decedent's family for up to 12 months.* If the allowance lasts more than 12 months, court approval is then required.

Family allowance payments are federally taxable income to the recipient to the extent an estate received income in the year the allowance is paid. However, they are not included as part of any possible estate tax marital deduction.** Finally, a family allowance can be levied on by creditors of the surviving spouse. (Those scoundrels!)

3. Exempt Property – Household Furnishings, Clothing, Etc.

The surviving family (spouse and minor children) are entitled to remain in possession of the household furniture and other personal property of the decedent exempt from "execution" by creditors until the probate inventory is filed.*** After the inventory is filed, the court "in its discretion" may set apart property of the decedent exempt from execution (i.e., the basics) for further use of the family.

4. The Family House

Owning the family home remains the American Dream, although it increasingly appears that those of us who don't already have a down payment made on our dream will have to labor for many years to save enough. In any case, assuming that a family does own a home (whether a separate house or a condominium), California probate law provides protection for it.

Forty days after the decedent's death, the surviving spouse has full power to sell, lease, mortgage or otherwise deal with the community real property, under Probate Code Section 203. No court order of any kind is required. Let me repeat: Once forty days have passed, the surviving spouse has full control over the disposition of all community real property. The proceeds of a sale of that property remain community property, of course, and half belongs to the decedent's estate. There is one limitation. If, before the surviving spouse attempts to dispose of the real property, someone else has recorded, at the County Recorder's office, a notice claiming an interest in the real property under the decedent's

---

* Notice of the allowance must be given to certain specified parties when the first payment is made.

** The estate tax marital deduction is discussed in more detail in Section G of this chapter and Chapter 3.

*** State law, California Civil Procedure Code Section 690 and sections following, specifies that certain types of property cannot be attached, seized, sold or "executed" on by creditors. This property includes most household furnishings, and such items as church pews. If you are experiencing debt problems and are interested in a run-down of assets exempt from attachment in California, see *The California Debtors' Handbook – Billpayers' Rights*, Honigsberg and Warner, Nolo Press.

will, the property cannot be transferred with clear title until that claim is resolved in probate proceedings.

5. The Family Homestead

A homestead may sound like an anachronism from days of sheepherders and pioneers, but in California homesteading is very much alive and important. If you don't have a declaration of homestead on your house, you should have one, as debt problems (say you were the victim of a large lawsuit) can creep up on anyone. Briefly, by recording with the County Recorder a simple declaration of homestead (usually only a page or two) on the family home, you can protect that house from the overwhelming majority of creditors, up to an equity of $45,000 (or $30,000 if the person recording the homestead is under 65 and is **not** the head of a family).* In other words, if your equity in your family house is less than $45,000, most types of creditors cannot foreclose on it once you file a homestead. If your equity is over $45,000, you should be able to refinance on that equity so that you can raise some cash and the equity drops beneath the protected amount.

The surviving family is legally entitled to have a homestead on the family house. If a homestead was recorded while both spouses were alive, this recorded homestead will be "set aside" by the probate court for the family. If no homestead was recorded while both spouses were alive,** the probate court will create one, if there is a need and it is requested to do so. This is called a "probate homestead." A probate homestead is better than none at all (particularly if creditors are pounding on the door, trying to foreclose on the family house***), but it is advisable to have declared a homestead before probate. Whether the homestead is "probate" or "declared" there must still be some probate court petition to establish or confirm its existence. However, if a probate homestead is needed, there can be complications regarding its duration, especially if it is selected from the decedent's separate property. Also, there can be a delay before a probate homestead is actually created, whereas a declared homestead is already recorded.

Another problem of a probate homestead has come about because of the rapid rise of California real estate prices and inflation. If a homesteaded property (probate or not) is appraised so that the equity is over $45,000 (the exempt amount), the property can be foreclosed on by creditors and the excess value over $45,000 can be taken (the owner of the property gets to keep the $45,000). If the homestead was filed while both spouses were alive and their equity becomes more than $45,000, the property could be refinanced. However, once one spouse is deceased, you are stuck with the appraisal.

IMPORTANT: No homestead protects you from foreclosure because of tax liens, certain contractor's liens, or defaults in mortgage payments.

6. Transfer of Community Property by Will

As I have often said, a decedent spouse has control over one-half the community property. The other one-half belongs automatically to the surviving spouse. If both spouses desire to leave their shares of the community property to the surviving spouse, there is, obviously, no problem with disposition. However, if a spouse desires to leave (all or some) of his or her interest in the community property to someone other than the surviving spouse, this may cause problems. First, there may be adverse tax consequences. Second, it may not be easy to pass certain community property by a will. Clearly, you can pass half of a community bank account by just dividing it up, but how do you pass a one-half interest in a car, a valuable painting, or any item which isn't cash, or easily divisible? You could just will it, and hope for the best, but that isn't wise, as it leaves lots of loose ends flying. Perhaps the other person you left the property to won't want it. Perhaps the probate court will order the item sold and the proceeds of the sale distributed. Perhaps the whole mess will end up in a nasty fight. None of this sounds good, does it? A little sensible planning is obviously called for.

Community property law doesn't require that each item be divided 50-50, but that the total worth of each party's share of the community property be equal. Determine, with your spouse, how your community property is to be treated in your wills. A simple

---

* See *Protect Your Home With A Declaration of Homestead*, Warner, Sherman and Ihara, Nolo Press, $5.95. This book contains homestead forms and shows you how to fill them out.

** Or if a homestead was created for a home that was the separate property of the decedent.

*** I repeat, in any well planned estate, this shouldn't occur because there are assets to pay all creditors.

solution to the picture problem would be to have your spouse give you his one-half interest in it and sign it over to you as your separate property. But remember, if his interest is more than $3,000, he'll be liable for gift tax (see Chapter 4). Or you could: 1) agree on a reasonable value for the picture; 2) agree that you are entitled to it in your estate, and 3) agree that your husband is to get something else of equal value in his half. This solution would not normally have gift tax consequences as there would be an equal trade and no gift.

7. Transfers of Community Property While Both Spouses Live

Until recently, the husband had the powers of management and control over all community property. Now, both spouses do. Either spouse can legally transfer any personal community property.* The proceeds for such transfer, of course, remain community property. Legally, written consent is required to make a gift of any community property and to transfer community real property.

8. Changing the Nature of Property from Separate to Community or Vice Versa

Community property can be changed into separate property or vice versa, if both spouses so desire. This can get a little tricky. First, there may be gift tax consequences. Second, changing title to real property may have adverse consequences under Proposition 13. The tax rules now are that a change in the form of ownership by husband and wife is not a transfer for Proposition 13 purposes; i.e., if title is changed from "joint tenancy" to "our community property," there is no Proposition 13 transfer.

Community property assets have traditionally been held by husband and wife in joint tenancy to avoid probate. This is no longer necessary because of the community property petition.

G.   The Marital Exemption

As explained in Chapter 3, Estate Taxes, section B, federal estate tax law now exempts **all** money transferred to a surviving spouse from tax. The complicated "marital deduction," which previously controlled the amount of property/money which could be given tax-free to a surviving spouse, has been repealed. Now, **any** amount of money/ property left to a surviving spouse is transferred free of tax, period.

WARNING! If your will contains a clause designed to minimize estate tax liability under the previous "marital deduction," you may well need your will re-written. The 1981 Tax Act provides that the **old** tax law continues to apply to any will written before September 13, 1981, when a "formula" will provision is used. For example, if your will (written before September 13, 1981) provides your spouse is to receive "whatever she/he can free of estate taxes," that surviving spouse will receive only the exempt amounts under the previous marital deduction, and estate tax exemption. This sum may well be far less than all of your property which can now be transferred to a surviving spouse free of estate tax. In this situation you probably need to revise and up-date your will(s).

IMPORTANT NOTE: Are you really married? For the marital exemption to be available, the surviving spouse must have been legally married to the decedent before death. If, for instance, a divorce decree of one spouse from a prior marriage was invalid or not properly entered, the marital exemption is not available, no matter what the understanding of the surviving spouse was.* Much to many people's surprise, common law marriage does not exist in California. No matter how long you have been living together, you are not married, if you haven't gone through the formalities.

---

* Because of oddities in California divorce law, many thousands of Californians who believe themselves to be married are not. For a full discussion of this area of the law, see *The People's Guide to California Marriage and Divorce Law,* Warner and Ihara, Nolo Press.

Also, for the marital exemption to apply, the surviving spouse must obtain rights and control over the assets transferred to her sufficient so she has the power to include them in her own estate upon her death. Thus, if a decedent's property is left in a trust for children, with the surviving spouse receiving only a "life estate" in that property (she receives only the income from the trust during her life), she cannot include the trust property in her estate, so no marital deduction for the trust property is allowed.

H.   Community Property and the "Second Estate Tax"

A major concern of estate planners is to minimize the "second" estate tax, the tax that will be imposed on the estate of the surviving spouse when he or she dies. Often, for large estates, there can be substantial estate tax savings in the long run if part of the estate of the first spouse to die is transferred to someone other than the surviving spouse. This transfer can be outright, or by means of a testamentary trust, where the surviving spouse has the right to receive the income from the trust during her life, but she cannot spend the trust "principal." It is all too easy for one spouse to leave all of his or her estate to the other spouse without thinking of the tax consequences of this decision. If the surviving spouse will have enough to take care of all his or her financial needs, there are good tax reasons to leave some money to others, especially if the surviving spouse has a short life expectancy. In Chapters 3 and 9, I give detailed examples of the use of trusts to reduce this "second" tax for married couples. Please turn to these chapters and study the examples to gain an idea of just how much money can be saved.

Determining what is precisely the right amount of property to leave to a surviving spouse can be complicated for estates that are well over the amount that can be transferred, to anyone, free of federal estate tax. The calculations can involve an interaction of the marital exemption, the estate tax credit, and the rules governing community and separate property, as well as knowing the surviving spouse's needs. You may be able to work out a good deal of this for yourself, but if a lot of money is involved, consultation with a tax expert (usually a lawyer or an accountant) makes excellent sense.

I.   Community Property and Estate Planning (Generally)

Numerous other aspects of estate planning are affected by the existence of community property, from life insurance to estate taxes. These matters are covered in chapters throughout the book and will not be repeated here.

8

Life Insurance and Flower Bonds

A. An Overview of Life Insurance

Life insurance has long been basic to much of estate planning in the United States. Indeed, one fear many people have of the phrase "estate planning" is that it's a cover for visits by life insurance agents and higher premium payments. Life insurance can create a relatively inexpensive means of providing ready cash to survivors and, as such, can be useful to people with dependents. As we will see, there are also several other common estate problems for which life insurance can be part of a sensible solution. But let me emphasize here at the beginning of this chapter, simply buying life insurance is not an adequate way to plan an estate. For many people, having no life insurance at all is sensible; those who probably should purchase some should be careful to buy no more than they really need. Before reading on, you may want to take a moment to consider your own beliefs about the necessities for life insurance. As a group, Americans certainly believe in it. They hold more than two trillion dollars of life insurance, far more per capita than any other nationality.

Here are some questions to consider regarding life insurance: How many persons are dependent on your earning capacity? How much money would they need, for how long, if you couldn't provide support? How much money would be available from public and private insurance plans that already provide coverage such as social security, union or management pensions, or life insurance plans? How much cash would any business you are involved in need on your death? What other sources of income, aside from life insurance proceeds, would your family have if you died? How much short-term cash would your family or other dependents require until your estate got straightened out? Are there other assets available for those immediate financial needs, such as money that can be left in joint bank accounts, marketable stocks and bonds that can be held in joint tenancy, or business funds?

In addition to making money available to dependent survivors, life insurance can be valuable for two of the basic estate planning goals:

❖ Normally, the proceeds of a life insurance policy avoid probate. This means that money can be transferred quickly to survivors with little red tape;

❖ In some circumstances, the proceeds are also excluded from the taxable estate, and thus reduce death tax liability.

Some examples of the use of life insurance in specific estate plans are given in the Appendix, *Sample Estate Plans,* at the end of the book.

B.   Types of Life Insurance

As any life insurance salesperson will be delighted to explain, there are an innumerable, bewildering array of different types of life insurance policies. It's all too easy to get caught up in insurance policy lingo and lose sight of the fact that, for estate planning purposes, there are three principal types of life insurance — "term," "whole life," and one or another type of "annuity." Let's look at each:

1. Term Insurance

Term insurance is usually the cheapest. It provides only a set amount of benefits upon the death of the insured during the term of the policy. If the insured lives beyond the end of the term, he or she gets nothing. There are many types of term insurance: annual, renewable, or convertible term; level renewable term (where premiums don't rise every year, but are averaged for a set period of years); deposit term; decreasing term, etc. But these are all details and don't change the basic fact that term insurance pays off if you die during the term and doesn't pay off anything if you live beyond that period of the policy. Term life insurance is particularly desirable for younger people with families, who desire substantial coverage at low cost. Since the risks of dying in your twenties or thirties is quite low, the cost of term insurance is not great. A man, age 25, in good health, might expect to pay about $55 per year for a ten-year term policy which would pay off $10,000 if he died during the term. At age 35, the same man would pay about $70 per year. If he were to purchase the same coverage at 45, still assuming good health, the annual premium would be in the neighborhood of $125 to $130. However, term insurance can become quite costly, considering the face value of the policy, if purchased in old age. Some policies are automatically renewable at the end of the term (often for higher premiums), and some are not. But again the basic feature of term that separates it from whole (or straight) life is that, if you outlive the term of the policy (say 5 years), there is no cash surrender value. This is probably a small disappointment compared to the pleasure of being alive. For the economy-minded, term insurance is usually the best buy.

2. Whole Life (Sometimes Called "Straight Life")

Whole life is almost always more expensive than term, especially in the early years of a policy. It provides a set dollar amount of coverage (say $10,000) if you die within the period covered by the policy (say 20 years). Whole life is usually renewable. The premiums are normally the same over the life of the policy. Because the policy charges of whole life, especially in the early years of a younger person's policy, are much greater than needed to cover the actuarial risk of death, these policies are designed to build up a "cash reserve" over time, which can be used for cash-surrender value, or as security for loans, etc. Thus, when you buy a whole life policy, you buy not only a life insurance policy, but also a savings account. Like a bank, the insurance company invests the money that you pay them and uses the profits not only to pay off the face value of the policy if you die, but also to provide you with the cash surrender value should you live. As you remember from the discussion above, term insurance has no value when the term of the policy runs out, which is why it is much cheaper.

However, and this is important—life insurance policies are not particularly efficient ways to save money. If you bought a ten-year term policy (as opposed to a ten-year whole life policy) and put the difference each month in a savings and loan, you would end up with considerably more in your account after ten years that you could get by surrendering your whole life policy. As with term, there are innumerable forms of "whole life" insurance. Premiums for a "whole life" policy are much higher than for term insurance since you are buying a savings account in addition to insurance. A man, age 25 and in good health, purchasing a ten-year "whole life" policy which would pay off $10,000 at death, would pay approximately $170 per year. Purchasing the same policy at age 35, his annual premium would be about $235, and at age 45, he could expect to pay about $340 per year.

3. Other Types of Insurance
There are other types of insurance, such as endowment policies, which are rarely used, or recommended, in estate planning.

4. Annuities
Basically, an annuity is a device whereby the insurance company pays the beneficiary of a policy a certain amount each year, or month, instead of one lump sum upon death. There are all sorts of types of annuity policies, and combinations of an annuity with a whole life policy. The estate planning advantage of an annuity is that it can provide periodic payments to those you believe are unable (too young, or too much of a wastrel, etc.) to handle one large lump sum insurance payment. Even if you have this kind of

situation, you will want to consider other alternatives before choosing an annuity policy. Often annuity policies are a relatively expensive way to meet your objective. Also, they are not flexible; if special needs of the beneficiary arise (illness, etc.), the payments normally cannot be increased. In many cases, a life insurance trust (see Section E) is a wiser choice, providing the control you want, but allowing the trustee to vary the payments in certain cases.

IMPORTANT: You may need to talk to an insurance salesperson to determine the specific type of life insurance policy that's right for your estate. However, you should have already determined the uses you want to make of insurance and the basic type you need. The salesperson should only be a technician. Always remember too that salespeople will probably not recommend that you buy term insurance, because they get a much higher commission from selling you whole life. And one final thing to remember— the cost of the same insurance can vary considerably from company to company. Often small (relatively) mutual companies charge lower rates than some of the giants of T.V. advertising.

C.   Life Insurance and Probate

The proceeds of a decedent's life insurance policy will be subject to probate, and included in the value of the probate estate, **only** if those proceeds are payable to his estate, i.e., if the decedent named his estate as beneficiary of his policy. If anyone else (including a trust) is the beneficiary of the policy, the proceeds are not included in the probate estate. This means that the proceeds of the policy pass directly to the beneficiary without the cost or delay of probate. Except in unusual cases, there is no sound reason for naming the estate, rather than another person (or trust for another person) as the beneficiary. One situation that can necessitate naming the estate as beneficiary is where there is a substantial probate estate, with substantial probate and tax costs, and no other asset in the estate that you want used to pay these costs, so that you must provide ready cash to do so. In most cases, though, there is enough cash, or other assets than can be sold for cash, in an estate, so there's no reason to name it as the insurance beneficiary. Unless life insurance proceeds are used for estate costs, they will be distributed to someone, eventually. Why reduce the amount your inheritors receive because of added probate costs? Why add to the time delay your inheritors must put up with before they get this money, because of probate?

D.   Life Insurance and Taxes

Whether life insurance proceeds are subject to death taxes or not depends on how the policy was controlled during the decedent's life. If, and only if, the decedent "owned" the policy, are the proceeds included in the taxable estate. If the decedent retained any "incidents of ownership" of an insurance policy on his life, he will be held to be the owner. The "incidents of owership" include any significant power over an insurance policy. If the decedent maintained any one of the following, the proceeds of the policy will be included in the taxable estate for tax purposes:

    1. the right to change, or name, beneficiaries of the policy;

    2. the right to borrow against the policy, or pledge any cash reserve it has, or cash it in;

    3. the right to surrender, convert, or cancel the policy;

    4. the right to select a payment option, i.e., the power to decide if payments to the beneficiary can be a lump sum, in installments, etc.

5. the right to make payments on the policy.

In most cases, there is nothing to be gained if the insured retains the incidents of ownership of a life insurance policy. The purpose of the policy is to protect and assist someone else upon the death of the insured. By making the beneficiary, or even a third person, the legal owner of the policy, death taxes can be significantly reduced. Many life insurance policies pay out substantial amounts of money. If this money is included in the taxable estate, it may increase the gross value of the estate high enough so that federal estate taxes will be imposed (or increase these taxes). Even if the face value of the policy will not increase the gross value of the estate to the federal tax level, it will, in almost all cases, insure that California inheritance taxes must be paid, or increase the amount of that tax.

There are two basic ways an insurance policy can be owned by someone other than the insured. First, a person having what's called an "insurable interest" (explained in Section D(1)(b) of this chapter) can take out and pay for a policy on the insured's life. Second, if the insured is the original owner, she can transfer ownership to another person, who does not have to have an "insurable interest." Usually, this type of transfer is made as a gift, so there may be gift taxes assessed, depending on the value of the policy at the time (see Chapter 4, *Gifts*). However, and this is where a lot of estate taxes can be saved, the value of the policy at the time it is given will always be substantially less than the face value of the policy (the amount it pays off on death). This means the amount of gift taxes paid will be far less than what would be paid at death if the insured remained the legal owner.

Before you decide for sure that you want to transfer your policies, consider two important factors. First, what is the size of your estate, and second, what is the size of your life insurance policies? Then you will want to ask yourself what the inclusion of the proceeds of your insurance policies in your taxable estate will do to your state inheritance tax, and federal estate tax liability. If there will be no tax consequences either way (highly unlikely), it isn't very important whether you transfer the policy or not. In the more usual case, however, there will be tax savings if you transfer the policy. Then the next question is, are these tax savings worth the loss of control over your insurance policy. Once the policy is transferred you can no longer cancel it, change the beneficiary, etc.

NOTE ON GIFTS OF LIFE INSURANCE AND GIFT TAXES: Suppose a husband gives his wife an insurance policy, with their son named as the beneficiary. When the husband dies, has the wife made a gift of the proceeds to their son? There are no cases on this in California, but courts in two other states have ruled there was a gift. The status of the law on this problem is simply not clear, so the conservative, lawyer-like advice is to have the person who is given the policy be the beneficiary—or see a lawyer. Sometimes a life insurance trust can be used in these circumstances to avoid gift taxes.

1. Avoiding the Incidents of Ownership of Life Insurance Policies
a. New Policies

If a new insurance policy is taken out, it should, where legally permissible, be originally owned by the beneficiary (or some other third person,) not the insured. The usual situation is a wife taking out a policy on her husband's life, or vice versa. The policy should specify that all the incidents of ownership are vested solely in the wife. This means that the person who takes out the policy should pay for it. If a spouse takes out a policy on her husband, she should pay for it all from her separate funds. If she has no separate funds or the desire is to use community property or the husband's separate property, the husband should "give" his wife enough money to cover the policy costs. This money should be placed in a bank account, clearly defined as the separate property of the wife, to prove the source of funds used for payment. The character of funds used to pay the insurance premiums determines the ownership of the policy, for both federal estate tax and California inheritance tax purposes. The will of the spouse who is the owner of the policy should provide that, if she predeceases her spouse, some third person, not the surviving spouse, inherits the policy. Finally, to keep everything consistent, the spouse who owns the policy should keep physical possession of it, rather than the insured.

b. Insurable Interest

California law requires that anyone taking out a life insurance policy as owner must have what's called an ''insurable interest'' on the life insured. If the person taking out the life insurance policy has no ''insurable interest,'' the policy is void. By state law, a person has an insurable interest in the life of:

1) himself;

2) any person on whom he depends wholly or in part for education or support;

3) any person under legal obligation to pay him money.

A person who has an insurable interest in a life can name anyone as beneficiary of the policy. This insurable interest must exist only when the insurance policy is issued. If the person who took out the policy has the necessary insurable interest at time of purchase, the policy can then be assigned or transferred to anyone. There is no requirement that the legal owner of the life insurance policy have an insurable interest at the time of the death of the insured. The purpose of the insurable interest requirement is to prevent insurance gambling (or worse, murder), by taking out a policy on the gamble that the insured will die, and a large return will be achieved.

c. Assignment of Life Insurance Policies

If there is an existing life insurance policy owned by the insured, the estate tax consequences of that ownership discussed above can be avoided by transferring, or assigning, the policy to someone else as owner. Assignments of life insurance policies to anyone are permitted by California law, whether or not the new owner would have had an ''insurable interest.'' The new owner should make all premium payments.

Legally, notice of the assignment need not be given the insurance company, unless the policy specifically requires it. Many do. In any case, it is a good idea to notify the insurance company. Many have printed transfer forms you can use. Also, the policy will usually have to be changed to specify that the insured no longer has any of the incidents of ownership. Policies can be transferred orally, but it's not advisable. If you transfer a policy, formalize that transfer in writing by use or adaptation of one of the following forms:

Husband and Wife Transfers:

Assignment of Life Insurance

The undersigned, husband and wife, hereby agree that the following insurance policy issued on the life of the husband is assigned to wife and is her separate property, that the husband releases and waives all rights to or incidents of ownership in said policy which now exist or may hereafter arise by virtue of the community property statutes of the State of California, including:

a) the right to change or name beneficiaries under the policy;

b) the right to borrow against the policy, or pledge any cash reserve it has, or cash it in;

c) the right to surrender, convert or cancel the policy;

d) the right to select a payment option;

e) the right to make payments on the policy.

Any future premium payments on said policy hereafter made with community property shall constitute a gift from the husband to the wife in the amount of one-half of the community funds so applied.*

Said policy is described as (identify policy by number, etc.) _____ Life Insurance Company.

Dated this _____ day of _____ , 19 _____ .

_____

_____

Transfers to Someone Other Than a Spouse:

Assignment of Life Insurance

The undersigned __(original owner)__ and __(new owner)__ , hereby agree that the following insurance policy issued to _____ on _(his/her)_ life is assigned to _____ as _(his/her)_ sole property, that _(original owner)_ releases and waives all rights to or incidents of ownership in said policy, including:

a) the right to change or name beneficiaries under the policy;

b) the right to borrow against the policy, or pledge any cash reserve it has, or cash it in;

c) the right to surrender, convert or cancel the policy;

d) the right to select a payment option.

e) the right to make payments on the policy.

Said policy is described as _(identify policy by numbers, etc.)_ Life Insurance Company.

Dated this _____ day of _____ , 19 _____ .

_____

_____

If the life insurance policy is transferred to someone who doesn't pay a reasonable market price for it, the transaction will be regarded as a gift by the tax authorities. So the transfer of a long-standing policy, with substantial present value, may require the payment of gift taxes. Even so, this will be, eventually, far more economical than leaving the policy in the estate.

NOTE: Any gift transfer within three years of death will automatically be set aside for federal estate tax purposes** (and probably be set aside, as a gift in contemplation of death, under California law as well). So insurance policies should be transferred as soon as possible, years before there is much likelihood of death.

---

* This alone might be sufficient, even if payments are made from community property, but establishment of a separate bank account for payments is safer.

** As I said in Chapter 4, *Gifts,* Section D(4)(a), the annual $3,000 gift exemption does *not* apply to gifts of life insurance made within three years of death. Int. Rev. Code Section 2035(a),(b)(2).

EXAMPLE: Louise gives her term life insurance policy to her friend, Leon, in 1979, two and a half years before she dies in 1981. The policy pays $100,000. Her taxable estate, aside from this policy, totals $175,000. Since the gift is disallowed, the full amount of the payments are included in her taxable estate, and it must pay federal taxes totalling $23,800. If she'd transferred the policy seven months earlier her estate would not have to pay any federal estate taxes, and gift taxes would be based on the value of the policy when transferred, not the pay-out amount (see Chapter 4, *Gifts*).

E. Life Insurance Trusts

Another means of transfer, for estate tax reduction, is to establish an irrevocable life insurance trust. Forms for a life insurance trust are given in Chapter 9, *Trusts*.* A simple life insurance trust has the settlor (the original insured), the trust "corpus" (the policy), a trustee, and a named beneficiary (the person named in the policy). A life insurance trust is often established where the beneficiary is a minor, or where the insured is, for whatever reason, concerned that the beneficiary will not wisely use the benefits of the policy if he

---

* Life insurance companies will frequently render help and forms for creating a life insurance trust. Check with your company.

receives them in lump sum. The insured could take out an annuity policy that provided for installment payments of some kind, but this is an inflexible approach and doesn't allow for extraordinary payments for the special needs (say an illness) of the beneficiary. Also, as we learned, someone other than the insured must own a policy, to remove it from the taxable estate. If the insured is worried about the beneficiary's prudence and judgment in the first place, she is unlikely to want to transfer ownership of the policy to that person. This means that some other third person must be found, and, if you have to do this, you may as well create a life insurance trust from the start.

If you want to gain the estate tax savings, a life insurance trust must be irrevocable. If you retain the right to revoke the trust, you will be considered the owner of the policy and the proceeds will be taxed in your estate upon death. You, of course, have the power to select the trustee who is the person responsible for supervising the trust and the distribution of the proceeds (the trust can establish different terms). Presumably, you will have the good sense to pick a trustee with mature judgment. Ideally, this should allow the flexibility to meet the real needs of the beneficiary, while insuring that mature supervision is also achieved.

Life insurance trusts can also be established that are revocable. The trustee is the legal owner of the policy, the beneficiary is whoever the settlor of the trust names. Upon death, the trust takes effect. However, the proceeds **will** be included in the taxable estate, but not the probate estate.

Once the trust is established, you can continue to make payments for policy premiums as long as that does not, by the terms of the policy or the trust, make you the legal owner. If there is any doubt, you can simply give the amount of the premium payment to the trust or trustee and let them pay it. You should arrange this type of trust in cooperation with your insurance company, or agent. They may well have trust forms for you to use, in addition to the ones provided in Chapter 9.

NOTE: There are some technical reporting requirements for a trust. If you're considering the establishment of one, be sure to read Chapter 9, *Trusts*, carefully. Also, you should know that there are many more sophisticated tax games and dodges that can be worked with life insurance—"crummey" trusts, etc. If you have the money and inclination for exploring how these trust devices can help you, see a lawyer.

LET ME REPEAT: Life insurance trusts can be particularly useful to protect minor children. In case of a disaster, they provide ready cash, and most importantly, continuity because of the existing trust and trustee without the necessity of any court papers or hearings.

This type of trust can also be used to pay funeral expenses, or any other cash benefits the settlor wants to provide for other people. If there is money remaining in the trust after all set benefits are paid as the trust defines, the remainder will be distributed to beneficiaries as the trust directs.

The costs of a life insurance trust can be higher than other forms of insurance. If your estate, even with all life insurance included, would not be subject to federal estate tax, there may not be any reason to bother with life insurance trusts. Determine the dollar value of the estate before you try such methods.

F. Loss of Ownership of Life Insurance Policies

Let me repeat a warning about life insurance and estate tax problems. Once you have transferred a life insurance policy, to a trust or by assignment to someone else, you have lost your power over it, forever. Suppose you have selected your husband as trustee in an irrevocable life insurance trust for your children or assigned him the policy, and you later get divorced. He will remain as trustee or owner of the policy. What does this mean? It means that you have a problem if you think that a divorce is possible. One solution would be to retain control over your life insurance policies and let them stay in your taxable estate. Or you can have them removed from your taxable estate and risk the consequences if you do divorce. You can't keep control and get the tax benefits too.

G. Other Points About Insurance Policies

1. Many people are members of group policies, through work. Sometimes these policies don't allow for transfer of ownership—you have to remain the owner. In other situations you can transfer ownership.

2. If an insured person designated one person as a beneficiary on a life insurance policy, but later names another person as the beneficiary on the same policy in her will, the first person will remain the legal beneficiary. You can't change a beneficiary simply by naming a new one in a will.

3. Under both California and federal tax law, a decedent's estate is taxed on policies the decedent owned on other's lives. The value of the policy is figured on the cash (surrender) value of it at the time of the decedent's death.

EXAMPLE: Harry assigns his life insurance policy to his good friend, Louise. Contrary to their mutual expectations, however, Louise dies before Harry. The value of the policy Louise owned on Harry's life is included in Louise's taxable estate. Usually this value, being only the surrender value of the policy, will not be immense.

4. If a policy has been paid for by community funds, one half the proceeds are owned by the surviving spouse, no matter what the policy states regarding the beneficiary.

H. Taxation of Insurance Proceeds Received After the Insured's Death

The principal (cash) proceeds payable after an insured's death are exempt from *all* federal taxes, both income taxes (to the recipient) and estate taxes (unless, as previously described, the deceased owned the policy or the proceeds were payable to his estate). However, if the proceeds are paid in installments, any interest paid is taxable income to the recipient.

Under California law, the proceeds of an insurance policy are likewise exempt from income tax. However, *only* the first $50,000 of life insurance proceeds are exempt from inheritance tax. Anything in excess of $50,000 is taxed to the beneficiary like any other property of the decedent would be.* If there are several beneficiaries, they share, pro-rata, in one $50,000 cumulative exemption. Survivorship benefits under public retirement systems are completely exempt from state taxes (annuities or not).

In some cases, the proceeds of life insurance will be exempt from attachments by creditors of the beneficiary. If the sole beneficiary is a surviving spouse or minor child, proceeds purchased by annual premium payments of less than $1,000 a year are exempt from creditors of the beneficiary. If anyone else is a beneficiary, proceeds purchased by annual payments of $500 or less are exempt from creditors.**

---

* Complete exemption from taxes is allowed for proceeds of government insurance on the lives of veterans of World War I, or II, if the proceeds are payable to an estate or creditor; the $50,000 limit still applies if the proceeds are payable to a named beneficiary.

** Proceeds of certain types of group life insurance are also exempt from execution by the decedent's creditors.

I. How to Collect the Proceeds of a Life Insurance Policy

To collect the proceeds of a life insurance policy, the first step is to notify the insurance company and get their claim form. Usually that form has to be sent to their home office. Also ask the life insurance company to send you U.S. Treasury Department form #712, which should be submitted with the claims form. This form is required by the state tax people, even if no state taxes are due. The form must also be submitted to the federal tax authorities, if federal estate taxes are due on the estate. When the beneficiary completes these forms, he files them and a certified copy of the insured's death certificate (see Chapter 2, *Funerals and Burials,* on how to obtain a death certificate) with the insurance company. The beneficiary may also have to file a copy of the policy, and proof that he is, in fact, the named beneficiary, if the insurance company so requires. It's simple and fast, but there can be one fly in the ointment. If the benefits are over $25,000, **or** if the life insurance company knows the total insurance payable (from all life insurance companies) on the decedent's life are in excess of $50,000, none of the proceeds can be released until the State Controller's office has issued a "consent to transfer." The State Controller's office, sometimes working through agents in the County Treasurer's office, is responsible for insuring that no property is transferred upon a death when death taxes might be due on that property. If the insurance proceeds will be part of the decedent's taxable estate, a consent to transfer will not be issued until the State Controller's office is satisfied that the estate has sufficient assets to pay state inheritance taxes, if the insurance proceeds are released to the beneficiary.

J. "Flower" Bonds

In certain cases, it may be advantageous to purchase a type of U.S. Treasury bond, colloquially called "flower bonds" (because they "flower" on the death of the owner).

These bonds become payable at their full face value at the death of the owner (and, also, like all other bonds, when the term of the bond itself expires). Flower bonds can be purchased through any bank or stock/bond broker. The purchase price will be less than the face value. The estate can use these bonds, which pay off at full value, at death, to pay estate taxes and costs. They are desirable in cases where an estate will need ready cash, and has no other source for it, often in cases where a person cannot acquire life insurance. Flower bonds are also advantageous if a person's life expectancy is short because of age or ill health.

Unlike life insurance, flower bonds, to be effective, must be retained by the owner to achieve their estate planning advantage. Therefore, they are always included in the taxable estate at par value.

There are drawbacks to the use of flower bonds. The interest these bonds pay is less than that of other U.S. government bonds. Until they are utilized, upon the death of the owner, they are not a good investment. Thus, they are usually purchased shortly before the death of the owner and are not commonly used when other investments would yield a better return.

Flower bonds are gradually being phased out. The Treasury Department has not issued any since 1971. The last series of flower bonds to mature will come due on November 15, 1998. If you believe it might be a good idea for you to purchase flower bonds, talk to your broker (if you have one) or a bank. They can tell you the exact current market price, effective yield and other facts about flower bonds.

To qualify for redemption at death, the flower bonds must be part of the decedent's (taxable) estate. It's not wise to buy flower bonds jointly. If the bonds are held in joint ownership, they can only be used (redeemed for full face value) in the amount that the surviving joint owner is required to pay to satisfy estate taxes on the bond, or other jointly held property with the decedent.

Community property bonds qualify for redemption at death only for one-half the payoff amount of each bond issued. So, if the bonds are bought specifically for redemption purposes, they should be bought from separate property, not community funds. Otherwise, double the amount of bonds need be bought.

9
Trusts

A.   A Little Background

The very word "trusts" has an impressive, slightly ominous, sound. "Trusts"—tools of the very rich, once used to monopolize, and dominate industries ("Standard Oil Trust," Teddy Roosevelt's "Trust Busting"). Trusts were also used to maintain family wealth. We know that somehow, by using elaborate "trusts," the duPonts, Rockefellers, Kennedys, et al. managed to preserve their wealth from generation to generation. (True, all true.) Yet despite their uses in monopolizing millions or billions, trusts are, in basic concept, rather simple: the "settlor" (the person who establishes the trust), puts something of value in a "trust." A written document establishes the trust, defining its terms and naming: 1) the "trustee," who manages the trust (who can be the settlor) and 2) the "beneficiary" of the trust. Legal title to the property in the trust is held by the trustee. Here is a valid trust: *"I, Cynthia Sims, hereby place in irrevocable trust for my minor son, Sam Sims, until he reaches majority . . . (trust property described) . . .and appoint Alice Sims, my sister, as the trustee of the trust."*

Trusts are an invention of medieval England. To escape death taxes and limitations on the willing of real estate, particularly the rule of primogeniture (only the eldest son could inherit real property) trusts were devised as a new means of transferring legal ownership. English common law, with its passion for forms of ownership (as opposed to the substance of what was really going on), accepted the fiction that a "trust" is a legally separate entity from the settlor.* Trusts have had a varied history since. At one time charitable trusts were greatly feared in the United States, and even banned in New York, because of opposition to the "dead hand" concentration of economic power in churches. Recently the use of trusts by the very rich to escape death taxes and maintain immense family fortunes has come under attack in the 1976 Federal Tax Reform Act.

---

* Similarly, the Supreme Court long ago ruled that the legal abstraction of a corporation is a "person" under the 14th amendment.

One of the standard tax dodges of the very wealthy has been to avoid estate taxes by leaving the bulk of their assets in trust for their grandchildren—with the income from the trusts (but not the trust principal) available for use by their children. The advantage of this strategy was that death taxes were avoided several times as, without a trust, taxes would be typically paid when the first grandparent died, then again when the second died and so on with the children until the amount of money that reached the grandchildren would be greatly diminished. The 1976 Tax Act adopted the concept of a tax on all "generation-skipping transfers" and has imposed death taxes on such trusts over $250,000 per child if the middle generation is skipped. Thus, for a generation-skipping trust over $250,000 per child, estate taxes are levied as if the trust didn't exist. There are some tax people who believe this will seriously curtail the ability of the immensely wealthy to pass on the bulk of their assets free of tax. The author is dubious—money has always found or bought holes in our tax system so far, and there seems little likelihood that this will change.

B.   Types of Trusts: Intervivos and Testamentary

There are two main types of trusts: intervivos and testamentary trusts. An intervivos ("among the living") trust is one where the settlor (to repeat, the person who set up the trust) is living; it can either be revocable, or irrevocable, depending on the desires of the trust settlor. A revocable trust can be revoked by the trust settlor, alone and at any time (unless the trust document contains other requirements). A testamentary trust is one established by will. Testamentary trusts can often be quite complicated; usually an estate that requires a testamentary trust is complicated enough so that a lawyer or estate planner should be consulted.

C.   Trusts and Estate Planning

There are two major uses of trusts in estate planning. First is probate avoidance. Property placed in an intervivos trust before the settlor dies is transferred to the beneficiary outside of probate. A probate avoidance trust is usually revocable during the settlor's lifetime, so that it **only** takes effect upon his death. Probate avoidance trusts can be relatively simple. If, after reading this chapter, you decide a probate avoidance trust is useful for your estate plan, you can prepare one from the forms given in this chapter.

The second major use of trusts in estate planning is for death tax reduction. In this case, the trust must be irrevocable, or established by will. These trusts are complicated, and I recommend you consult a lawyer if you decide you need one (with the possible exception of an irrevocable life insurance trust). Often tax-reduction trusts have other purposes as well, such as to protect minor children of the trust settlors. The fiendishly clever minds of generations of estate planners (mostly lawyers) have created trusts of incredible complexity out of what appears to be a simple matter—reduce death taxes and protect my children.

EXAMPLE: John and Mary have four children, and a substantial estate. As part of their estate plan, they decide, in case they both die before the children become adults, to leave their assets in trust for the children, and reduce estate taxes as low as possible. Sounds simple enough, but it won't be after the estate planners get through. Should the trusts be left to the children, or the childrens' children, John and Mary's grandchildren? What happens if the oldest child dies? If the oldest child dies after being married and having two children? If two of the children are adults when both parents are deceased, and two are still children? How much discretion should the trustee have to use the trust assets up for benefit of the children?

    The questions, and permutations, are nearly endless, especially when, as is often the case, there are different tax consequences for each option. Suppose the trustee is given power to control distribution of funds? Suppose the surviving spouse is given some interest in the trust? Suppose the settlors decide that they want to revoke the trust, or change the provisions? All these choices may affect the estate tax implications of the trust. Likewise, there are many types of trust—"sprinkling" trusts, family pot trusts, short-term reversionary trusts, also known as "Clifford" trusts (no relation), pour-over trusts, etc., etc.

    As this brief discussion indicates, most testamentary or tax-reduction trusts are so complicated that they should be prepared by a professional estate planner. Trusts designed to minimize estate taxes are rarely desirable for estates under (roughly) $250,000, and don't often come into serious use unless at least $300,000—$500,000 is involved.

Fortunately, trusts are flexible, and in simpler forms can be very useful for a moderate estate. Don't be frightened off by the word "trust" or by the fact that they can be complicated. Read on, and see if a trust—especially a probate avoidance trust—can be useful for your estate plan.

D.   Intervivos Trusts (among the living)

IN SOUTHERN MELANESIA THE HOUSES, FISHING NETS AND OTHER POSSESSIONS OF A PERSON WHO HAS DIED ARE DESTROYED. EVEN THE CROPS AND FIELDS ARE PUT TO THE TORCH.

1. Avoiding Probate

A revocable intervivos trust has one noticeable advantage, from the estate planner's point of view. It does not take effect until death of the settlor, and can be revoked by him at any time, and for any reason, before death. This means that the person setting up the trust does not have to lose any control over his money or other property as would be the case with an irrevocable trust or a joint tenancy situation. When the settlor dies, the trust becomes fully effective, and the property in the trust is transferred outside of probate. Revocable intervivos trusts do not have tax advantages—just probate avoidance advantages.

EXAMPLE: James wants to leave his valuable painting collection to his son, but wants total control over it until he dies. He doesn't want the value of his collection, several million dollars, included in his probate estate. So he establishes a revocable intervivos trust for the paintings, naming himself a trustee while he lives, with his son the beneficiary. When James dies, his son receives the paintings outside of probate.

James wants to know if it will reduce his estate taxes when he establishes this trust. The answer is no, this trust will not reduce his death taxes at all.

EXAMPLE: James thinks he will leave his motorcycle collection to his niece, but he isn't certain. So he establishes a revocable intervivos trust for the motorcycles, naming himself as trustee while he lives, and his niece as the beneficiary. If he changes his mind and later decides to leave his motorcycles to someone else, he simply revokes the trust.

Generally, a revocable intervivos trust is a useful means to transfer assets of significant value outside of probate. The bother and expense of establishing and maintaining a trust seem unnecessary for items of lesser value, but for major assets—such as a house, land, blocks of stock and such items, you should consider using a revocable intervivos trust.

This probate-avoidance feature of revocable intervivos trusts was widely publicized by Norman Dacy, in his well-known book, *How To Avoid Probate*. Essentially, Dacy recommends that a person put **all** his property in different revocable intervivos trusts, so that when he dies, there is no probate estate whatsoever. I do not recommend such a complete and indiscriminate use of revocable intervivos trusts. Why? First, because the value of property in such trusts will be included in the settlor's taxable estate, even though probate is avoided, so this trust won't solve **all** estate planning problems. Even without probate, the estate will often incur obligations to file complicated tax and property transfer forms. I do recommend that the simplest way to get these forms and transfers taken care of is through the probate of a small part of the total estate (see Chapter 5). In addition, there are costs and inconveniences to establishing and maintaining an intervivos trust. The trust, legally, is a separate entity from the settlor. It must be managed by the trustee (even if this is the same person as the settlor) as a separate entity and income received by the trust reported in tax returns (if the income is accumulated in the trust). Other technicalities in the maintenance of the trust must be observed.

Revocable intervivos trusts are **one** means to transfer property on death outside of probate. They can be, and often are, valuable, but there are other means to achieve the same result, including holding property in joint tenancy, making gifts, leaving your half interest in community property to your spouse, setting up a simple savings bank trust, etc.

To plan an estate you should understand the advantages and drawbacks of all these forms of probate-avoidance transfer. I do not believe that intervivos trusts are a "legal wonder drug" that should be used for all property in all cases. But they can be simple and, if they fit the overall estate plan, they are often the best means of transferring property outside of probate.

2. Other Advantages of an Intervivos Trust

There are some situations where the establishment of a revocable intervivos trust is a most desirable form of estate planning. For example, there may be reasons someone, or a couple, doesn't want the responsibility of management of their property, but don't want to lose final control over it. Perhaps a person is old, ill and weary of the struggle of the marketplace, and wants to be relieved of that burden.

Example: George and Martha have a substantial community estate, consisting mostly of stocks. They are both ill, and tired of managing their stock "portfolio." They both want the surviving spouse to receive the decedent spouse's share of their community property, and they want to reduce probate fees. So they each transfer their shares of the community property stocks into a (separate) revocable intervivos trust, naming the other spouse as beneficiary. They each name the trust department of their bank as trustee, to manage their stocks.

Also, if there are any problems concerning mental competency (of the settlors), a trust can be advisable, because the appointed trustee can then manage the assets. Otherwise there might be court proceedings, the painful problems of establishing incompetency, and the appointment by the court of a conservator to control the person's money. Similarly, revocable intervivos trusts are advisable if the beneficiary is a minor (or fiscally irresponsible, whatever his age). Upon the death of the settlor, the trust continues without the necessity for a court appointed guardian, court reportings, etc.

Example: J. Ferguson Plessy thinks he wants to leave a large amount of money to his 6-year-old niece, Alicia (once again, as in all these examples, the settlor — here Mr. Plessy — wants to reduce probate fees). So he leaves her the money by a revocable intervivos trust. He names himself as trustee while he lives, and appoints his younger brother, good old reliable Bob, as trustee once he dies; he specifies that the trustee can control the distribution of the money to Alicia, with whatever limits he chooses, until she reaches age 18. Thus there will be no need for a court appointed guardian for the money Alicia receives, and it will have been transferred outside of probate.

Another common situation is where it is impossible or undesirable to hold shared property in joint tenancy, or as community property. In many non-corporate businesses with more than one owner, such as a partnership or joint venture, each owner wants to exclude his interest from being probated, and to insure continuity of the business upon his death. At the same time, it is undesirable to make irrevocable commitments regarding the business — there may be a falling out of partners, or a need for one to sell. So each puts his interest in a revocable intervivos trust naming himself as trustee. If needs change, the trust can be instantly revoked or amended. If death strikes, the trust becomes effective.

Example: Carol, Kal and Joanne are partners in a consulting business. They all want to insure continuity of the business if one of them die, but want their financial interest in the business to be inherited by other persons. They are all somewhat volatile and don't want to make any irrevocable commitments regarding the business if they don't have to. So each partner creates a revocable intervivos trust for their share of ownership of the business. They each name themselves as trustees of their trust while they live, and name the other two partners as trustees once they die. They name whoever they've chosen as beneficiaries of the trust, but specify that these people only have the right to their share of profits from the business. The right to manage the business is given to the trustees, the two surviving partners. (See Chapter 11 for a further discussion of estate planning problems concerning business.)

Joint tenancy, as is explained in Chapter 10, is another method of holding title that provides for automatic transfer to the surviving owner(s) on the death of one owner. However, joint tenancy has the limitation that each joint owner can sell his half interest while living.* If you want a person to receive a valuable asset upon your death, but do not want him to have any control over the property while you're alive, a revocable intervivos trust is the best means to accomplish this goal and avoid probate. Also, if you transfer property you own into joint tenancy with yourself and another person, you are in effect making a gift of that interest, and there may be gift taxes assessed. As a general rule, if you use a revocable trust, there will be no actual transfer until your death, and so no transfer taxes until then, when the property transferred will be included in your taxable estate.

Other advantages to a revocable intervivos trust:

1. If the settlor is not also the trustee, the trust provides a "testing ground" for the settlor. While she lives, she can see if the trust (and the trustee) is working as she desires. In effect, this would give the settlor a chance to see how part of her will works on a trial run. If it doesn't work suitably to the settlor, she can simply revoke the trust or remove the trustee and start again.

Example: Maeve wants to leave her money to assist worthy poets. She hopes her friend Padraic could manage this money, but she's worried—he's such a dreamer. So she transfers the money to a revocable intervivos trust, and names Padraic as trustee, with the power to distribute income from the trust to help poets. Maeve can see, while she's alive, if Padraic can manage the trust property well, and if he helps poets she thinks merit assistance. If she decides Padraic can't hack it, she simply revokes the trust.

2. Funds or property transferred to a revocable intervivos trust are protected from creditors of the settlor, unless there was fraud in the creation of the trust (e.g., he was insolvent at the time).

Notice that there really are two very separate functions for which a revocable intervivos trust can be used. The first is to avoid probate, or at least to reduce the probate estate. In such a case, any property at all may be put in the trust—a car, a house, a boat, or cash. Sufficient records of the trust should be maintained so that its validity, on death of the settlor, isn't questioned by the State Controller's office when the "consent to transfer" the property is eventually requested by the beneficiary. However, when the settlor is also the trustee, this type of trust is essentially a paper trust, effective because of the traditional respect Anglo-Saxon law pays to paper form.

The second function of a revocable intervivos trust is to allow the management of money or stocks by the trustee who is **not** the settlor. In this situation probate avoidance may be a secondary goal, but basically the settlor wants to hire someone reliable, often a "professional," to handle investment/fiscal responsibilities. The trustee may be a financial institution, such as the trust department of a bank, a business colleague, a trusted friend, etc. Many of the larger California banks are not enthusiastic about handling "small" trusts—anything less than $250,000. Even smaller banks, which will handle smaller trusts, want the assets to be "liquid" (cash, stocks, bonds); if not, there isn't much use for the bank's financial management services. A financial-management intervivos trust is a rarity for the non-rich. It is advisable only for persons gravely ill, or functionally incompetent, who do not have family or friends who can manage their financial affairs. If you want this type of trust, see a lawyer.

Clearly, the establishment of even a "paper" probate-avoidance revocable intervivos trust requires some work. And while such a trust can be revoked at any time, this means more work. Accordingly, you shouldn't establish any intervivos trusts until you are sure

IMPROVISED LYRICS ARE SUNG ABOUT THE DEAD AT WAKES IN THE PHIL-IPINES. SOMETIMES SINGERS COMPETE WITH EACH OTHER FOR THE BEST SONGS TO THE DELIGHT OF THE ASSEMBLED. TALENT-ED SINGERS ARE MUCH IN DEMAND.

---

* After which, the new owners hold title as "tenants in common" **without** rights of survivorship.

that: 1) you definitely have chosen the beneficiary (or beneficiaries); 2) the overall plan of your estate has been determined; 3) you don't foresee any reasonable likelihood there will be reason to change your estate plans, and the intervivos trusts, in the near future. Trusts can be revised and brought up to date with changing circumstances, but you don't want to have to do this every week, or month. In sum, revocable intervivos trusts are normally for the long term (or, if you procrastinate, for a last minute probate avoidance device if death is imminent). Otherwise, for a short term, a power of attorney is preferable.

Important Note—Power of Attorney

A "power of attorney" is not a trust, but it can be used to allow someone to manage your property. A power of attorney is a written authorization by one person (the principal) authorizing another person (the "attorney in fact") to perform certain acts for him. The attorney in fact becomes an agent of the principal. It is important to know that:

1) A power of attorney terminates automatically upon the death of the principal. 2) A power of attorney thus has no real function in estate planning. 3) A power of attorney cannot be used to give a person authority over your assets, or the decision on how you are to be buried, once you die.

However, if you want to authorize someone to manage some, or all, of your affairs while you are alive, for whatever reason (e.g., you're taking a long trip, you don't want the responsibility) it's often best to achieve this by a power of attorney, not by a revocable intervivos trust. Why? Because the power of attorney is a much simpler device better fitted to this limited objective.

3. How to Establish Revocable Intervivos Trusts

Any revocable intervivos trust should be in writing. Legally, a valid intervivos trust can be created orally for personal property (not real property), but it is not a good idea. The trust should state that it is revocable, upon written notice from the settlor to the trustee. All intervivos trusts in California are legally revocable unless the trust agreement specifies otherwise, but there's no reason not to make it explicit. This will serve to avoid any conflict on how it can be revoked, and whether, in fact, it was revoked.

The trust document names the trustee and beneficiary(ies) of the trust, specifies the asset(s) transferred to the trust (the trust "corpus") and defines the administrative and distributive provisions of the trust. You should also provide for what you want to occur if, by any chance, the beneficiary or trustee dies before you do. Do you want that to automatically terminate the trust? Or, do you want it to continue? If so, you should identify successor beneficiaries and/or trustees.

Formalities of a Revocable Intervivos Trust

To be sure the trust will be honored by the authorities, you must observe certain formalities. Specifically, the settlor/trustee should:

1. transfer the trust property to the trust. If real property is transferred, the deed of transfer should be recorded with the County Recorder;

2. have a written trust document and keep that writing in a safe place, usually a safety deposit box rented in the name of the trustee;

3. keep a trust bank account and a set of books for all trust transactions;

4. register the trust assets in the trustee's name.

If the person establishing the trust is also the trustee (called a "grantor trust"), which is normal for probate avoidance trusts, there is no requirement that a taxpayer I.D. number be obtained for the trust. Likewise, for grantor trusts, income received by the trust does not have to be reported on a separate fiduciary trust return (I.R.S. form #1041) but can be reported on the grantor's 1040 form. However, if the person establishing the trust is **not** also the trustee, then a taxpayer I.D. number must be obtained for the trust (by filing I.R.S. form #4), and fiduciary trust tax returns (form #1041) filed with the I.R.S. if the trust's yearly gross income exceeds $600.00.

Writing the Revocable Intervivos Trust

If the only purpose to establishing the trust is to avoid probate of the trust property, the settlor usually names himself as trustee. If the settlor is the trustee, it's particularly important to keep separate trust records and bank accounts. If the trust is established for an on-going business, this can get complicated: if you face this problem, it's advisable to see an accountant, or a lawyer. If another person is desired as the trustee, the settlor can select any person or organization he desires, excluding non-California corporations.* The beneficiary can also be the trustee, unless he's both the sole beneficiary and the sole trustee. If co-trustees are chosen, their decision regarding management of the trust must be unanimous, unless the trust specifies otherwise.

Unless the trust so requires, the trust does not terminate if the named trustee vacates his function (because of death, illness, lack of interest or whatever reason). Instead, the settlor, or the probate court, if the settlor has died (even if the trust is not subject to probate) can appoint a successor trustee. Generally, it is wise to name a successor trustee or two in the trust document. Banks or other financial institutions are commonly named as successor trustees, especially for trusts that require the management and investing of funds. If a bank is to be a successor trustee, it is important that the original trustee keep proper records of the trust management. If the trust is a mess, the bank (fearing liability for claimed mismanagement of trust assets) may decline to serve as the successor trustee.

There is no set schedule for the fees charged by trustees of a revocable intervivos trust. Some banks charge a lesser fee if they have no investment responsibility under the trust. The usual annual fees charged are 3/4 of 1% of the value of all real property in the trust, and 4/5 of 1% of the value of all other property in the trust.

A revocable intervivos trust, like all other trusts in California, can be managed without any reports to judicial officials, unless the trust specifically requires otherwise. Lawsuits can arise over trusts, as they can anytime money is involved. The legal grounds for contesting the validity of a trust are similar to those for contesting a will: fraud, undue influence, incompetency, etc. For any intervivos trust created after July 1, 1971, anyone with a financial interest in that trust who has legal objections to actions by the trustee can petition the local probate court to resolve the matter.

4. Creating a Trust Corpus

A trust has to contain some asset, the "corpus." A funded trust may be funded with anything having cash value—real estate, stocks, art works, or money itself.** An "un-"unfunded trust" is one which does not contain any significant asset. A common example

---

* Except national banking corporations licensed to do business in California.

** The current tax status of business interests transferred to an intervivos trust is less clear. Private corporate stock, such as in "subchapter S" corporations, may be placed in a revocable "grantor" trust, but the tax advantages of the subchapter S corporation may end on the settlor's death. Also, the impact of the 1976 Tax Reform Act on the transfer of a partnership interest to an intervivos trust can be complicated. If you're planning to establish an intervivos trust with a business asset in the corpus, you should discuss this with a lawyer.

is a trust whose only asset is a life insurance policy on the life of the settlor. (Funds for the payment of premiums, alone, without an actual policy do not by themselves create a "corpus.") Another example is a written designation of a beneficiary to the rights of the settlor in a profit sharing or pension plan.

Placing property into a revocable trust is not a gift, for gift tax purposes as the trust can be revoked at any time. But when the settlor dies, estate taxes will be due if the estate is of sufficient value. If community property is placed in trust, the terms of the trust should make it clear that neither party has made a gift of their community property interest to the other. In one California lawsuit, where the trust instrument stated that only the husband had the right to amend or revoke the trust, the I.R.S. contended (on the husband's death) that **all** of the trust property was included in the husband's estate because the wife gave her half of the community property to the husband, and it all became his separate property.*
To protect against this, an intervivos trust instrument of community property should state:

1. Neither party intends to make a gift in the trust;

2. **Either** the husband or wife can revoke or amend the trust as to his/her interest (or require BOTH of them to do it);

3. State that property put in the trust retains the character it had before — if it was community property it remains so, etc.

5. Transfers of Real Property to Trusts and Proposition 13

As all Californians know, Proposition 13 imposed restrictions on the property taxes that can be imposed on real property. Whatever the overall merits of Proposition 13,** it has created new problems regarding transfers of real property in estate planning. Proposition 13 imposed, as of the date of passage, a roll back on all property taxes to the levels of 1975-1976 assessment year. If, after the effective date of Proposition 13 (June 1978), there is a "change of ownership" of real property, the property is re-assessed on its current market value. With the drastic rise in prices of California real estate since 1975-76, this means there is a major financial deterrent to changes of ownership of real property owned before passage of Proposition 13. Even if you purchase property after the effective date of Proposition 13 (and so it was assessed on the market value at the time you bought it) it soon becomes undesirable to change ownership of the property. Under Proposition 13, appraisals cannot rise more than 2% a year. If you bought real property in November 1979, and had it assessed as of that date, it will almost surely result in a considerable

---

* The Appeals Court ruled there was no gift, as the wife had not intended to make a gift.

** Among the other consequences of Proposition 13 are that business real property, which is sold less often than residential real property, will gradually provide less and less of the overall revenue from property taxes. As Bart Maverick said, "you can fool some of the people all of the time, and all of the people some of the time, and that's pretty good odds."

increase in property taxes to transfer it a few years later, as actual real estate prices will have increased far in excess of 2% a year.

But now suppose you own real property and as part of your estate plan you want to pass it outside of probate. One means to do this is to transfer the property to a revocable intervivos trust. Does this constitute a "change of ownership" for Proposition 13? The answer is no, at least at the time this book is published. Proposition 13 was not clearly worded, and did not define what a "change of ownership" (which allows a new property tax assessment) was. But a 1979 California statute* defines a "change of ownership" as a "transfer of a **present interest** in real property . . ." Since there is normally no transfer of any "present interest" in real property transferred to a revocable intervivos trust, there is no "change of ownership" requiring reassessment. The statute specifically provides that transfers of real property to intervivos trusts are not changes of ownership, so long as: 1) the "transferor" (i.e. the settlor) is the present beneficiary of the trust (which is usually the case in probate-avoidance trusts); or 2) the trust is revocable.

Important: Transfers from the trust back to the settlor are likewise not changes of ownership. When the trust takes effect, on the death of the settlor, the property will be reassessed, but this would have happened anyway.**

6. Revoking a Revocable Intervivos Trust

Unless the trust document specifies otherwise(and there's no reason for it to), a revocable intervivos trust can be terminated at any time by the decision of the settlor. No reason for the termination need be given. However, the revocation must be in writing if the trust document is written as it should be. In addition, the revocation should be recorded with the County Recorder (if the trust document was recorded). A copy of the revocation must also be given to the trustee, or, practically, the trust will not be terminated.*** A form for the revocation of an intervivos trust is provided in Section E(2) of this Chapter.

E. Intervivos Trust Forms

The following form may be used, or adapted, for a **revocable intervivos trust** used for a "probate avoidance" purpose. The goal of the trust is to transfer property outside of probate on the death of the settlor. This is a simple trust form, since there is no need for complex administrative provisions. If substantial amounts of money are involved, you may want to have the trust you prepare reviewed by a knowledgeable attorney. The fees for this should not be immense, and it might add to your peace of mind.

Real Property Reminder: If real estate is transferred into (or from) a revocable intervivos trust, there must be a deed actually transferring the property. The deed must be recorded with the County Recorder's office. A simple quitclaim deed form will suffice.

The "probate avoidance" intervivos trust can be used for several different beneficiaries and/or different forms of property. You can place several different types of property—a house, car and boat—in one trust for one beneficiary, or you could place them in 3 separate trusts for one beneficiary (making it easier to revoke a trust for any one item) or you could place them in 3 trusts for 3 different beneficiaries.

---

* A.B. 1488

**There may be an exception to this reassessment rule if the beneficiary is also the surviving spouse. The statute is so confusingly worded it's hard to be sure what it means. If this area matters to you, check with an attorney and find out how the new law has been interpreted.

*** If the trustee is the settlor, as is usual, this is no problem.

This trust form is for a trust where the settlor names himself as trustee. If you wish to set up a probate-avoidance trust, but you don't want to be your own trustee, use the alternative form in Section I(a). The trust should be typed on 8½ × 11 typing paper (again, handwriting is not recommended).

Declaration and Instrument of Revocable
Intervivos Trust

Section I Trustees and Beneficiary

(a) __(name of settlor)__ , called the "settlor" and/or the "trustee" declares that __he/she__ has set aside and holds in trust all that property described in Schedule A, attached to this trust instrument, for the use and benefit of __(beneficiary)__ . The trustee of this trust shall be __(name of settlor)__ . Upon my death the trustee of this trust shall be __(name and address)__ .

Alternative paragraph I(a) — if settlor is **not** trustee:

(a) __(name of settlor)__ , the "settlor" declares that __he/she__ has transferred to this trust all that property described in Schedule A, attached to this trust instrument, for the use and benefit of __(beneficiary)__ . The trustee of this trust shall be __(trustee's name and address)__ .

(b) Each person designated or acting as a trustee of any trust shall have the power to designate successor trustees to act when he or she shall become unable or unwilling to act as trustee of the trust. Each person may designate the same or different persons or entities, including corporate fiduciaries, to act as successor trustee of the trust. If all individuals appointed as trustee and any successors designated by them shall be unable or unwilling to act as trustees __(name successor trustee, possibly a bank)__ shall act as trustee. Any person acting as trustee of the trust may revoke any previous designation of any successor to himself; and appoint other successor trustees; all such revocations or designations shall be made in writing and are effective on delivery of the writing to __(person selected, normally a beneficiary of the trust)__ .

(c) All trustees shall serve without bond.

Section II The Trust Estate

(a) The property subject to this intervivos trust, as listed in Schedule A, is referred to as the "trust estate" and shall be held, administered, and distributed in accordance with this instrument.

(b) Until the property listed in Schedule A is transferred to ___(beneficiary)___ , pursuant to the terms of this trust, all income or profits which may accrue from said property shall be distributed to the settlor during ___(his/her)___ lifetime. (If community property is transferred to the trust, specify whether a gift has been made from one spouse to the other or not.)

Section III   Transfer of Trust Property to Beneficiary

Upon my death, my successor trustee is hereby directed to transfer all property of this trust to the beneficiary ___(name)___ , and thereby terminate this trust.

[If the beneficiary is a minor, add:]

If the beneficiary is under 18, the successor trustee shall hold the trust assets in trust, under the California Uniform Gift to Minors Act, and administer the trust in the best interests of ___(name of beneficiary)___.

Section IV   Reserved Powers of Settlor

(a) I reserve unto myself the power to amend or revoke this intervivos trust, at any time during my lifetime, without the necessity of obtaining the consent of the beneficiary.

(b) I reserve unto myself the power to name a new beneficiary, should _____ (beneficiary) predecease me; should I fail to name a new beneficiary, following the death of ___(beneficiary)___ , this trust shall terminate on my death, and the trust property revert to my estate (**or** if you wish to name further successor beneficiaries, do so here).

_____
(signature)

Dated: _____   [have signature notarized; it's safer.]

Schedule A – Property Transferred to Trust
[List all property transferred to this specific intervivos trust. List the property with detail, e.g., if real estate is transferred to the trust, identify that real estate as it is identified on the property ownership deed. Be sure to staple this schedule to the trust document.]

Revocation Form:

Revocation of Intervivos Trust

Whereas, on _____(date)_____ , I created a written revocable intervivos trust, with _____(name)_____ as the beneficiary of the trust and _____(name)_____ as the trustee;

and **Whereas,** pursuant to Art IV(a) of said trust, I reserved to myself the full power to revoke the trust;

Now therefore, pursuant to Art IV(a) of the trust, and the laws of the State of California, I hereby revoke the trust created by me in the document "Declaration and Instrument of Revocable Intervivos Trust," and state that said trust is completely revoked and all property transferred by me to said trust shall be forthwith returned to me and legally owned by me.

Dated: _____

_____
(signature)

[It's safer to have this notarized]

F. "Managerial" Revocable Intervivos Trusts

Managerial intervivos trusts are far more complicated than a "probate-avoidance" trust. In a managerial trust, actual control over the trust property vests in a trustee separate from the settlor. Since there is usually a substantial amount of property involved, the trust should be carefully drafted. Managerial intervivos trusts are usually wordy, and complicated. Anyone considering such a trust should discuss it with an attorney. You can learn how to draft this type of trust yourself,* but it's a lot of work, and the penalties for mistakes can be severe.

---

* The best book on the subject is by the Continuing Education of the Bar (C.E.B.), *Drafting California Revocable Intervivos Trusts,* available at all law libraries.

G. Irrevocable Intervivos Trusts; Life Insurance Trusts

1. Uses of Irrevocable Intervivos Trusts

An "irrevocable" trust means what it says: once you create it, that's it. You have no legal right to terminate or change it later. Obviously, the fact that you can't revoke a trust could be inconvenient (things change) so why set one up when a revocable trust will avoid probate just as well? Because people who set up an irrevocable trust have other goals, in addition to probate avoidance.

The main uses of an irrevocable intervivos trust are:

1. tax savings—to transfer property so it will not be included in the taxable estate of the trust settlor;

2. to allow a beneficiary to count on the assets; an irrevocable trust allows the settlor to make a permanent transfer without necessarily allowing the beneficiary (rather than the trustee) full control over the assets.

3. to make a permanent gift now, to take effect in the future.

To achieve one or more of these goals, the settlor must normally have a lot of money. Why? Because those with less money are unlikely to give away large sums irrevocably to a trust during their lifetime. An irrevocable intervivos trust is a form of a gift, and the trust settlor is subject to the gift taxes on any assets he transfers to the trust. The main tax advantage to the establishment of an irrevocable intervivos trust is that the income of the trust is **not** taxable to the trust settlor during his lifetime. Also, the value of the trust is not included in the settlor's estate, if 1) the settlor does not retain a "life interest" in the trust corpus (i.e., the power to invade the trust, or receive money it makes); 2) the trust settlor does not have the power to shift benefits, or re-name the beneficiaries, of the trust; 3) the transfer to the trust was made more than 3 years before death. The trust itself must pay taxes on its income, but the trust will be in a lower income bracket than the settlor. However, the income from the trust will be taxed to the settlor if it is required to be used to pay a legal obligation of his, such as child support or alimony.

There are many sophisticated tax games that can be played with irrevocable trusts. There is a "Clifford" trust, which is particularly useful to provide support for an aging parent or low-income minor or relative who you'd be supporting in any case. There are charitable trusts, reversionary trusts, all sorts of complexities designed by clever tax lawyers. If you have a lot of extra cash that you do not need and don't believe you will need in the future—at least $250,000 and preferably $500,000 or more—you should see a lawyer/estate planner and consider the creation of irrevocable trusts. Of course, if you have a spare quarter of a million dollars or more, you've probably already done that.

2. Irrevocable Life Insurance Trusts

Creation of an Irrevocable Life Insurance Trust is one use of this type of trust that can be helpful to people with moderate estates. The purpose of an irrevocable life insurance trust is to exclude the proceeds of a life insurance policy on the decedent's life from both his probate and taxable estate. (see Chapter 8, Life Insurance.)

Example: Elizabeth, a single parent of children ages 2 and 4, does not want the proceeds of her life insurance included in either her probate or taxable estate when she dies. Her children are the beneficiaries of the policy. There is no adult she trusts enough to be willing to transfer the ownership of the life insurance policy to. So she establishes an irrevocable life insurance trust, assigning her policy to the trust. She names herself as trustee of the trust while she lives, and the trustee of her will as trustee when she dies. Thus, on her death, the proceeds of the policy, being owned by the irrevocable trust, are excluded from both her probate and taxable estate. Her children don't need a court-appointed guardian for the insurance proceeds, because the trust can manage their money.

If you decide that you prefer, or need, the bother of such a trust, rather than the outright assignment of a life insurance policy on your life to someone else, the following form can be used, or adapted, to create an irrevocable life insurance trust. These trusts can become tricky, especially if community property is involved, or if a spouse is a beneficiary of the policy. If so, check the trust with a lawyer. (It's probably a good idea to check an irrevocable life insurance trust with a lawyer anyway.)

A reminder: In most cases, there is no real need for a life insurance trust. A simple assignment of the life insurance policy is sufficient (see Chapter 8, Life Insurance). Be sure you really want, and need, a life insurance trust before bothering with one.

If you do create an irrevocable life insurance trust, you should also observe the formalities I've previously described that are applicable to all trusts. Specifically, you should:

- keep trust documents in a safe deposit box;
- transfer a life insurance policy to the trust (and money for payment of insurance premiums if desired);
- keep a trust bank account, and a set of books for all trust transactions, e.g., premium payments;
- notify the insurance company of the establishment of the trust; and
- obtain a federal taxpayer number for the trust (call your local I.R.S. office for details) and file the appropriate tax returns.

Declaration and Instrument of Irrevocable Intervivos Trust

Section I   Settlor

(a) __(settlor's name)__ , called the "settlor" declares that __(he/she)__ has set aside and holds in trust the life insurance policy and property described in Schedule A, attached to this trust agreement.

(b) This trust is irrevocable and may not be altered or amended in any respect, and may only be terminated by distribution of the life insurance proceeds of the life insurance policy described in Schedule A to the beneficiaries of this trust.

Section II   Trustee

(a) __(settlor's name)__ , hereby appoints __(name and address of trustee)__ , to serve as trustee under this trust agreement.

(b) If __(trustee's name)__ , shall for any reason fail to qualify or cease to act as trustee, then __(successor trustee and address)__ , shall act as trustee.

(c) Notwithstanding the last preceding paragraph, each person designated or acting from time to time as a trustee of any trust(s) established by this instrument shall have the power to designate successor trustees to act when he or she shall become unable or unwilling to act as trustee of the trust(s). Each person may designate the same or different persons or entities, including corporate fiduciaries, to act as successor trustee of the trust(s). If all individuals appointed as trustee and any successors designated by them shall be unable or unwilling to act as trustee, _____(name of bank or trust co.)_____ shall act as trustee of the trust. Any person acting as trustee of any trust may from time to time revoke any designation of any successor to himself (whether that designation shall have been made by him or by his antecedent in interest), and that person may designate other persons or entities, or one or more of the same persons or entities, or all the same persons or entities previously designated in a different order, as successor trustee to him. All such designations or revocations shall be exercised in writing and shall be effective on delivery to the _(settlor and/or beneficiaries of the trust)_.

(d) No bond shall be required of any person named in this instrument as trustee, or of any person appointed as the trustee in the manner specified here, for the faithful performance of his duties as trustee.

(e) The trustee shall be entitled to pay himself reasonable compensation from time to time without prior court order.

(f) The trustee is authorized to perform all legal acts necessary, in his judgment, to carry out this trust.

Section III   Beneficiaries

(a) The beneficiaries of this trust are _____ , also named as beneficiaries of the life insurance policy listed in Schedule A.

(b) Should any beneficiary of the trust predecease the settlor, said beneficiary's interest in the trust shall _____ .
[Specify what you want done if a beneficiary dies before you, e.g., his interest shall be divided equally between the other beneficiaries, or shall pass to his heirs, or lawful issue, etc.]

Section IV   The Trust Estate

(a) The life insurance policy and property subject to this instrument listed in Schedule A is referred to as the "trust estate" and shall be held, administered, and distributed in accordance with this instrument.

(b) Any funds or property transferred to this trust by the settlor for payments of life insurance premiums shall be irrevocable gifts to the trust.

(c) The trustee shall retain all incidents of ownership of the life insurance policy listed in Schedule A, and _____(settlor)_____ shall have no incidents of ownership of that policy, and shall not act as trustee for that policy or of this trust.

(d) [add if trust is funded to pay insurance premiums]: The trustee shall pay any net amount of premium, assessment, or other charge, after deducting any dividend or other credit against the charge, on the life insurance policy of which the trust is the owner that are required to keep it in a binding insurance contract.

Section V   Distribution of Trust Assets

(a) On receipt of proof of death of the insured, the trustee shall use reasonable efforts to collect all sums payable under policy terms. All sums received shall become principal of the trust estate, except for interest paid by the insurer, which shall be income. Subject to any contrary provision in the beneficiary designation of any policy, all sums payable under any policy shall be allocated _____ .
[Specify how proceeds are to be allocated, if desired.]

(b) The trustee shall have full power to compromise, arbitrate, or otherwise adjust any claim, dispute, or controversy arising under any insurance policy subject to this trust, and shall have authority to initiate, defend, settle, and compromise any legal proceeding necessary in the trustee's opinion to collect the proceeds of any such policy.

(c) The trustee's receipt to any insurer shall be considered full discharge, and the insurer shall not be under any duty to inquire concerning the trustee's application of policy proceeds.

(d) If any person entitled to outright distribution of a trust or a portion of a trust is under age 18, the trustee shall hold and administer the minor's portion of the trust estate for the minor's benefit. Income of the minor's portion shall be added to principal and the trustee shall pay to or apply for the benefit of the minor as much of the minor's trust as the trustee in the trustee's discretion considers necessary for the minor's proper health, education, support, and maintenance. When the minor attains the age of 18, the trustee shall distribute to the minor his or her entire share of the trust estate.

(e) If after the death of the settlor, a beneficiary who is a minor dies before attaining age 18, the minor's portion of the trust shall be distributed subject _____
_____
                                    (specify what happens)

(e.g., to the minor's issue, or if there are none, to the other beneficiaries of the trust, etc., or under the Uniform Gifts to Minors Act; see Chapter 4, Gifts.)

Section VI   Interpretive Provisions

(a) The validity of this trust and the construction of its provisions shall be governed by the laws of the State of California. This paragraph shall apply regardless of any change of residence of the trustee or any beneficiary, or the appointment or substitution of a trustee residing or doing business in another state.

(b) In this instrument, the term "issue" shall refer to lawful lineal descendants of all degrees, and the terms "child," "children," and "issue" shall include adopted children who were minors at the date of adoption.

(c) As used in this instrument, the masculine, feminine, or neuter gender, the singular or plural number, shall each include the others whenever the context so indicates.

(d) If any provision of this trust instrument is unenforceable, the remaining provisions shall nevertheless be carried into effect.

Section VII   No Contest Clause

In the event any beneficiary under this trust shall, singly or in conjunction with any other person or persons, contest in any court the validity of this trust or of the deceased settlor's last will or shall seek to obtain an adjudication in any proceeding in any court that this trust or any of its provisions is void, or seek otherwise to void, nullify, or set aside this trust or any of its provisions, then the right of that person to take any interest given to him by this trust shall be determined as if that person had predeceased the execution of this Declaration of Trust without surviving issue.

The trustee is hereby authorized to defend, at the expense of the trust estate, any contest or other attack of any nature on this trust or any of its provisions.

Section VIII   Trust Names

The trust created in this instrument may be referred to as the _____
(Full names of settlor, and year trust established)   (e.g. James Jones, 1980 Trust)
_____

Signature

_____

Executed at _____ , California, on _____ , 19 _____ .

(Individual trustee)

(signature of trustee)
_____
(typed name of individual trustee)

(Corporate trustee, if needed)

_____
(typed corporate name)

By <u>(signature of corporate trustee, if needed)</u>

(typed name of signator, and
capacity, e.g.) Secretary

I certify that I have read the foregoing Declaration of Trust and that it correctly states the terms and conditions under which the trust estate is to be held, managed, and disposed of by the trustee. I approve the Declaration of Trust in all particulars and request that the trustee execute it.

Dated: _____

_____
(signature of settlor)

(typed name of settlor)

[Attach "Schedule A" identifying the life insurance policy, and any other assets transferred to the trust.]

H.   Testamentary Trusts

Testamentary trusts are those established by a will, and obviously do not avoid probate because, as I hope you remember, all property left by will (or intestate succession) automatically goes through probate. Testamentary trusts are normally used to reduce subsequent death taxes, not those on the settlor's estate. An example of the uses of a testamentary trust by a husband or wife to reduce death taxes on the death of the second spouse was given in Chapter 3, Taxes. Another example is given shortly in this section. this section.

Testamentary trusts can also be used to control bequests, because:

1) some form of control is inevitable, i.e. the beneficiary is a minor, or incompetent, so that the law requires some supervision of money left to that person. Providing for a trust and trustee normally allows much more discretion than a court-appointed guardian or conservator. A trustee does not have to get court approval for spending trust money.

2) the testator (the writer of the will) wants to exert control; e.g. he's worried that the recipient is a wastrel, and wants the trustee to control spending the trust money, or only wants him to receive a bequest until he's 21, after which the money will go to someone else.

Once a testamentary trust is established, it must be managed by the trustee with the same formalities required of all trusts. The trustee is entitled to a fee for his services, which is fixed by the probate court. Traditionally, the annual fee is ¾ of 1% of the fair market value of the trust assets.

THE CANELOS INDIANS OF THE ANDES PLAY A DICE GAME DURING A WAKE. THE PURPOSE IS TO REMOVE THE TABOO SO PROPERTY CAN BE DISTRIBUTED TO THE SURVIVORS.

Testamentary trusts can become very complicated indeed. If, when you plan your estate, you decide you have sufficient assets so that a testamentary trust might be valuable (at a minimumm the estate should have over $250,000), see an attorney.

In one type of situation, testamentary trusts can be very advisable: when there is an elderly couple with substantial assets. If they each leave all their property to each other, with the surviving spouse leaving the entire estate to other inheritors, the total estate taxes paid may be significantly more than if trusts are used (see discussion in Chapter 3, Estate Taxes, section B(5)). As explained in Chapter 3, no federal estate taxes are assessed for property transferred to a surviving spouse. However, when the second spouse dies, all the estate will be subject to federal estate tax, which can, in the case of large estates, be substantial. One way to lessen the amount of estate taxes imposed on the death of the second spouse is for the first spouse to die to establish a testamentary trust (usually for their children) of all, or some portion, of his or her assets. The surviving spouse can be given the right to receive the income from the trust for his or her life. Also, the trustee can be given the right to invade the principal of the trust for needs of the surviving spouse, if the trustee determines that the money is needed.

Here's an example of how the use of testamentary trusts can result in substantial overall estate tax savings.

Example: Husband and wife own $2,100,000 of community property. Wife dies in 1983. Husband dies in 1984.

If wife leaves her estate ($1,050,000) to her husband, who then leaves all the estate to their children, here are the estate tax consequences:

On Wife's death:

Gross estate (½ of community) . . . . $ 1,050,000

Less: administration expenses(burial, etc.) . . . .   <50,000>

Net estate   1,000,000

No estate tax assessed . . . .

On Husband's death:

Gross estate . . . . $ 2,050,000

Less: administration expenses . . . .   <50,000>

Net estate   2,000,000

Tentative estate tax   780,800

Less: 1984 unified tax credit   96,300

Estate tax payable . . . . $ 684,500

Now assume wife leaves her estate to her children. Husband receives the income from the trust for his life. When he dies, the principal of the trust is turned over to the children. Note that the income to the husband can be quite substantial. If wife's $1,000,000 estate is placed in a trust, it should earn at least 10% interest under current economic conditions. Thus, husband will receive a minimum of $100,000 income per year from the trust. Assume husband has spent all his trust income before he dies. Here are the estate tax consequences of using trusts here:

On Wife's death:

Gross estate (½ of community)	$ 1,050,000
Less: administration expenses(burial, etc.)	<50,000>
Net estate	1,000,000
Tentative estate tax	345,800
Less: 1983 unified tax credit	79,300
Estate tax payable	266,500

On Husband's death:

Gross estate	$ 1,050,000
Less: administration expenses (burial, etc.)	<50,000>
Net estate	1,000,000
Tentative estate tax	345,800
Less: 1984 unified tax credit	96,300
Estate tax payable	$ 249,500

Total estate taxes paid using trusts	$ 516,000
Total estate taxes paid without trusts	$ 684,500
Tax savings from using trusts	$ 168,500

Even greater ultimate estate tax savings can sometimes be achieved by use of "generation skipping trusts" (see section J of this chapter) or by other sophisticated trusts.

Given the troubles that can arise if a testamentary trust is not prudently and properly drafted, and the substantial tax savings that can be achieved, I can't recommend drafting such a complex document yourself. If you decide you need one, see an attorney. This does not mean that you should blindly find a lawyer and drop all your problems on her desk with no thought. It does mean you should try to understand your situation yourself, plan as much of your estate as you can, and only then, if you believe a testamentary trust might be desirable in your case, discuss it with an attorney who can do the technical work involved and precise dollar calculations of the tax saving to your estate.

I. Powers of Appointment

A ''power of appointment'' means the authorization of one person by another to decide what shall be done with that second person's property. A simple example in a will is ''I appoint Henry Neale with the general power of appointment to distribute all my paintings as he sees fit.'' The reason a ''power of appointment'' is sometimes used, rather than a testamentary or irrevocable intervivos trust, is that the grantor wants another person to have maximum flexibility to decide what should be done with his property. Powers of Appointment are used mainly with large estates.

J. Generation Skipping Trusts

At the beginning of this chapter I discussed the fact that for years, the rich could reduce the total estate taxes paid on their wealth over several generations using ''generation-skipping'' testamentary trusts. The bulk of the rich man's wealth was left in trust for his grandchildren, while his widow and his children received only the income from the trust. The wealth was subject to the estate tax when the rich man died, but when his widow died, and then when his children died, there were no death taxes imposed, as the money remained in trust for the grandchildren. The 1976 Tax Reform Act contains provisions supposedly curtailing these ''generation skipping transfers.'' Under the new law, the full value of the trust assets **are** subject to federal estate taxes upon the death of the children. However, there is an exclusion of the first $250,000 of trust assets for every child (not grandchild) of the trust settlor. In other words, if the trust settlor has two children, and they each have three children, the trust settlor can leave a total of $500,000 in trust for his grandchildren tax free. This can be done by setting up two separate $250,000 trusts. Each child receives the income from one of the trusts for life, and on his or her death the trust monies are transferred tax free to the grandchildren, to be divided as the grandfather's will provided.

Generation-skipping trusts should be prepared by someone knowledgeable in estate planning. These trusts are designed to have affect for at least two generations after the settlor's life, i.e. well over 50 years. There are many contingencies that should be considered, and a trust of that complexity is difficult to prepare yourself. Also, there are requirements regarding the age of the trustee and the time the estate tax on this transfer will be assessed.

Important: The $250,000 exemption for generation-skipping trusts applies **only** to trusts for children and grandchildren. Trusts for anyone else, even other relatives— nephews, great-grandchildren—are not eligible for this exemption.

Even if you have a spare quarter of a million dollars for a generation-skipping trust, it may well not be advisable to establish one. This type of trust means your children cannot obtain the bulk of the money in the trust. They can only receive the interest or profits from the trust money. This is all well and good if you will leave other money to your children, or if they have earned plenty on their own, but may be a mistake if there are no other resources. So, before you decide to establish such a trust, be sure you understand the restrictions they place on your children. Of course, if you have an estate of several million, it is certainly advisable to establish generation-skipping trusts, as the balance of your estate should suffice for your children (and all other inheritors) and these trusts can substantially save on taxes.

10
Joint Tenancy

A. Joint Tenancy and Probate

One of the traditional ways to avoid probate of property is to own that property "in joint tenancy" or as "joint tenants" with another person or persons. Use of these words in the property ownership documents creates a "right of survivorship." This means that the property "automatically" is transferred to, and becomes owned by, the surviving joint tenant upon the death of the other joint tenant. Since, legally, the deceased owner lost all his ownership of property at the moment he died, the transfer to the surviving owner occurs outside of probate. Joint tenancy can be a particularly desirable means to transfer ownership of one or two major items of property outside of probate, thus greatly reducing probate fees. Joint tenancy does not reduce death taxes.

Important: Property owned in joint tenancy passes automatically to the surviving joint tenant(s) even if a deceased joint tenant leaves a will with contrary instructions.

The reason property held in joint tenancy has a right of survivorship is based on ancient English law. The words "joint tenants" are what lawyers call "terms of art" — magic legal words that, when used, have a defined legal affect. Any property, not just land, can be owned in joint tenancy. Because the ritual of "joint tenants" is accepted by the American legal system, property owned in joint tenancy is not part of a probate estate.

To own property in joint tenancy, the ownership document must contain words which clearly demonstrate the intention of the owners to own the property in that legal manner. There is no presumption that shared ownership is joint tenancy; it must be clearly spelled out. The most simple and effective way to do this is to state, in the ownership document that the property is owned ". . .as joint tenants" or "in joint tenancy." Legal "terms of art" are useful, at times, because once the magic words are used, the legal position is clear.

The other major means of shared ownership in California is a tenancy-in-common. The major legal difference between joint tenancy and tenancy-in-common is that tenants-in-common have **no** right to survivorship. If one tenant-in-common dies, his interest in that property passes by will, or, if there is no will, by intestate succession. Either way, unless you use a device like an inter-vivos trust, the property becomes part of the probate estate. Joint tenancy is the reverse; as you should now know, a joint tenant cannot pass any interest in the jointly held property by will.

Most readers probably know the way they hold title to property. If you aren't sure, you should check it out. If, after weighing the advantages and disadvantages of joint property ownership, you decide you do want to hold certain property as joint tenants, this section presents the forms you need to do it.

Any number of persons can co-own property in joint tenancy, but they must own the property in equal shares. Each joint tenant owns an individual equal interest in joint tenancy property with the other owner(s). If there are three joint tenancy owners of an item of property, and one dies, the property is "automatically" transferred to the **two** survivors, who remain joint tenant owners, now each owning one-half of the property, rather than one-third. All joint tenant owners share equally in all income, profits (and losses) from the property.

NOTE: If you wish to own property with others in unequal shares, joint tenancy is not for you; you should consider tenancy-in-common (another set of magic words) along with a contract setting out the shares. People living together commonly wish to own property in unequal shares. Contracts and forms to bring about this result are contained in the *Living Together Kit,* Nolo Press.

B.   Joint Tenancy and Estate Taxes

Owning property as joint tenants does not reduce the taxable estate for federal estate tax purposes. The federal government includes the value of the decedent's jointly owned property in his taxable estate. The amount of that interest is based on his financial contribution to the acquisition of the jointly owned property. If the decedent put up all the money to purchase an item of joint property, the full market value of the property is included in his taxable estate. Moreover, the tax authorities will **presume** that the first joint tenant to die contributed **all** of the cash for the purchase (and maintenance, if additional costs were required for that) of jointly owned property. The burden of proof is on the surviving tenant(s) to overturn this presumption by establishing that the survivors made cash (or other) contributions, toward purchase and/or upkeep of the jointly held property. To the extent the surviving tenants can prove that they put up part of the purchase price, or expenses, the value of the joint tenancy property included in the decedent's taxable estate will be reduced proportionately. One risk with holding property in joint tenancy is that the jointly owned property will be subject to death taxes twice for its full market value, unless good records are kept.

Example: Years ago, Phil and Patsy, who are brother and sister, bought a house as joint tenants. They each contributed half the purchase price, but any records that can prove that have long vanished. Patsy dies in 1982. The full 1982 market value of the house is included in her taxable estate, since it is "presumed" she contributed all the purchase price. Phil, the surviving joint tenant, owns the entire house. He dies in 1983. The full 1983 market value of the house is included in his taxable estate. Had Phil and Patsy kept records, only half the value of the house would have been included in Patsy's taxable estate.

However, where a husband and wife are involved in a joint tenancy the rules are different; under the 1976 Tax Reform Act **only one-half of the value of marital joint tenancy property is included in the estate of the first spouse to die no matter who put up the money to buy the property originally.** These rules apply to joint tenancies in either real or personal property created since January 1, 1977, as long as gift taxes are paid at the time of the transfer, if a gift is involved, and there are no joint tenants in addition to the spouses.

The creation of a joint tenancy may involve a gift. If one person puts up all the money to purchase the property, but another is listed with her as a joint tenant, the purchaser is making a gift of half-ownership of the property; a gift tax return must be filed, and any gift taxes due must be paid.* Likewise, if a sole owner of property transfers ownership into joint tenancy, a gift has been made. There are some limited exceptions to this rule. First, if a bank account, savings bonds, or securities are bought in joint tenancy, with one person actually paying all or most of the cost (or deposit), there is no taxable gift at the time of creation of the joint tenancy. Only when the person who did not contribute half the cost takes possession of more than his original contribution (i.e., by withdrawing money from the bank account, or selling his interest in the stock or bond) is there a gift with gift taxes due. Second, if property is placed in joint tenancy ''for convenience only,'' for example, to avoid probate, and there is no donative intent to make a present gift, it is possible no completed gift has been made. However, this exception is tricky, and should not be used without consulting a lawyer. In normal cases, you must declare there has been a gift, and pay any gift taxes due, at the time of the transaction creating the joint tenancy.

C. Creating a Joint Tenancy in Personal Property

To create a joint tenancy for any type of personal property, all you have to do is declare in a **written** ownership document, that you and the co-owner(s) own the property ''in joint tenancy'' or ''as joint tenants.'' The document does not need to be recorded, unlike joint tenancy for real property, which should be.

---

* If the value of the gift was over $10,000, and no combined estate-gift tax credit is used to avoid the imposition of gift taxes (see Chapter 4, Gifts and Taxes). However, the creation of a joint tenancy between a husband and wife will not be treated as a gift, unless the donor expressly provides it **is** to be treated as a gift.

1. Joint Bank Accounts

Bank accounts can be a very useful means of avoiding probate, especially for making smaller bequests. There are two principal types of accounts that will serve to transfer money outside of probate: joint bank accounts, and "Totten trusts" which are discussed below under (2).

Any bank account may be held in joint tenancy. To open such an account, all you have to do is have both persons sign the account papers as "joint tenants." California banks have joint tenancy account forms and are familiar with those types of accounts. When one person dies the other can (within the limits on the account and by the procedures described below) obtain all the money in the account.

In a joint tenancy bank account either party can withdraw any or all of the money in the account at any time. If the purpose of the account is for shared expenses—as the family account of a husband and wife—this is not a problem. However, if what you desire is **just** to have the money in the account given to someone else on your death, a joint tenancy account exposes you to the risk that the other person can remove the money while you are alive. If the joint account consists of community funds of a married couple, there is never a gift problem, because both husband and wife already own the funds equally. Otherwise, though, there is a taxable gift **if,** and when, one joint tenant withdraws money deposited by another tenant. To put it another way: there is no "gift" made if you deposit money in a joint account, only when the other person takes it out.

2. Totten Trusts

There is a simple means of avoiding loss of control of your money while you live, while at the same time allowing you to pass it free of probate when you die. It is commonly called a "Totten trust." You simply open a savings account* in your name as the depositor, "as trustee for the benefit of _____" (whomever you choose). Banks have standard forms for opening Totten trust accounts. No other trust forms are required.

The beneficiary of a Totten trust account has absolutely no right to it while the depositor is alive. After death of the depositor, the beneficiary takes full title to the account without it passing through probate. The depositor can close the account whenever he likes and he can change the beneficiary at any time. Also he can withdraw (or deposit) any amount he wants from the account.

Because the depositor retains complete control over the account until his death, the establishment of a Totten trust is not a completed gift and so is not subject to gift taxes. Only when the beneficiary withdraws the money does title to it change. So, the amount in a Totten trust will be included in the taxable, but **not** probate estate of the original depositor. Any federal estate tax due must be paid by the depositor (from his estate).

3. Safety Deposit Boxes

Safety deposit boxes can be useful items to own in joint tenancy. A safety deposit box is a sensible place to keep important papers—wills, instructions on funeral, burial or body donation, veteran, union death benefits or pension documents, etc. If the safety deposit box is jointly owned, either co-owner can obtain instant access to the documents when they are needed.

---

* Checking accounts can legally be used as Totten trusts, but rarely are.

Until January 1, 1981, safety deposit boxes were sealed by the bank upon notification of the death of any owner. The contents could not legally be released until the box was inventoried by the County Treasurer. Even before the repeal of California's inheritance tax, the legislature adopted a statute eliminating the sealing and inventorying of safety deposit boxes. So now the surviving owner can legally remove all jointly-owned contents of a safety deposit box at any time.

Important: If you decide to get a jointly-held safety deposit box, be sure to specify on the bank account cards that the co-owners share ownership of all contents of the box. Joint tenancy rental of a safety deposit box does not create ownership rights in that box's contents unless it is clearly spelled out. The bank (or a disgruntled heir) might claim you are co-owner of the box alone—but the contents remained separate property, unless you clearly indicate otherwise.

If there's substantial property involved or if there is some separate property and some community property, it is wiser to rent separate safety deposit boxes.

4. Other Personal Property

For a few other types of personal property, there are standard forms for creating joint tenancy ownership. For example, the Department of Motor Vehicles has a form for registering joint ownership of a car.*   Likewise, stocks can simply be re-registered in the names of the new joint owner. For most other types of personal property—from art objects to furniture to clothes, whatever—you must create your own joint tenancy document. Suppose you own a very valuable painting, a Renoir your astute grandmother bought in 1870 for a few francs when she passed through Paris on a "grand tour." It is now worth a few million. Certainly you want to exclude this painting from your probate estate. You know that you wish to leave the painting to your cousin Kendell. So, you create a written joint tenancy of that painting now. When you die, the painting "automatically" becomes Kendell's property. Your estate has saved many thousand dollars of probate fees.

5. Joint Tenancy Documents for Personal Property

The following forms can be used to create joint tenancy ownership of personal property. The first form is used when you are making a gift of ownership to the new joint tenant(s). The second form is for the less common occurrence of actually selling one half (or two-thirds, etc.) interest to others. Finally, the third form is for newly acquired property, to document that it was bought in joint tenancy.

---

*   If you want to hold a car in joint tenancy, you should state so specifically. The law states that if the pink slip says only "A **or** B" as owners, there's a presumption this is a joint tenancy, but if it says only "A **and** B" are owners, the presumption is that it is **not** held in joint tenancy (and don't ask me **why** that's the rule; I have no idea. Maybe no one does).

FORM #1   Joint Tenancy Ownership Document

Ownership of the personal property identified below, previously owned by (your name) _____ , is hereby transferred to ___(your name)___ and (joint tenant's name) as joint tenants. Said joint tenancy property is described as:

(list and clearly identify the property).

Dated: _____

_____
(your name)

Dated: _____

_____
(joint tenant's name)

FORM #2   Joint Tenancy Ownership Document

Ownership of the personal property identified below, previously owned by (your name) _____ , is hereby transferred to ___(your name)___ and (joint-tenant's name) as joint tenants, for consideration paid of (purchase price) by (joint-tenant's name) to _____ (your name). Said joint tenancy property is described as:

[list and clearly identify the property]

Dated: _____

_____
(your name)

Dated: _____

_____
(joint-tenant's name)

FORM #3   Joint Tenancy Ownership Document

Ownership of the personal property identified below is held by _____(your name)_____ and _(joint tenant's name)_ as joint tenants.

Said joint tenancy property is described as: (list and clearly identify the property).

Said joint tenancy property was purchased on _____, 19____ for a purchase price of $_____, of which _____ contributed $_____ and _____ contributed $_____ of the purchase price.

Dated: _____

_____
(your name)

Dated: _____

_____
(joint tenant's name)

D.   Creating a Joint Tenancy in Real Property

Since real estate prices have become so high throughout California, it is particularly desirable to transfer a home, often the major asset of a moderate estate, outside of probate. Any real estate, home or not, can be owned in joint tenancy. Use of the words "joint tenancy" or "as joint tenants" after the owners' names in the deed to the real property will create a joint tenancy, with "automatic" rights of survivorship. Thus, joint tenancy ownership of real estate can substantially reduce probate fees and allow the surviving owner to continue full use of the property. For this reason, some estate planners recommend you transfer most separately-held title to real estate into joint tenancy where you're married and/or know who you want to receive that real estate upon your death. Once again, I cannot recommend the indiscriminate transfer of all your property (here real estate) into any one form of ownership. There are risks to holding property as joint tenants, which I cover in Section E of this chapter.

After weighing the pros and cons, if you decide you want to hold title to real property as joint tenants with one or more other persons, the procedures for doing so are simple.

❖If you buy real estate in the future, you can own it as joint tenants simply by instructing the title company to list you and the other owner(s) as joint tenants on the ownership deed.

❖If you now own real estate property in sole ownership, you can transfer that ownership into joint tenancy yourself, by creating a deed listing the new owners and reciting that they hold title as "joint tenants." (This type of transaction will either be a gift to the new owner(s),* or, less likely, a sale if the new owner(s) actually pay(s) you money for the creation of the joint tenancy interest.) The new joint tenancy deed should be recorded as soon as possible with the County Recorder's Office.

---

* Once again, no gift taxes will be due on transfer if the new joint tenant doesn't cash in, somehow, on his new ownership interest.

❖If you now own property as a tenant-in-common, you can convert ownership into joint tenancy if, and only if, all the tenants-in-common agree to do so. If they do, then you all simply sign a new deed, stating that the property has been transferred to ''joint tenancy'' ownership; this document should be recorded.

❖If you own community real property, it likewise can be transferred to joint tenancy by the husband and wife executing (and recording) a new joint tenancy deed.

Following is a sample joint tenancy deed for real property. Standard real estate deed forms, such as blank Quit Claim deeds, are available at many stationery stores. In this deed, Alfred Smythe has created a joint tenancy in real property between himself and his son Anthony, by giving Anthony a ''joint ownership'' interest in the real property.

RECORDING REQUESTED BY

AND WHEN RECORDED MAIL TO

NAME Alfred Smythe
ADDRESS Easy Street
CITY & STATE El Dorado Hills, Ca.

Title Order No.________ Escrow No.________

SPACE ABOVE THIS LINE FOR RECORDER'S USE

MAIL TAX STATEMENTS TO

NAME Alfred Smythe
ADDRESS Easy Street
CITY & STATE El Dorado Hills, Ca.

Individual Grant Deed

~~FOR VALUE RECEIVED~~

Alfred Smythe
GRANTS to

Anthony Smythe and Alfred Smythe, as Joint Tenants

all that real property situate in the City of El Dorado Hills

County of Dreams, State of California, described as follows

(property described and identified)

Said property to be owned in joint tenancy by Alfred Smythe and Anthony Smythe

Dated July 1, 1980 XXXXXX

/s/ Alfred Smythe

/s/ Anthony Smythe

STATE OF CALIFORNIA }
________ County of ________ } ss.

On________, 19____, before me, the undersigned, a Notary Public, in and for said State, personally appeared________
____

known to me to be the person whose name ________ subscribed to the within instrument, and acknowledged to me that __he__ executed the same.

____
Notary Public

FOR NOTARY SEAL OR STAMP

MAIL TAX STATEMENTS AS DIRECTED ABOVE

1. Joint Tenancy of Real Property and Proposition 13

Proposition 13 provides that real property taxes will be reassessed on the basis of current market value at the time of a "change of ownership" of that property. Under a 1979 California statute* interpreting Proposition 13 the creation of a transfer of a joint tenancy interest in real property is **not** a "change of ownership" if the original owner is one of the (new) joint tenants. However, if the original owner is not one of the new joint tenants, then any "creation, transfer or termination" of a joint tenancy interest is a "change of ownership."

Example: Mrs. Jefferson has two pieces of separately owned real estate. She transfers title to the first piece to herself and her husband, Raymond, as "joint tenants." She transfers title to the second piece to herself and her daughter, Lila, as "joint tenants." There has been no "change of ownership" for Proposition 13 purposes.

Example: Mrs. Jefferson transfers (by gift or sale) a third piece of real estate (formerly separately owned by her) to her son and his wife "Raymond Jefferson and Lila Jefferson, as joint tenants." There has been a "change of ownership" for Proposition 13 purposes, since the original owner, Mrs. Jefferson is not one of the joint tenants.

Warning: The law governing what is a "change of ownership" for Proposition 13 purposes is subject to change (it changed completely during the preparation of this book). If you're considering the transfer of real property into joint tenancy, check with someone knowledgeable to make sure the law hasn't been changed again.

E. Limitations of Joint Tenancy

Joint tenancy can be created **only** by a written document (not orally) and should be used prudently, with full knowledge of its consequences. As long as both joint tenants are alive, the joint tenancy ownership can be destroyed by either owner, whether or not the other owner consents to it, or even knows about it. Either joint tenant has the power to sell his interest in the jointly owned property at any time. The new owner takes that interest as a tenant-in-common with the remaining original owner.** If the remaining (original) owner, and the new (tenant-in-common) owner conflict, either party can seek, and obtain, a court ordered partition of the property into two equal halves; if that is impossible, the court will order a foreclosure sale with the proceeds divided inhalf. Thus, if Kendell sells her joint interest in the Renoir painting, you may co-own it with a total stranger, or someone you hate. Perhaps worse, Kendell could force a sale of the painting.

---

* A.B. 1488

** Remember, people who own property as tenants-in-common don't automatically inherit from one another and, unless a trust is created, the share held by the deceased tenant-in-common will go through probate.

A joint tenant can "sell" her one-half interest in joint tenancy property to a third person, who then owns the interest as a tenant-in-common. A recent court decision held that a joint tenant can transform his interest into tenancy-in-common without using a straw man transfer to a third person. The owner simply changes title, transferring his interest in the property to himself as a tenant-in-common; now there is no right of survivorship.

There can be other problems with joint tenancy. If one joint tenant becomes incompetent, it will be difficult and time consuming for the other owner(s) to operate and control the property. Further, creditors of either joint tenant may attach that tenant's interest (not both tenants' interest), and obtain a judicial foreclosure sale if necessary. Thus if Kendell acquires a lot of debts, her creditors can attach her one-half interest in "your" painting (or maybe Kendell assigned her interest in the painting to them). In either case, your painting winds up co-owned by a stranger, and if you can't work out mutually satisfactory methods of possession with the new owner, he can seek a court-ordered sale of the property.

Thus while holding property in joint tenancy often is an extremely attractive probate avoidance device, it is only recommended with people you deeply trust. If you want to exclude property from probate, but still retain complete control over it while you live, a revocable inter-vivos trust (see Chapter 9, *Trusts*) is preferable, although more cumbersome and costly to establish and maintain.

F.   Creditors

As I stated above, joint tenancy property can be levied on by any creditor of either owner, while both owners live. However, upon the death of one owner, the surviving owner takes the property free of any responsibility for the decedent's debts. There are exceptions where:

1. the decedent pledged his (then existing) interest in the joint tenancy property as security for a loan, etc.

2. a creditor has sued, gotten a judgment and has initiated legal steps to collect the money prior to the decedent's death.

3. a creditor can show that the joint tenancy arrangement was a scheme set up solely to defraud creditors. This might be the case if you were about to die, had a lot of creditors, and then suddenly put all your property in joint tenancy so as to avoid paying the debts.

G.   Joint Tenancies Outside of California

If real property is held in joint tenancy in California by residents of another state, they will be accorded the "automatic" right of survivorship all resident joint tenants have. However, California requires legal proceedings of some kind to terminate such joint tenancies. This should be a minor hassle compared to probate, however.

If you hold real property in another state, you should strongly consider having it in joint tenancy (or a revocable inter-vivos trust). Otherwise, while your estate is subject to probate in California, many other states require "ancillary administration" for the real property (or personal) in their state. What this means is extra expenses—not only is there a California lawyer, but there must be a lawyer, and legal proceedings in another state as well. There shouldn't be any property tax reason not to transfer out-of-state real property into joint tenancy although it's worthwhile checking this out with a local realtor or lawyer to be sure. Even if a California resident holds out-of-state property in joint tenancy, there will be some legal costs for transfer of title to the surviving owner. Even the "automatic" right of survivorship takes paperwork, and requires taxes to be paid. This is normally not difficult and can be done by a non-lawyer, but usually fees for this sort of transfer are low and it is often easier to hire someone who knows the procedure.

H.   How "Automatic" Are the Automatic Rights of Survivorship?

The legal cliche that joint tenants have an "automatic" right of survivorship doesn't tell you anything about what really happens when one joint tenant dies. Obviously the words on a deed to real property do not magically change the day a joint tenant takes his last breath. Until someone acts, the legal title will remain recorded in the joint tenants' names. What "automatic" means is that it is possible to transfer title to the surviving owner fairly easily and fairly quickly without the necessity of probate. This is true for all joint tenancies, whether of real or personal property. Notice I used the word "fairly." There is some paperwork involved.

You can hire a lawyer to terminate a joint tenancy after the other joint tenant's death. There is no set statutory fee for this, and the fees lawyers charge for it can vary widely. The practice I'm familiar with is for a lawyer to charge one-third of what the probate fee would be for property of the same value. Often this expense isn't really necessary. Joint tenancies can be simply terminated, by non-lawyers. The procedures for terminating joint tenancies are summarized here, even though obtaining rights of survivorship is not technically part of the "planning" of an estate, because it may be a big help, and save money, for you to show your inheritors how they themselves can obtain title to your jointly held property. Your inheritors may decide it's wiser to hire a lawyer.

1. General Principles and Methods for Termination of Joint Tenancy

The main hassle to actually winding up a joint tenancy after one owner dies used to be getting a release of death tax liens on the property. The "automatic" transfer of joint tenancy property to a surviving owner couldn't, in fact, occur until the tax man was sure he'd get his bite. The actual lien was imposed by California law as part of the state inheritance tax system. Since, to repeat it once more, the inheritance tax was repealed by Proposition 6, the state lien will no longer be imposed. Federal liens may still be imposed, but in most cases, because of the size of the federal estate tax credit (and/or the marital exemption), no federal estate tax will be due on the decedent's estate at all, so in reality no federal lien will be imposed.

There can be a real hooker here, though. The taxes "due" will depend on the size of the taxable estate, but the actual value of that probably won't be determined for quite a while, usually in a probate proceeding. But if the surviving owner must wait until the full estate taxes are known (or even worse, paid) there's no practical, effective right of automatic survivorship. So, federal estate tax people will usually accept a general statement of the property in the estate, with a clear indication that the estate has enough other assets to pay off all liens and taxes. The proof required that all taxes due can be paid from the remaining taxable estate will vary depending on the size, complexity and liquidity of the estate.

Once you obtain the tax release, the rest is easy. You attach that release and a certified copy of the death certificate* to the ownership form, and re-register full legal title in your own name.

2. Changing Title to Real Property

Termination of joint tenancy title to real property can be done by using an affidavit or declaration under penalty of perjury stating that the surviving joint tenant has a right to the property.** Since some county recorders do not accept declarations relating to real property, local custom must be checked. You file with the County Recorder's office: 1) a certified copy of the deceased joint tenant's death certificate, 2) a certificate of release of federal tax lien, if any, and 3) an affidavit executed by the surviving joint tenant, and 4) the new deed listing the (new, sole) owner.

---

* If, for some unusual reason, a death certificate isn't available, there has to be a legal proceeding to "establish the fact of death." In that case, see a lawyer.

** An affidavit must be notarized; a declaration under penalty of perjury does not have to be notarized, and has the same legal affect.

Following is a form that can be used or adapted for the declaration of the surviving joint tenant; if you adapt this form be sure to specify how you and the decedent became joint tenants. Similar forms are also available at many stationery stores.

Declaration [or Affidavit] of Death of Joint Tenant

State of California

County of _____

    I, (surviving joint tenant's name) , ["being duly sworn," if Declaration is to be notarized] say:

    I am 18 years of age or over; (decedent's name) , the decedent mentioned in the attached certified copy of Certificate of Death, is the same person as (name of decedent) , named as one of the parties in the deed dated _____ , 19 ____ , executed by (name of grantor) to (name of decedent) and the undersigned, as joint tenants, recorded on _____ , 19 ____ , in Book ____ , Page ____ , of the Official Records of _____ County, California, covering the property situated in _____ , County of _____ , State of California, described as follows:

[legal description of property]

_____
(signature of affiant)
_____
(typed name of affiant)

<table>
<tr><td rowspan="3">if
notarized</td><td>Subscribed and sworn to before me

on _____ , 19 ____

_____
(signature of notary public)</td><td>

(seal of notary public)</td></tr>
</table>

    I declare under penalty of perjury that the foregoing is true and correct. [Omit this if a notary is used.]

    Executed on this _____ day of _____ , in _____ , California.

_____
(signature)

---

3. Release Procedures for Joint Bank Accounts and Totten Trusts

To obtain the money in either a joint bank account or a Totten trust, the survivor must submit to the appropriate bank officials:

1) a certified copy of the death certificate;

2) release of any federal estate tax lien imposed;

3) no other forms appear to be required. The "Consent to Transfer" forms previously needed from the State Controller's Office are not needed now that the California inheritance tax law has been abolished.

4. Release Procedures for Safety Deposit Boxes

As I stated in Section C(3) of this chapter, safety deposit boxes no longer must be inventoried by the County Treasurer after the death of one owner. The contents of a safety deposit box can be obtained by any of the listed owners, even after the death of a co-owner. However, any property in the deposit box owned by the deceased owner must, by law, be included as part of his federally taxable estate.

5. Transfer of Automobile Title

To re-register a car in the name of the surviving joint owner, the DMV requires:

1. the pink slip signed by the new owner, and the registration card;

2. a new smog compliance certificate; and

3. a certified copy of the death certificate. Submit these documents and the DMV will record the transfer and issue a new pink slip and registration card. An inheritance tax release is normally not required.

6. Transfer of Title to Bonds

Jointly owned savings bonds, or bonds owned in "beneficiary form" (where one person buys the bonds and lists another as the beneficiary who is entitled to redeem them when they mature) are transferred to the surviving owner or beneficiary by:

1. "surrendering" (turning over) the bond, with the surviving owner's signature, at the nearest office of the U.S. Treasury Department;

2. submitting a certified copy of the decedent's death certificate; and

3. submitting Treasury form PD 1787 (available at Federal Reserve banks, commercial banks, as well as the Treasury Department itself). The Treasury Department will then issue a new bond, with the surviving owner (or beneficiary) listed as the sole owner.

When the original bond is "redeemed" for the new one it will be worth more than it was when purchased, as it is nearer to maturity. This increment in value is treated by the IRS as income taxable to the surviving joint tenant.

Your local bank can assist you with all this, including providing the necessary forms.

7. Transfer of Stock

If jointly-owned stocks are securities in a California corporation submit a certified copy of the death certificate to the corporation. New stock will be issued listing the surviving tenant as sole owner.

If the jointly-owned stocks are those of a non-California corporation, it's a little more difficult. To the issuing corporation, you submit:

1. the original jointly-owned stock certificate;

2. a copy of the death certificate;

3. a "signature guarantee" card. This is a signed statement by a bank officer that you, and (especially) your signature are authentic. Banks provide forms for signature guarantees;

4. as with joint bank accounts, "Consent to Transfer" forms are no longer needed.

11

Two Special Types of Estate Planning
Problems: Benefit Programs and Businesses

Many special estate planning problems can arise for those entitled to retirement or death benefits (including the family of the decedent) and for those who own their own businesses. Of course, the two can be intertwined, and a sensible estate plan will require the determination of death benefits from the business. Both of these problems require careful attention to the facts of one particular situation and can't easily be generalized into rules.

Start by asking yourself the following questions: What does your particular pension plan say about survivor's payments? Does your business have any limits such as corporation by-laws or partnership papers that limit the type of payments that may be made to the owners' survivors? These problems are lumped together here because I can give only rudimentary information on how to handle them. They are on the fringes of the type of estate planning I feel a non-lawyer can do by himself. Often, especially in the case of small businesses, there are complex and unique financial situations which require careful scrutinizing by sophisticated (expensive) estate planners. For example, the co-owner of a multimillion dollar corporation might need a lawyer to arrange trusts so as to leave her wealth to her grandchildren, while also insuring managerial continuity of the business. Similarly, many executives can arrange for complicated deferred salary/stock payments that may be available to inheritors. This Chapter does not presume to cover these types of problems. However, it does give a rough outline of the basic benefits available, especially Social Security, and of some types of business problems, that can arise. If professional help is still needed, hopefully you'll be better equipped to ask the right questions after studying the informaion provided here.

A.   Retirement Benefit Programs

Most people are entitled, upon retirement, to payments from one or more retirement programs they have accrued (earned) during their lifetime. These benefits are usually designed to provide support for people who are no longer able to work or who no longer wish to work once they have reached a certain age (this can vary from 55 to 70) or who have worked at a job for a set period of time (usually 20–40 years) or some combination of both. We are all familiar with social security payments, veterans' benefits, private and public employee pension plans and other sorts of retirement payments. Retirement rights, and planning for retirement, is a complicated field separate frome estate planning. I don't pretend to cover it here. There are many good books on the subject, particularly Sylvia Porter's book, *Money*.*

However, retirement rights and estate planning can be interrelated. A sensible estate plan must consider such things as survivor's rights under pension plans or social security, as well as whether the survivor has any pension benefits of her own. Why? Well, suppose a surviving spouse can expect to get regular monthly pension checks that will cover most living expenses. In this situation it may be unwise and unnecessary to leave that person a large sum of cash, when some of the money could be passed to others at lower tax rates (see Chapter 3). Also, there may be different options available to you to provide money for survivors. Suppose you own a small business and have a few thousand dollars a year you want to use for your retirement, and also for your family after you die. Should you put all of your money into some type of retirement plan, or some into (perhaps additional) life insurance? Are you adequately insured now? Again, this type of problem becomes very personal. How much income tax will you save now by deferring taxes on the money put into the retirement plan? What other options do you have for retirement?

Then there is the question of what happens if the family breadwinner dies before he is sixty-five, or whatever the established age is for him to be eligible for retirement benefits? What happens to the benefits he would have received if he'd lived? Do you know? Are his survivors (i.e., especially his spouse) entitled to any portion of these benefits? For how long? What about minor children? If you can't answer these questions, check the particular program's benefit provisions. There is no legal requirement that a pension plan **must** pay benefits to the widow (or any person). Some are generous; some are miserly, and some don't even bother to say "tough luck, friend." Obviously, any sensible estate plan must take into consideration whether or not pension benefits will be available to survivors.

Social security does provide payments to family survivors of covered wage earners. These survivors benefits are established by law, and are excluded from probate, as are all death benefits payable directly to a designated person. However, if death benefits under a retirement program are payable to the decedent's estate, they are subject to probate. So, obviously, if you have any choice in the matter, be sure to state that death benefits are to be paid **not** to your estate, but directly to some other named beneficiary, such as your spouse. Death benefits, including social security payments payable to a designated person, are also excluded from the decedent's federally taxable estate. However, these types of benefits are often subject to California inheritance taxes. Whether a particular benefit will be subject to state taxes depends on the nature of the benefit contract provisions. State and other civil service retirement plan payments are exempt from state taxes.

1. Social Security

a. There is a lump-sum payment for actual funeral expenses (for fully or currently insured workers) up to a maximum of $225 (See Chapter 2, Burials).

b. A widower or widow (or surviving divorced wife or husband)** receives 100% of the deceased spouse's social security benefits if he or she is over 65 **AND** the deceased

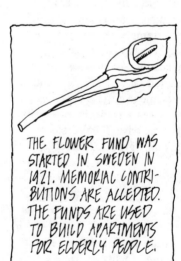

THE FLOWER FUND WAS STARTED IN SWEDEN IN 1921. MEMORIAL CONTRIBUTIONS ARE ACCEPTED. THE FUNDS ARE USED TO BUILD APARTMENTS FOR ELDERLY PEOPLE.

---

* I also recommend *The Rights of the Elderly and Retired*, which is available from Nolo Press. This book gives an in-depth review of social security and pension rules. (See the back of this book for order information.)

** The first (divorced) marriage must have lasted 10 years.

spouse was over 65 and had already started receiving social security benefits. If either was less than age 65, there will be a reduction in benefits paid according to a set formula.*

---

* If the deceased spouse's benefits began before age 65, the widow (or surviving divorced wife) if age 65 on application, will get benefits equal to the greater of what the deceased spouse was getting or 82½% of the deceased spouse's primary insurance amounts. If the application is made between age 60 and 65, a reduced benefit will be payable based on the deceased spouse's benefit amount. (Benefit would be reduced by 19/40 of 1% for each month before age 65.) In no case, however, would the benefit be less than 71½% of the deceased spouse's amount.

If a widow or widower age 60 or over remarries, his or her benefit is reduced to 50% of the deceased spouse's primary insurance amount. If the widow or widower will receive a larger benefit based on the new spouse's earning recored, the larger benefit will be paid. A widow's or widower's remarriage before age 60 (or surviving divorced spouse's remarriage at any age) prevents benefits based on the prior deceased spouse's earnings record, except when the subsequent marriage ends. (Contact Social Security for detailed regulations.)

A widow's or widower's benefit will not be terminated because of a remarriage if the marriage is to an individual entitled to a widower's or widow's mother's or disabled child's benefit. If a widow remarries and her husband is entitled to a disabled child's benefit, her benefit ends when he is no longer entitled to such benefit (unless by death). The benefits of a widow who remarries will be reinstated if her second marriage ends.

A disabled widow, surviving divorced wife or widower can get a reduced disability benefit age age 50, based on the work record of the deceased spouse. At age 50, the benefit is 50% of the deceased spouse's primary insurance amount. If the widow, surviving divorced wife, or widower is older than 50 when the benefits begin, the benefits will be larger, ranging up to a maximum of 100% of the deceased spouse's primary insurance amount at age 65 or older.

(Anyone who reads this deserves a medal!)

Other survivors are also entitled to monthly payments based on the social security rights, including the decedent's:

— unmarried children under 18 (or 22 if full-time student);

— unmarried son or daughter 18 or over who was severely disabled before age 22 and who continues to be disabled;

— dependent parents 62 or older;

— widow (including surviving divorced mother), under 60 if she's caring for the insured worker's child who is either under 18 or disabled, who is getting a benefit based on the earnings of the deceased worker;

— widow or dependent widower 50 or older who becomes disabled not later than seven (7) years after she stops getting checks as a widow caring for worker's children.

IMPORTANT: Under federal law the decedent's own last monthly social security check must be returned to the Social Security Administration. The amount is not pro-rated. Thus, even though a person receives her social security check on the first of the month, but dies on the 20th of that month, her estate cannot keep any of her last check.* The full monthly check must be given back to Social Security. (Who knows why?)

For children to be eligible for social security benefits, the parent must have been fully, currently insured. to be eligible, the child must be (1) unmarried, and under 18, or only if a full-time student, under 22;** (2) be dependent on the decedent when the parent died. The benefits paid to each child of the decedent are 75% of the decedent's own social security benefits, subject to an over-all family maximum.

2. "Keogh" and "IRA" Retirement Programs

As you doubtless know, these are programs that can be established by self-employed persons who have no other pension-retirement programs. *** Taxes are due upon retirement, but this should be at a much lower rate than during earning years.

You can use money in a Keogh or IRA plan to provide for others upon your death. You can direct that some or all of the money in the plan be paid to survivors after your death. The money can be paid in a lump sum, or in installments, i.e. in the form of an annuity. It is normally advisable to have the money paid in installments. The value of an annuity, established under an IRA plan, receivable by a beneficiary will be excluded from the decedent's gross taxable estate to the extent the decedent's payments to the IRA account were deductible for income tax purposes. In other words, only if the decedent put more into his IRA plan than was tax-exempt will there be any federal estate taxes, and these only on the excess over the IRA tax limits. The annuity must last for at least 36 months after the decedent's death to escape inclusion in the taxable estate. If the annuity is for less than 36 months, or payment is made in a lump sum, that amount may be included in the taxable estate. Finally, if IRA or Keogh payments are payable to the decedent's estate they will be included in his taxable and probate estate, so avoid this. Incidentally, lump sum payments to a named beneficiary from corporation contributed pension plans are **included** in the decedent's gross taxable estate.

3. Other Retirement Programs

There are many other types of benefits, and accompanying problems: veterans benefits, railroad retirement benefits, state and federal employment retirement, union

---

* Thus the state, acting wisely for once, encourages you to spend **all** of your last check, as soon as you get it.

** **or** have been disabled before age 22.

*** This means no other retirement plan they are presently involved in. They can have accrued rights under early retirement programs, and can also receive social security.

pension plans, and so on. The benefits (if any) these programs provide family survivors depend on the exact nature of each program. Check the regulations and precise program that applies to you.

The federal government has pamphlets which explain its programs, including Keogh and IRA and all other retirement programs. Fact Sheet IS-1 contains information on Federal Benefits for veterans and dependents.

B.   Business Ownership

If a person is sole or part owner of a business, his death will normally cause serious disruption of that business. With a small business, the death of one owner can produce drastic results, especially if no planning has been done. The main problems revolve around the surviving owners insuring managerial continuity, and financial solvency,* while enabling the deceased owner's heirs to receive the value of his share of the business. There are so many different kinds of businesses that precise rules cannot be given that cover all situations. Some factors are common:

1.   There should be some planning for who will receive the ownership interest of any deceased owner;

2.   It should be determined how managerial control and continuity will be maintained;

3.   A method for determining the worth of the deceased owner's interest should be decided on. This is particularly necessary in the case of a small business, as it is often difficult (and needlessly expensive) to have outside ''experts'' determine the worth of a deceased owner's interest;

4.   Some means of paying the decedent's survivors and inheritors for his interest should be selected. Life insurance is one possible way to do this.

Determining how to coordinate the business with an estate plan varies depending on the circumstances of each situation. In one case, use of a revocable inter-vivos trust may be advisable. For example, Jackson is the sole proprietor of a small thriving printing company. He wants to leave it to his friend and employee, Brown, but only if Brown is still around when he dies. He creates a revocable inter-vivos trust, names himself as trustee and transfers ownership of the printing company to it. Brown is named as the beneficiary. When Jackson dies, the business automatically becomes owned by Brown. While Jackson lives, he can change his plan any time he wants to.

Another way to provide for continuity is by creating a corporation. ''Close'' corporations, where there are fewer than ten (10) stockholders, are not difficult to create. The great advantage of a corporation is that they have achieved what has eluded all humans — corporations live forever (until dissolved). **

The shares in a ''close'' corporation can be transferred by any of the methods available for other property. Usually, there should be an agreement on how the shares are to be valued. And if the inheritors of the shares are not going to continue the business there should also be agreement on how the corporation can buy them. It is particularly difficult with ''close'' corporations to determine the value of one owner's stock where there is no ready market to determine the value of the stock generally. The safest method is to have all owners agree to a means for determining this worth. A set dollar figure can

---

* Incidentally, all lawsuits against the decedent, as the owner of a business, survive his death and can be prosecuted against that business and/or his estate.

** See Mancusco, *How To Form Your Own California Corporation,* (Nolo Press). (Order information at back of this book.)

be provided, or there can be some percentage figure, or formula used, or a named third person selected to make a binding determination of the value of the decedent's interest.

If the business is run as a corporation, the agreements can become complicated. For instance, if the business buys the decedent's stock, is that purchase price taxed to the decedent's estate as a dividend? It can be. If your business is a corporation, it is wise to discuss your estate-planning with a lawyer.

The '76 Federal Tax Reform Act created new special provisions for the valuation of, and tax payments by small businesses. First, under specified circumstances, farms and closely held businesses can be valued for their current use, not market value. For example, a farm does not have to be valued for its (possibly much higher) worth as a potential location for a shopping center, or high-rise office building, but can be valued as a farm. There are many restrictions on sale or mortgage and financial reporting for up to 15 years. The consensus of estate planners seems to be that, except in rare cases, these restrictions are so severe that this valuation option is not desirable. A more useful option is the new provisions that estate taxes on a family farm or closely held business (where that is a principal asset of the estate) can have tax payments extended over 15 years (at interest of 4%); the first payment due can be delayed up to five years after death.

Partnerships

By law, the decedent's surviving business partners are required to wind up that partnership business without delay (i.e. to end the business). This legal requirement can be avoided by a previous written agreement by all the partners that the death of any partner does not require the dissolution of the business. The partnership agreement should also state what is to occur upon the death of a partner. Property, both real and personal, that is owned by a partnership can be transferred by all the normal probate avoidance means, such as joint tenancy or inter-vivos trusts. Other methods suggested in this book are also appropriate. If the partners take out life insurance to protect the business, no partner should own his own policy; it should be transferred to other partners.

No matter what type of business you have, there should be some written agreement providing for managerial continuity. Otherwise, the probate court must be petitioned to appoint a "special administrator" to continue the business during probate. Such strangers are expensive and there is no reason to allow the probate court to decide what is far better decided by the actual owners. Finally, the methods previously described to avoid or reduce estate taxes should be used for businesses if possible. A life insurance policy on the owner of a business should be owned by that business itself, not the owner. This is one reason it may be advisable to form a corporation so that, legally, there will be a separate entity to own that life insurance.

12
Wills

A. Introduction

"Who needs a will? You do!" a Bar Association pamphlet urges. Indeed, lawyers invariably advise almost everyone that they need a will. "Need" is a peculiar word to apply to your will. Perhaps your would-be inheritors need you to make a will so they can receive property they want. Perhaps a lawyer needs you to make a will in order to collect a fee. Perhaps some charity needs you to make a will so that they can carry on their work. But does this mean that you "need" a will? It is true that a will is one way for you to insure that certain portions of your property go to specific persons on your death, but at the risk of disturbing the legal establishment, let me give you my opinion that, in the normal sense of the word, no one "needs" a will. After all, it won't help you — will it?

Even though it is a little silly to say you need a will, drafting one is usually desirable, as well as being rather easy. I imagine many people avoid preparing their will because they are afraid a will may be costly, and perhaps because they would just as soon believe that their will won't be necessary for a long time to come. Lurking behind this reluctance to prepare a will is the superstition that thinking about a will, or preparing one, might somehow hasten death, or acknowledge its inevitability. For some reason, wills didn't frighten our cultural ancestors as much as they do us; they were commonly used by both the ancient Greeks and Romans. Wills were much less used in feudal times, since most property passed automatically by primogeniture (the eldest son inherits all). The English adopted a "Statute of Wills" in 1540, the first Anglo-Saxon law requiring the formalities we now associate with wills.

What about the basic fact that property which passes by use of a will must go through probate? Isn't probate avoidance a major goal of estate planning? Yes, as I said, probate avoidance is an important goal, and for this reason I've recommended not using a will to pass the bulk of your property. Totten trusts (Chapter 10), inter vivos trusts (Chapter 9) and Gifts (Chapter 4) are some of the sensible ways to pass property that do not involve either wills or probate. But does this mean that wills are really so old-fashioned that they are unnecessary? No. For reasons that will soon become clear, wills are still useful to pass significant amounts of property.

If you decide you want a will, draft it soon. There are no benefits obtained by postponing drafting your will. Just as it is true that everyone will die someday, it is also true that no one can be sure when they will die. A will is simply legal writing which states who gets your property when you die. With a will, your property that hasn't been taken care of in other ways will be distributed in exactly the manner you choose. If you do not leave a will, this property will be distributed according to the California law of "intestate succession" (see Chapter 5, *Probate*). The intestate succession law will very likely not distribute your property in exactly the way you would prefer.

Anyone over the age of eighteen* and of "sound mind" can make a will. If you reside in California, you can make a valid will here even if you are not a United States citizen. Having property distributed under the intestacy provisions is almost always unwise. A will not only allows you to handpick your beneficiaries and the amounts and types of property they will receive, but also allows you to provide for any special family or other needs and to select the person you want to supervise the handling of your estate. Also, planning the distribution as opposed to letting the intestate laws take care of it gives you a chance to plan to minimize death taxes. Even if you attempt to transfer all

---

* Anyone under 18 who dies and owns property will have it distributed to his or her family heirs by the intestate succession law, and cannot pass property by will.

your property outside of probate, a will is usually desirable as there may be assets you hadn't considered or discovered or owned, at the time you made your probate avoidance plans.

The process of drafting your own will requires an understanding of probate avoidance methods and your estate tax situation. Once you comprehend this information, you can decide what property you want to pass by will, and then learn how to draft your own will. A will is one part of an estate plan, and you should draft it understanding how your will works with your over-all plan.

Here's one simple example of how a will can be used in a sensible estate plan. Mathilda has an estate of roughly $500,000, including a house worth $350,000, savings of $120,000, and miscellaneous heirlooms, loved by various relations worth $30,000. She wants to leave the house to her son James and his family. She wants all estate taxes paid from her savings (not pro-rated according to the worth of property received because James is strapped, and, if he has to pay a share of estate taxes, he won't be able to keep the house). She wants to leave the rest of her savings to her niece, Emily. And she wants to leave her heirlooms to over a dozen relations. How can she best accomplish this plan?

To keep the probate costs down, she first creates a revocable inter vivos trust leaving the house to James (see Chapter 9). She next determines what the estate taxes on her $500,000 estate may be and sets this amount aside in a bank account.* Then she transfers her remaining savings into a joint bank account with Emily, which removes this money from her probate estate. And then she writes a will specifying who should get each heirloom, that all estate taxes are to be paid from her own separate bank account, and that the "residue" of her estate is to go to her friend, Martha.

In drafting your will, you aren't limited to just the technical provisions explained in this chapter. After all, it's your will, and you can say anything you want without fear of reprisal, although if you libel someone in your will, your estate can be sued for damages. Short of libel though, your scope is limited only by your imagination and interest. For example, the German poet Heinrich Heine wrote a will leaving his property to his wife on one condition, that she remarry. "Because," the will stated, "then there will be at least one man to regret my death." William Shakespeare cryptically left his wife his "second best bed," a bequest that has intrigued Shakespearean scholars for centuries. If you're without malice, you could include some humor in your will, or perhaps, after naming an inheritor, you could write a poetic description of your love for him or her.

B. Information Necessary to Draft Your Will

1. A Few Definitions, and Some Words of Encouragement
The language of wills (e.g., "devise," "per stirpes," "codicil," "pretermitted heirs," etc., etc.) is one of the more jargon-ridden areas of law (rather an achievement). Some of this language will be used here, since inventing new words usually becomes even more cumbersome than using the traditional ones. Thus, the "testator" is the person making the will. The "estate" is all the property of the testator that can pass by will. The "executor" is the person appointed in the will by the testator to control and supervise the estate while it, and the will, are in probate. Other technical words-of-art will be defined as they are used. I realize that learning this lingo can be a frustrating job, but be patient and you will quickly realize that the concepts behind the mumbo jumbo are usually quite simple.

---

* If Mathilda plans on living a while, it'll be hard for her to estimate future estate taxes with any certainty. So she should set aside a generous amount to pay those taxes.

Despite the use of some technical language, simple wills, sufficient for most situations, can readily be prepared by a non-lawyer. If you have a large estate, and desire extensive estate planning ("pour-over" wills, "generation skipping" trusts, that sort of thing), your will should be prepared by a lawyer. But if you have an average-sized estate and no particularly intricate desires for it, drafting your own will isn't going to be a problem. Lawyers try to scare people into buying their services by claiming that each will needs "expert, professional" care. They then routinely have their secretaries use the same form wills over and over.

This chapter provides you with the information and language necessary to draft your own will, and should allow you to judge whether you can do it yourself or if you need "professional" help. I don't mean to say that having a lawyer do your will or check your work is never needed. Sometimes you do need help. Most of all, as you go through this chapter, please relax and take your time. Drafting a will is not a ten minute job.

2. Types of Wills

There are two types of wills valid in California* — a holographic (handwritten) will, and a formal, typed will.

a. The Holographic Will

A holographic will must be written, dated and signed entirely in the handwriting of the person making the will. Courts have been strict when examining holographic wills, so they must be prepared correctly. The handwritten document must show a clear intent to be a will and to dispose of the writer's property on his or her death. The best way to do this is to be sure that the document clearly states that it is a will. It is absolutely crucial that a holographic will be entirely in the handwriting of the person making it. Any printing on the document can invalidate the whole will. ** The law is very strict on this point. For example, if an intended will is written on paper that has the year 1982 printed on it, the will may not be accepted as valid because the testator did not write the date in his or her own hand. A holographic will does not have to be witnessed, but it can be.

---

* Technically, there is also a "noncupative will," an **oral** will that can only be made by someone serving in the Armed Forces, just before death, where the amount left is all personal property and is less than $1,000. Hopefully, this type of will is as outmoded as the cross-bow.

** One recent California case, *Estate of Black* did take a more tolerant attitude towards handwritten wills, validating one which was a partially pre-printed stationer's form.

Last Will & Testament

I, Felix Finnegan, a resident of Alameda County, California, declare this to be my Last Will and Testament. I revoke all prior wills and codicils:

First: I leave my 1965 Volkswagon to my only child, Joyce Finnegan.

Second: I leave no property to my former wife, Sue Finnegan.

Third: I leave my collection of bumper stickers to the Berkeley Public Library.

Fourth: I leave my dog Beagle, to Delilah Washington who resides at 1442 Wood Ave, Oakland, California.

Fifth: I leave my 350 cc Honda motor-cycle to Sara Tamura, who resides at 2342 Penn Street, Oakland, California.

Sixth: I leave the remainder of my estate to my companion of many years, Keija Adams. If she is not then living, I leave the remainder of my property to my parents, Herbert Finnegan, and Mary Finnegan, in equal shares. If my parents do not survive me, I leave the remainder of my property to the American Civil Liberties Union of Northern California.

Seventh: I nominate Keija Adams as executrix of my will. If she is not then living, I nominate Delilah Washington to act in her place. I direct that no bond be required of my executrix.

Executed at Berkeley, California
on March 15, 1980.

Felix Finnegan

IMPORTANT: Let me emphasize — A holographic will should be letter perfect. If you make a mistake writing one, do it over. Courts have rejected holographic wills that had crossouts, additions, etc.

A holographic will is admitted to probate just like a typed, formal will. In both cases, the will must be "proved." This means that it must be established that the will is truly what it purports to be. For a formal will, this is usually done by the testimony of the witnesses to the will. In the case of a holographic will, it can be proved by a witness who saw the will prepared or by someone who knows the writing of the decedent, or by a handwriting expert. (This can be a problem — remember Howard Hughes?)

Holographic wills are not valid in a majority of states, so if you've drafted one and you move, check the law of your new state. Also, joint holographic wills cannot be made. A joint holographic will is not valid for the person who merely signs it (but is for the person who wrote it out **and** signed it).

A holographic will is not for regular use. Why American society suspects handwriting and prefers the form neatness of a typewriter is to the author an interesting question, but the fact is that handwriting is suspect, and a will is no place to be provocative. The chances of someone raising serious questions about the validity of a will are greater when a holographic will is used. But the holographic will does have its place. If you get trapped in the woods, or face some other immediate disaster, a holographic will is far better than none. Also, if you have only a very small amount of property or if almost all of your property has been taken care of by probate avoidance devices, a holographic will is probably adequate and certainly better than no will at all. Still, it is almost always better to prepare a typed, witnessed will according to the instructions set out below.

b. The Formal (Typed) Will

There are not many legal requirements for a formal will. A lay person can easily prepare one for a fairly simple estate. The requirements for a valid formal will in California are:

- It must be typed or printed (it does not need to be notarized);
- It must state in some manner that it's the testator's will ("This is my will" suffices);
- It must be signed and dated by the testator;
- It must be witnessed by at least two witnesses (who, normally, must be disinterested in the estate) who sign and date it after watching you sign and date it;
- The testator is supposed to declare to the witnesses at the time he or she signs the will that it is his or her will.

Other than these, there are no specific requirements for a valid formal will. In our law office we usually staple our wills to a blue cover-binder, sometimes attaching a red ribbon and a seal. We have found that people prefer that their wills look like impressive documents. Blue-backing paper (called blue backs) are available at most office supply stores.

c. Joint Wills

A joint will is one document involving two people who are usually married. Each leaves everything to the other when the first one dies, and then the will goes on to specify what happens to the property when the second person dies. In effect, a joint will prevents the surviving person from deciding what should happen to the parties' property on the second death. I feel that it is normally better for a husband and wife to make two separate wills with the same provisions rather than a joint will. That way, after the death of one spouse, the surviving spouse can revise his or her will if he/she feels there is reason to do so.

There may, however, be cases where a joint will might make sense for you. Suppose a married couple, Fred and Ida, want to leave their money first to each other, but on Ida's death, Fred wants the remainder of the estate to go to cousin Duane. Fred knows that Ida detests Duane and is likely to leave him nothing if she gets the chance. To solve this problem, Fred convinces Ida to draft and sign a joint will, leaving the estate to Duane no matter which of them dies first. Logically, in a situation where a joint will is felt to be needed by one person, the other will probably oppose it. I believe that coercion is rarely good karma. In this case, I feel it would make more sense for Fred to set up a trust leaving his wife a ''life interest'' in his estate with the residue to go to Duane. In this way Duane would be guaranteed of getting Fred's money, but would almost certainly not get Ida's. And why should he? Ida thinks he's mean as a tiger with thorns in its toes.

Whether or not a joint will can be revoked by one of the makers, as to her, is often unclear. If the joint will is regarded as a contract between the two makers, both must consent for revocation to be effective. This potential source of litigation is another reason to avoid joint wills.

d. Wills Drafted Out-of-State

A will made out-of-state is valid and can be probated in California if:

1) It was prepared so as to be valid under California law, i.e., signed by the testator, witnessed by two witnesses, etc. (see Section B1b above); or

2) It was valid under the laws of the state where it was made; or

3) It is valid under the laws of the state or country where the testator was domiciled* at the time of death or at the time of the making of the will.

A will admitted to probate in another state or country will be effectuated in California. If the will has been established and validated in the courts of another state or country, no probate contest will normally be allowed here.

e. Contracts to Make a Will and Conditional Wills

A contract to make a will (and leave certain property to the other party to the contract) is valid. A valid contract in which you agree to leave your car to Fred will take precedence over a subsequent will (one that breaches that contract) which does not mention Fred and leaves the car to Sam. Of course, the contract with Fred could be mutually rescinded or Fred could breach it, in which case Sam would inherit under the will. Tying up your property so you cannot change your will is not desirable for more reasons than I can list here. Lawyers and other financial advisors invariably advise against a contract to make a will. The usual case in which they are made is where someone provides services—care, live-in nursing, etc.—in return for an agreement that the person receiving the care will leave all or some of his/her property to the person providing the care. Most lawyers prefer to establish some form of trust for these situations.

Finally, a conditional will, one which by its own terms is conditioned on some event or circumstances to be valid, will be granted or denied probate depending on whether the condition has occurred or been satisfied.

---

* Domicile is a legal term of art; it is the place where you have your legal home. Usually that means your residence, but domicile is a matter of intent, so you can reside primarily in Florida, but still be domiciled in your rarely seen Manhattan apartment if it is your intent that New York is your basic home. You can only have **one** domicile at a time.

3. Preparing a Will
a. What You Can and Can't Do in Your Will

In your will, you can give your property away in almost any conceivable way you desire. You can leave all you've acquired to a foundation, or to your favorite grandchild, or to your lover, or in trust for your cats.* You can leave bequests to non-citizens. You can exclude, or disinherit, anyone you want to, within the limits of community property law and the family allowance.

But there are some limits. The most important one applies to married couples. One-half of the community property is not yours to give away. Why? Because it belongs to your spouse and may be left to whomever your spouse wants to have it. Another limit that applies to everyone states that you cannot attempt to encourage or restrain certain types of conduct of your beneficiaries. For example, you cannot make a gift contingent on the marriage, divorce, or change of religion of a recipient. You can, however, make a gift contingent on other behavior, i.e., "to John, if and when he goes to college." Common sense should tell you whether you can make a gift contingent on any particular criterion or act; if you have doubts about such a bequest, consult a lawyer. Also, a provision in a will that leaves money for an illegal purpose, e.g., to establish the Institute for the Murdering of Orphans, will not be probated by the courts.

Another limit of the power of the testator is the selection of an attorney to handle the probate estate. As I said in Chapter 5, *Probate,* the final determination of who that attorney is to be is made by the executor. The testator can indicate his or her desires for a particular attorney, and the executor presumably will follow that request, but the executor cannot be legally bound to do so, no matter what the will says or the testator wanted.

An obvious limit concerns property you no longer own at the time of death. A will is not binding until the death of the will writer. Before then, you can give away, or sell, any asset mentioned in your will. Even if the will is not thereafter amended or re-written, the gift or sale is valid. If a piece of property left to someone in your will is not part of your estate at death, that particular bequest is not valid. Of course, if you do give away, or sell, property that you've specified in your will, it's advisable to amend or re-write your will to reflect that change.

DISINHERITANCE NOTE: As all readers of murder mysteries doubtlessly know, you can disinherit anyone you please from receiving any property (subject, of course, to community property and family allowance limitations). If you decide to disinherit a child or spouse, you must specifically state so in your will (e.g., "I disinherit my son, Nero, and declare he shall receive nothing from my estate."). Anyone else can be disinherited simply by omitting to name him or her as a beneficiary of the will. **

---

* But the trust must be measured by a human's life, not a cat's.

** If you fail to mention a spouse or living children in your will (in legalese called pretermitted heirs), the spouse or child is entitled to receive what portion of the estate he would be entitled to if you died without a will.

There are very few limits as to whom you can leave property to. Some felons and anyone who unlawfully caused the death of the person who wrote the will can't inherit under its terms, but otherwise you can leave your property to whomever you please.

There are limits as to how long you can control what happens to property after you die. These are more important. A "future interest" is created when I leave my house to John for his life, and then to his son Fred. Fred has no present right to the property, only a "future interest" in it. The property doesn't "vest" in Fred until John dies. John can't sell Fred's interest, or will it. The main legal rule concerning "future interests" is the ancient one known as "the rule against perpetuities."* This rule is designed to protect against "remoteness in vesting" because it is inconvenient for society as a whole to have too many future interests around. Society has decided that there should be only a finite time period during which the desires and instructions of the deceased can control the disposition of property, and there should be limits on the uncertainties as to when, or if, someone will acquire full title to property. The rule's intricacies have baffled law students for generations. If you desire to have complicated bequests in your will, with a gift that will not "vest" (i.e., become definite and fully owned by one person) for some time in the future, you should see a lawyer who's experienced in the technicalities of future interests.

---

* A rough statement of the rule, for whatever help it might be, is that an interest must vest, if it can vest at all, no longer than a time of a life in being (at the time the will is probated) plus 21 years.

In most cases, the testator simply wants to leave his property to certain persons, outright and without restrictions or limits, so you probably don't have to worry about the rule against perpetuities much, but I do want you to know that it exists.

A NOTE ON INVALIDATING WILLS: Your will can be invalidated for lack of testamentary capacity, undue influence or fraud. All these concepts have legal definitions and ramifications, which are mostly elaborations of what common sense tells you the words mean. For instance, to have the "capacity" to make a will, the testator must be of "sound mind," which means he must know that he's making a will and what a will is. A person has to be pretty far gone before a court will declare that he lacked the capacity to make a will. For example, forgetfulness or inability to recognize friends does not by itself establish incapacity. If you believe a testator wrote a will invalidated by fraud, duress or lack of capacity, see a lawyer. And be prepared to spend some money.

If the testator is too ill to sign his own will, he can direct that a witness sign it for him;* the witness should sign the testator's name and add his own name and address.

As for your own will, if you can read this book, you certainly have the capacity to write a valid will.

b. Prepare and Type Your Will Neatly and Carefully

Once you've studied this chapter and have formed your over-all estate plan, do a rough draft of your will, using or adapting the will form provided in Section 3(e) below. Once you are satisfied that you have covered everything, have the will carefully typed. Normally, this is done on regular 8" × 11" white typing paper. You then proceed to date and sign the will at the end and have it properly witnessed. You don't have to sign each page. Then store the original (executed) will in a safe place; a safety deposit box is the traditional storage place. You can make copies of the will if you want some, but **do not** sign the copies. If you and the witnesses sign the "copies," they then become additional "originals" of the will, and, if you later decide to change your will, you have to change each original.

It is legal, though never advisable, to make alterations on your will by yourself only before it is witnessed.**Once your will has been witnessed, you can't simply cross out a provision or add a new one. The legal methods for amending or revoking a will are described in Section C of this chapter. In any case, it's obviously not desirable to leave a will full of corrections. Your will is an important document; have a completely clean copy typed before you sign it and have it witnessed.

IMPORTANT: If a will does not comply with the technical requirements—say you had only one witness to a formal will—the will cannot be validated by the probate court and property will pass intestate. It's not hard to do a will right. But it is wise to check and double check to be sure you do!

c. Have Your Will Witnessed

A formal, typed will must be witnessed by two witnesses to be valid in California. Many people feel that adding a third witness makes the whole procedure that much safer. Certainly it can't hurt, especially as some other states require three witnesses and this could avoid the necessity of re-doing your will if you move to such a state. The Probate Code is specific as to how the witnesses are to witness the will.***The testator signs the will

---

* This may be a situation where you would want to have a lawyer present if substantial amounts of property are involved. It could always be claimed that someone too ill to sign his name wasn't mentally competent. In a subsequent challenge as part of a probate proceeding, the fact that a lawyer presided over the ceremony and could testify that the testator appeared to be in full possession of all faculties could be important. California has adopted the Uniform International Wills Act, Section 60–60.8 of the Probate Code, which expressly authorizes certain persons, including lawyers, to sign a will if the will-writer is unable to sign himself.

** If so, both the testator and both witnesses should initial the alterations at the signing.

*** Probate Code Section 350 and those following.

at the end, in the presence of both witnesses, "present at the same time." At the time the testator signs the will, he "must declare to the attesting witnesses that it is his will." Some authorities suggest a little ritual when the will is signed. The writer of the will says, "This is my will." The witnesses answer, "He says it's his will." It sounds like Gilbert and Sullivan, but it does satisfy the technicalities of the law. The testator does not have to disclose the contents of the will to the witnesses. Then the two (or three, if you wish) attesting witnesses sign (and date) the will, at the end, below where the testator signed. The Probate Code adds "the witnesses should give their places of residence" and it is wise to do so. However, failure to put in names and addresses "will not affect the validity of the will."

Your witnesses should ideally be people who know you and are likely to be around and available to testify when the will is probated. In an uncontested probate proceeding, as most all of them are, a will may be "proved" (established as genuine) by the testimony of one witness to it, either in person, or, if none of the witnesses resides in the county, by another deposition. Only if there is a lawsuit over the will (e.g., was it forged?), will the testimony and character of your witness be crucial. This is very unusual. If none of the witnesses can be found, after a reasonable search, the court can accept other means— handwriting analysis, etc.—of verifying their signatures. However, this adds to the delay and cost of a probate proceeding, so do try to select witnesses who are likely to be around.

The truth is that wills are routinely "witnessed" in law offices by secretaries, lawyers or associates who don't know the testator from Adam, so the ideal is not always achieved, even by lawyers. The vital thing is to have at least two witnesses. **The witnesses must be at least 18 and should not be beneficiaries of your will. This is crucial as the Probate Code states that any will provision leaving something to a subscribing witness is void,** * unless there are two other disinterested and subscribing witnesses. However, a mere creditor of the testator can be a witness.

d. A Few Words About Technical, Legal Language in Wills

There can be as many distinct wills as there are separate individuals. Your first job is to decide how you want your property distributed. Once you have done that, you can use, or adapt, the language and forms provided in Section 3(e) to draft the will that achieves your goals. Remember, we are only concerned here with that portion of your property which you decide to pass by will; as you already well know, this book is full of suggestions of other ways to pass property which avoid probate. If the will provisions set out here do not cover all of your desires, you can either research the matter further yourself,** or consult a lawyer.

If you do make any alterations or additions to the provisions in Section 3(e), be careful and use your common sense. California law does try to give effect to the intent of the testator, but sloppy words can make that intent hard to discern. We have all heard of wills such as the one where someone left a large yearly sum to a young man "as long as he attends school," which allowed him a lifetime of loafing as a subsidized student. If the meaning of the will's words is clear, a court cannot ignore that meaning, just because it suspects that meaning was not the testator's real intent.

Wills often employ much unnecessary traditional legal language. Where possible, I have omitted such phrases, as many other lawyers do now. For example, the phrase

---

* There is a qualification to this rule. If an interested witness would have been entitled to a share in the estate had the testator died without leaving a will, the interested witness can take as much under the will as he would have received in intestate proceedings.

** In any decent sized law library, at a law school or county courthouse, there will be several large books on will drafting; in particular, the California CEB (Continuing Education of the Bar) book on *California Will Drafting* is recommended.

"being of sound mind and without undue influence" is not used. This phrase adds nothing, from a legal point of view. There is a legal presumption that any writer of a will was of sound mind and not under undue influence. This presumption can be overcome, at a probate hearing on the validity of the will, by specific facts proving (to the court's satisfaction) that the writer was really not of sound mind, or was under undue influence. Saying you are of sound mind if, in truth you are not, does not make it so.

Likewise, this will does not include any provision to "pay my just debts" or the like. The Probate Code requires that the decedent's estate pay all debts for which the decedent would have been liable during life, and for funeral/last illness expenses. A direction to pay "just" debts is either unnecessary or could possibly revive debts that the estate is not legally liable for, e.g., gambling debts, debts where the statute of limitations has run, etc. Provisions for payment of debts you owe and for the forgiving of debts owed to you can be included in your will by using or adapting the language in the third clause of the sample will set out below.

Two matters that may be desirable for you to include in your will are not covered in these provisions—testamentary trusts and business dispositions. As described in Chapter 9, *Trusts,* a larger estate can possibly reduce subsequent estate taxes by the establishment of testamentary trusts. Also, you may want the continuing control of what happens to the assets that a testamentary trust allows, rather than leaving a bequest outright to a beneficiary. And, if you own a business and don't arrange for the full transfer of it outside of probate, you should make provision for it in your will. Both testamentary trusts and business dispositions through wills are often technically complicated. Rather than urge you to try to learn these difficult will drafting areas, I suggest that you consult a lawyer to draft these provisions for you. But even where some legal help is advisable, there is no reason to turn all the drafting of your will over to the lawyer. Before you see her, you should:

1. Carefully review the information provided here and draft provisions for what you want for the rest of your will; and

2. Know the substance, if not the legal form, of what you want the trust and/or business disposition provisions to accomplish.

A Note About The Completion of Your Will

Your will is your own business. You don't have to reveal its contents to anyone, even your witnesses. Giving close family members or other loved ones a summary of your will may be a good idea if all is peace and harmony, but there is no legal reason to do this and sometimes lots of practical reasons not to. On the other hand, a party celebrating the completion of your will could be fun. You've done a tough job; why not gather those you love, break out some good brandy, reveal as much of your will as you want to, and enjoy.

e. Will Clauses for Most Normal Situations

The following clauses are typical of provisions used in drafting a will for a moderate estate. The actual will clauses are printed on the left hand pages; explanatory comments are printed on the right hand pages. The comments, keyed to the will provisions, are divided into sections by headings such as "Prior Marriage and Children," "Estate Taxes," etc. In several of these areas, I provide more than one alternative as to what specific provision you might want for your will. The comments explain the differences each alternative provision will make. The Appendix contains a tear-out short form will with instructions and a sample. Also in the Appendix there are some completed sample wills, so you can see how the pieces look when put together.

The Will

WILL OF ___YOUR NAME___

I, _____ , a resident of _____ County , California, declare that this is my will.

FIRST: I revoke all wills and codicils that I have previously made.

SECOND: I am married to _____ , and all references in this will to ''my husband/wife'' are to him/her. I have never been married before. I have two children now living, whose names and dates of birth are:

_____	_____
Name	Date of Birth
_____	_____
Name	Date of Birth

The terms ''my children'' as used in this will shall include any other children hereafter born to or adopted by me.

THIRD:

A. I make the following gifts of money or personal property:

[Use one of the following for #1]

1. I give the sum of $ _____ to _____ if _____ (he/she) survives me by 180 days; if ___(he/she)___ does not, this gift shall be made to _____ (e.g., ''his/her issue who survive me by 180 days, etc.).

OR

1. I give the sum of $ _____ to _____ if _____ (he/she) survives me by 180 days; if ___(he/she)___ does not, the gift shall lapse and become part of my estate.

2. I give my standing Tiffany lamp to . . .

3. I forgive and cancel the debt of $4000 owed to me by _____ _____ .

Your Name and Address

Normally, use your full name and use the same form of your name throughout.

Your estate could get in trouble if you had ties with another state and more than one state tried to tax the full worth of your estate, even if you lived only in California. Giving your residence is also helpful to establish in which county the will is to be probated (it is probated in the county of your domicile, at death).

First: Revocation

This clause applies to and covers all wills including any holographic writings that might be construed as a will. This phrase avoids possible litigation over how much inconsistency in a past will is enough to be "wholly inconsistent" with the new one.

Second: Prior Marriages and Children

If you have been married before, it is wiser to mention the other marriage(s), how it (they) ended, and that you do not mean to refer to your previous spouse(s) as your "husband/wife." In referring to your children, list all of them, including any who are deceased. If there are any children of previous marriages — or relationships — you should mention them too, and state whether in using the phrase "my child" or "my children" you mean to include or exclude them. If a child is not specifically excluded, he/she has the right to inherit his/her intestate share of the estate. This means that, if you do wish to exclude one or more children (perhaps because they have been provided for in some other way), you should say so.

Third: A Survivorship Periods

A 180 day survivor period is used for many bequests to avoid double estate taxes. If the person to whom you left the property dies soon after you do, the property will be included in his or her estate too, and the property you'd hoped someone would use and enjoy would merely raise the dollar value of another estate and increase its taxes. You can select any reasonable survival period you want instead of 180 days, e.g., 30 days, 60 days, etc. Determine what you want to happen to the property if the person you willed it to does not survive you for 180 days, assuming you want to impose this limit on the bequest. If you don't say what happens to a will gift if the beneficiary dies before you, or before a survivorship period expires, it will automatically go back to the residue of the probate estate, unless the gift is to a kin of the testator, in which case it goes to the kin's lineal descendants.

Gifts of Personal Property

If you are giving specific items of property, be sure to describe them with sufficient detail so that there can be no question as to what property is meant. All major items of property should be handled in this way. However, if you also have all sorts of minor personal items, and don't want to bother itemizing them in your will, you can add a provision stating, for example, that "all my dolls, or baseball cards or records, etc. are to go to _____." Or as another alternative, you can state that minor pieces of personal property "are to be distributed as my executor deems proper." You could then leave a note for your executor, stating what you want done. This is obviously not recommended for anything of any significant value.

You can also forgive any debts you want to, by specifying here that you do so; it helps to specify any writing or promissory note that identifies the debt.

4. etc. (other specific gifts of personal property, including survivorship periods and specifications as to what happens if the beneficiary does not survive you for that period)

B. I make the following gifts of real property:

1. I give my real property in _____ County, California, and commonly known as ___(address and street)___ , _____ , California, together with any insurance on that property to ____(name)____ , if ___(he/she)___ survives me for 180 days. If ___(he/she)___ does not survive me for 180 days, that property shall be given to . . .

[Use one of the following for (a)]

(a) I direct my executor to pay any encumbrances on that property at the time of my death, including any mortgage, deed of trust, and real property taxes and assessment.

OR

(a) I give the property to ____(name)____ , subject to any emcumbrances on it at the time of my death, including any mortgage, deed of trust and real property taxes and assessments which shall be paid by him/her and not from my estate.

2. etc. (any other gifts of real property)

Fourth:

A. I give all my jewelry, clothing and household furniture and furnishings, auto-mobiles, (etc.), and other tangible articles of a personal nature, or my interest in all such property, not otherwise specifically disbursed by this will or in any other manner, to ____(name)____ if ___(he/she)___ survives me for 180 days, and if ___(name)___ _____ does not, to ____(name)____ if ___(he/she)___ survives me for that period. (If to your children, consider adding ''in equal shares as they shall agree on, or as my executor shall in my executor's discretion determine if my children do not agree.'')

B. I give the residue of my estate and property as follows:

[Example]

1. To _____ , if ___(he/she)___ survives me by 180 days;

2. If not, to _____ if ___(he/she)___ survives me by 180 days;

3. If neither _____ nor _____ survives me by 180 days, then to _____ .

Finally, if you give monetary gifts, it might be wise to add to the bequest "but in no event more than _____ % of my (net or probate) estate" just in case there's not as much there as you'd planned.

Third: B   Real Property

Again, it is wise to include a 180 day survivorship period, and to state what you desire done with the property if the person you leave it to doesn't survive that 180 days.

Encumbrances on Real Property

When you are giving real property, there is a question of who pays encumbrances on it. Are mortgages, taxes, any liens, or other debts on that property paid from the estate, or by the receiver of the property? The will should specify what you desire.

Fourth: A   Other Property

This provision determines what happens to your personal belongings not specifically given away and can be adapted however you desire. You can leave them to a lover, friend, etc. The provision for the executor to decide on distribution of this property in case of any disagreement among those receiving it is recommended because it will encourage agreement and provide a ready, non-litigious solution if agreement isn't achieved.

Fourth: B   Residue

The "residue" of your estate is exactly what it sounds like — all that remains after all specific bequests have been distributed, and all fees, costs, taxes, etc. have been paid. Again, you can select anyone you want to receive the "residue" of your estate.

Fifth: I leave the following property in trust for _____ .

(describe trust, etc.)

Sixth: [Use one of the following alternatives]

Alternative #1

I give all those gifts described in Paragraph Three (or whatever is desired, e.g., ''Paragraphs Three, Four, etc.'') free of all inheritance, estate or other death taxes, and I direct that my executor shall pay all such taxes out of the residue of my estate.

Alternative #2

I direct that all death taxes due (on either ''my probate estate'' or on ''my taxable estate'') be paid by _____ .

Alternative #3

I direct that all inheritance, estate, or other death taxes that may, by reason of my death, be attributable to my probate estate or any portion of it, including any property received by any person as a family allowance or homestead, shall be paid by my executor as follows: out of the residue of my estate disposed of by this will (or any other means of payment you choose).

Alternative #4

I direct that all inheritance, estate, or other death taxes that may, by reason of my death, be assessed against my estate or any portion of it, whether passing by probate or not, shall be paid by my executor as follows: out of the residue of my probate estate (or any other means of payment you choose).

Seventh:

A. I nominate _____ as executor of this will, to serve without bond. If _____ shall for any reason fail to qualify or cease to act as executor, I nominate _____ , also to serve without bond. (and so on)

B. I direct that my executor petition the court for an order to administer my estate under the provisions of the Independent Administration of Estates Act. (See Chapter 5, *Probate*.)

C. I authorize my executor to sell, either at public or private sale, any assets or property of the estate not mentioned in Section _____ of this will, (1) as he/she deems proper to pay for the costs of probating the estate, and maintaining my family after my

Fifth: Trusts

Trusts can be desirable; aside from tax savings, they can give a lot of flexibility for caring for young children. However, as I've said, establishing and maintaining a trust is beyond the scope of this book. If you are interested in this, re-read Chapter 9. There are some simple trusts such as a "totten trust" and an "insurance trust" which you can handle yourself, but these are designed to avoid probate and thus are not made part of your will.

Sixth: Death Taxes

Before you decide how any estate taxes are to be paid, you obviously need to have estimated what they will be. If no federal estate taxes are due (see Chapter 3), there is much less to worry about here, although the will writer can still include these provisions so as to relieve any inheritor from any state inheritance taxes due. The will writer can direct that the death taxes assessed on his/her estate can be paid in any manner he/she chooses, as long as the means he/she chooses provide sufficient cash to pay those taxes. If there is no provision for the payment of federal estate taxes, the IRS will proportion the taxes on the percentage of the estate inherited by each inheritor (or joint tenant, trust beneficiary, etc.), so the executor normally deducts from each inheritor's share of the estate his/her proportionate share of the taxes due.

If you want to relieve certain bequests of any tax liability, you should use Alternative #1.

If you want all estate taxes paid from one or more set sources (sufficient to pay all those taxes, of course), you should use Alternative #2, 3, or 4, or some variation of them.

Particularly if many assets are transferred outside of probate, it is desirable to state how the death taxes on that portion of the taxable estate are to be paid. Unless a specific source for the payment of taxes is set up, it is common to provide that taxes be paid from the "residue" of the estate. You can, however, specify any other asset sufficient to pay these taxes.

If you want your probate estate to pay death taxes only on that portion of your total estate passing through probate, and you don't want it to pay death taxes on any property passing outside of probate, use Alternative #3.

If you want your probate estate to pay for all your estate and inheritance taxes even for property not passing by will, use Alternative #4. If the death taxes are not to be paid by the "residue," and/or if the residue isn't sufficient to pay these taxes, you must specify other assets in the **probate** estate sufficient to pay these taxes.

Seventh: Executors

If the phrase "to serve without bond" is not used, the court must require the executor to post a bond. This results either in the tying up of large amounts of cash, or means that the estate must pay a bondsman's fee which is usually 10% of the face value of the bond.

The court may require a bond, even if the testator directs that it be waived. In practice, this is not likely to occur unless you select a non-Californian as your executor.

As I have previously described (in Chapter 5, *Probate*), the executor is the person who handles your estate while it is in probate. The executor should be someone you can trust and rely on, and who will be available and competent when you die. A spouse is often named as the other spouse's executor. It is not advisable to name someone who lives far from you to be your executor. Successor executors should be named, just in case the original one predeceases you or declines to serve, etc. To be certain there will be some executor, it is wise to make arrangements with a bank or other financial organization to serve as successor executor if, for some unforeseen reason, it becomes necessary. Even if a will names no executor who can or will serve, the will must still be probated, and the court will appoint an executor, called an "Administrator with Will Annexed."

Provisions B and C are all designed to allow the estate to be managed and probated as efficiently as possible. There is no reason to restrict the executor's powers any more than death, **or** (2) as he/she in his/her discretion deems it necessary for the proper administration and distribution of my estate.

Eighth: If any beneficiary under this will in any manner, directly or indirectly, contests or attacks this will or any of its provisions, any share or interest in my estate given to the contesting beneficiary under this will is revoked and shall be disposed of in the same manner provided herein as if that contesting beneficiary had predeceased me without issue.

Ninth: I declare that I have made and paid for funeral arrangements with _____ , and I direct my executor to take all steps necessary to carry out such arrangements.

Tenth: If my wife/my husband and I should die simultaneously, or under such circumstances as to render it difficult or impossible to determine who predeceased the other, I shall be conclusively presumed to have survived my wife/husband for purposes of this will.

Eleventh:

A. I give the following property _____(describe property)_____ to __(name of guardian)__ , an adult Californian (or appropriate financial institution), as custodian for _____(name of minor)_____ under the California Uniform Gift to Minors Act.

B. [Alternative #1]

If at my death anyone who takes property from me by will or by succession is a minor, I appoint ___(name and relationship if any, to testator)___ of ___(full address)___ , California, as guardian of any of the property the minor takes from me. If_____ shall for any reason fail to qualify or cease to act as guardian, I appoint _____ _____ of_____(full address)_____ , California, as such guardian in his/her place.

[Alternative #2]

My executor shall represent any child under age 18 in matters relating to any distribution under this Paragraph Eleven, including the selecting of the assets that shall constitute that child's share, and my executor may in my executor's discretion sell for the

is legally required. If you can't trust him/her, don't use him/her. However, if there is certain property you want to make absolutely certain he/she can't sell, identify that property.

Eighth: Disinheritance and Will Contests

Clearly, this is designed to discourage will contests. If you don't mind if a will contestant's children inherit from you, strike ''without issue'' from this clause.

I have not included any general disinheritance clause, or a clause giving $1 to all nieces and nephews, etc. Your spouse and child(ren) are special cases and should be disinherited specifically if that is your wish. There is no need to mention other people just to say they are excluded; most will-drafters and contemporary California will form books prefer to omit a general disinheritance clause.

Ninth: Body Disposition

If you've made provision for your body, or parts, to be given to a scientific or medical institution, this should also be specified here. As stated in Chapter 2, a provision in a will declaring what the testator desires done with his/her body will legally be given immediate effect, even if the will is not otherwise valid.

Tenth: Simultaneous Death

If it cannot be determined who died first, the law that applies without this provision can increase the death taxes. People often wonder what happens if they die at the same time as their spouse, or at the same time as one of the other people who would inherit money from them or from whom they would stand to inherit. California has adopted the Uniform Simultaneous Death Act (Probate Code Section 296). It applies to situations where people have died in some way (i.e., car or plane wreck) where it is likely that they died simultaneously; if the disposition of property would depend on who died first, the property of each person is disposed of as if he or she died last. This avoids all sorts of complications including double probate.

Example: A parent and two of the parent's children die in a plane wreck. Absent clear proof that one or more person(s) survived the other(s), each person's property will be disposed of as if he or she survived. Thus, the parent's property would go under the intestate succession law, or under a will to his or her other heirs and it would not go to the children who also died in the wreck.

Where two or more beneficiaries are designated to take successively in a will by reason of surviving the person making the will and they die simultaneously, the property is divided in as many equal portions as there are successive beneficiaries, and portions are distributed to those who would have taken if that beneficiary had survived.

Example: In your will, you leave money to Aunt Alice and if she died before you, to Uncle Dan, and if they both died before you, to Cousin Gail. If you die and, on the way to your funeral, Alice, Dan, and Gail die simultaneously when a semi-truck wipes out their motorcycles, the money gets divided into three piles and one-third goes to those who take from each of them, either under their wills, or, if there are no wills, by intestate succession.

Where husband and wife die simultaneously, one-half of the community property is treated as if the husband had survived, and one-half as if the wife survived.

Where two or more joint tenants die simultaneously, the property is divided into as many shares as there are joint tenants. Then, the shares are divided as if each of the joint tenants had survived.

Where insurance is involved and the insured and the beneficiaries of a life or accident insurance policy are killed simultaneously, the proceeds of the policy will be distributed as if the beneficiary had died before the insured.

child's account any part of that child's share. Any property or its proceeds distributable to a child under age 18 pursuant to this Paragraph Eleven may be delivered without bond to any suitable person with whom he/she resides or who has the care or control of him/her.

    C. If my ___(husband/wife)___ does not survive me and at my death any of my children are minors, I appoint ___(name and relationship to testator)___ of _____ ___(full address)___ , California, as guardian of the estate of my minor child or children, and recommend that _____ be appointed as guardian of the person(s) of those children. (If you believe it wise to have two guardians, one for the child personally, and one to supervise his or her estate, you should draft two separate guardian paragraphs, 11C and 11D).

    If _____ shall for any reason fail to qualify or cease to act as such guardian, I appoint _____ of _____ ___(full address)___ , California, as such guardian.

    D. I request that no bond be required of any guardian named in Clause 11, Paragraphs A, B or C.

    I subscribe my name to this will this _____ day of _____ , 19_____ , at _____ , California.

_____
(full name)

    On the date last written above (or, ''on this _____ day of _____ , 19 _____ '') ___(testator's full name)___ declared to us, the undersigned, that this instrument, consisting of _____ pages, including this page signed by us, was ___(his/her)___ will, and requested us to act as witnesses to it. ___(He/she)___ thereupon signed this will in our presence, all of us being present at the time. We now, at ___(his/her)___ request, in ___(his/her)___ presence, and in the presence of each other, subscribe our names as witnesses.

    We declare under penalty of perjury that the foregoing is true and correct.

_____ residing at _____

_____ residing at _____

_____ residing at _____

Eleventh: A   Minors

Gifts to minors are specifically authorized under the Probate Code. If a gift is made to a minor, use this phrasing. If these magic words are used, all the provisions of the Gift to Minors Act apply (see Chapter 4 for details on the workings of this act). If these magic words are not used, a will bequest ''shall be deemed'' a direct bequest to a minor, and there will be no custodian, ''unless the will clearly requires otherwise.''

Eleventh: B   Guardians of Minor's Property

Minors cannot own estates over $2500 without a guardian being appointed. This means that court proceedings to appoint a guardian will be necessary if any significant bequest is made to a minor. The testator may, in the will, name alternate custodians, and specify the amount or rate of compensation (if any) for the custodian. If you want to name someone other than the executor as the minor's guardian, use Alternative #1. If the executor is also to be the guardian, use Alternative #2.

Eleventh: C   Guardians of Minor

The guardian of the **property** of a minor can be named in a will, but not a guardian of the minor himself/herself, although courts often follow the wishes of a deceased parent expressed in a will, if there is no compelling reason to do otherwise. In very brief outline, the rules are as follows: A divorced parent who has legal custody of the children of the marriage cannot will that custody of the children to someone other than his/her ex-spouse, unless the ex-spouse gives written consent to such a custody arrangement (or is dead or incapable of giving consent). Even if you don't like your ex-spouse, he or she is the one who will get custody under California law unless he or she is unfit or doesn't want custody. But what happens when the surviving natural parent is out of the picture? A divorced parent* can designate a guardian in his/her will, and that guardian will normally (if the court agrees that the person named is fit to be a guardian) acquire legal custody if the parent is 1) not alive, 2) has no interest in gaining custody of the children, 3) is unfit. The court's duty is to appoint a guardian on the basis of what is best for the interest of the child. If a child is over 14, he or she may nominate his/her own personal guardian, who will be appointed by the court, unless disapproved.

Eleventh: D

This clause may avoid the necessity of a guardian for the minor obtaining a bond in order for the executor to deliver the assets, obtain receipts and secure an order of final discharge.

Signature Clause

Be sure you understand the formalities required (see Section B of this chapter) before signing your will and having it witnessed.

---

* Unmarried couples face some special problems here, which can vary depending on whether a paternity statement was, or was not, signed. See *The Living Together Kit,* Ihara and Warner, Nolo Press.

C. After Your Will is Drafted

1. Changing Your Will

Suppose you decide to change your will in one regard only. Aunt Mary died, so you decide to leave the silver tea set that was to go to her to Cousin Martha. Do you have to redo the entire will? Suppose you decide to change your will drastically (you just got divorced). How can you change or revoke it? Does any change require an entirely new will? Do you have to have the two original witnesses present? Obviously, anyone who drafts a will should know the rules regarding changes or revocations. These are discussed separately in the next several sections.

When you should change your will is a matter of common sense. Surely after marriage or divorce, and perhaps after other major events in your life and family life, a change is appropriate. However, impromptu changes are not desirable. People who change their wills as often as they change their clothes obviously have problems. Remember, you can't just ink out a provision or a bequest in your will. Changes must be made as discussed below. It is normally a chore and a bore to revise a will, so it makes sense to draft a will that will need as little revision as possible (e.g., leave property "my children" rather than one or two specifically named children.) If you do change a will, be sure to change all the copies.

The legal jargon used to describe a change or addition to a will is "codicil." A codicil is an addition, amendment, or alteration made to a will after the will has been drafted, signed and witnessed. A codicil is a sort of legal "P.S." to the will and is executed with all of the formalities of a will. This means that it is typed on the will itself, if there's room on the last page, and/or on additional pages, below the signatures. Then the new material is dated and signed by the testator and two witnesses* (additional page(s) can be used if needed). Codicils are frequently used for minor matters like changes of individual gifts. If a major revision of the entire will is desired, it is not advisable to attempt this by codicil. Why? Because a will which has been substantially re-written by a codicil is a confusing document and awkward to read. It may not be clear what the relationship of the codicil to the original will provisions means. For major revisions, draft a new will and revoke the old one.

IMPORTANT: A codicil should be typed on **all** copies of the will. This may be a nuisance, but will prevent confusion, or even conflict, later. The codicil does not have to be part of the same page as the signature page of the will. It must, however, refer to the previous will. This can be simply accomplished by labelling the change "first codicil of the will of . . .[testator's name], dated . . .[giving date]." The codicil then "has the effect to republish the will as modified by the codicil." The entire will is now considered to have been prepared as of the date of the codicil.

Following is a sample form you can use or adapt if it becomes necessary to make a codicil to your will.

---

* They don't have to be the same two witnesses of the will, but it's better to use them if they're available.

FIRST CODICIL TO THE WILL

OF

JOHN ANDREW JONES

I JOHN ANDREW JONES, a resident of _____ County, California, declare this to be the first codicil to my will dated _____, 19_____.

FIRST: I revoke Section _____ of Paragraph _____, and substitute the following: (Add whatever new provision is desired).

SECOND: I add the following new Section _____ to Paragraph _____: (Add whatever is desired.)

THIRD: In all other respects I confirm and republish my will dated _____, 19_____, this _____ day of _____, 19_____, at _____, California.

_____
(Testator's Full Name)

On the date written below, _____(testator's full name)_____ declared to us, the undersigned, that this instrument, consisting of _____ pages, including this page signed by us as witnesses, was the first codicil to his will and requested us to act as witnesses to it. He thereupon signed this codicil in our presence, all of us being present at the same time. We now, at his request, in his presence, and in the presence of each other, subscribe our names as witnesses.

Executed on _____, 19_____, at _____, California.

We declare under penalty of perjury that the foregoing is true and correct.

_____ residing at _____

_____

_____ residing at _____

_____

_____ residing at _____

_____

2. Revocation

Wills can be revoked by two basic means. First, the testator decides to revoke it, and legally does so. Second, by marriage, after making a will; in this case, the revocation only applies to the new spouse.

A testator who wants to revoke his or her existing will has two means of doing so. He or she can write a new will, expressly stating that he or she is revoking all previous wills. If the new will doesn't expressly state that it revokes all the previous wills, they are not revoked unless their terms are "wholly inconsistent" with the new will. Determining how much inconsistency it takes to be "wholly inconsistent" can be a tedious (and expensive) legal task, so if a will revokes earlier wills, that fact should always be stated.

An existing will (or codicil) is also revoked by being "burnt, torn, concealed, defaced, obliterated or destroyed" if the testator intended to revoke it. If someone other than the testator physically destroys the will, the fact that it was done at the at the testator's direction and intention must be proved by two witnesses. Even if you destroy your own will, it is advisable to do it before witnesses; otherwise, once you are deceased, it may well be difficult to determine what your intent was.

The revocation of a subsequent will does not revive an earlier one, unless the terms of the revocation state that it is the testator's intent to revive the first will, or if the first will is "republished" (i.e., signed and witnessed anew). Thus, if Marguerite makes one will and then sometime later makes a second will expressly revoking the first will, the first will does not become valid of Marguerite tears up the second.

Marriage has certain automatic affects on wills drafted before that union was entered into. If the (new) spouse survives the other spouse and that spouse had made a will prior to the marriage, and the will has not been changed, the will is revoked as the the (new) spouse and he/she will take his/her intestate share of the estate unless:

1. "Provision" is made for the (new) spouse in a marriage contract;

2. The new spouse is provided for in the will (i.e., was covered in the will even before marriage); or

3. The new spouse is mentioned in the will in such a was "as to show an intention not to make such provision."

EXAMPLE 1: Betty, a wealthy woman, had her will drafted several years ago. On a vacation to Paris, she meets and marries Pierre. A couple of months later she leaves him, deciding he was a gigolo and a bounder. Betty dies before she can file for divorce or thinks to change her will. Pierre is entitled to his intestate share of her estate as her lawful husband.

EXAMPLE 2: The same example, except that this time Betty was more cautious. She had Pierre sign a marital contract stating that, aside from the money in their joint bank account, he is not to inherit from her estate. In this situation Pierre is not entitled to any intestate share in Betty's estate.

The rules as to children are similar. If there are any children or further descendants of the new marriage and any of them survive the person making a will, the will is revoked as to them unless they are provided for, or mentioned in the will so as to show the testator's intention not to provide for them.

EXAMPLE 1: After Betty and Pierre married, they had a daughter Cassandra, who Betty was not very fond of. However, Betty did establish an annuity for Cassandra in case of her own death. Betty dies leaving the child nothing in her will. Cassandra does not inherit her intestate share, even if Betty had never changed her will after the marriage. Why? Because Betty did make a specific provision for Cassandra in the form of an annuity. If this confuses you, read the following.

EXAMPLE 2: Betty and Pierre also had a son, Yves, whom Betty regarded as a bigger scoundrel than Pierre. Betty re-wrote her will after Yves' birth, specifically providing that Yves was disinherited and not to receive anything from her estate. Yves has been legally excluded from Betty's estate and inherits nothing.

Planning ahead so as to exclude a future spouse or any future children from a will certainly seems undesirable. Why would anyone want to state ''in case I ever marry (again), I exclude my new pouse from my estate?'' Not too romantic. Obviously, the sensible way to handle this problem is to keep your will up-to-date. If you decide to exclude a spouse or child from your estate, re-draft your will to say so.

DIVORCE NOTE: A divorce has no effect on the will of either party, unless changing a will is part of the written divorce settlement. So, if you get a divorce and don't want your ex-spouse to inherit from your estate, draft a new will.

3. Lost Wills

I include this section more because you may be curious than because you will need it. Losing a will is one of those things that shouldn't happen. If you do lose yours while you're alive, write a new one, revoking all previous ones.

But what happens if the will of a decedent cannot be found? The contents of the lost will can still be given effect by the probate court **if:**

1. The lost will is proven to have been in existence at the death of the testator, or was destroyed in a public calamity, or was fraudulently destroyed without the testator's knowledge;

2. The contents of the will are proved by (at least) two credible witnesses.

However, if a will cannot be found after the testator's death, and when last seen or known to exist was in the **testator's exclusive possession,** a presumption (rebuttable by evidence) arises that the testator destroyed it with the intent to revoke it.

It is certainly cumbersome to prove the contents of a lost will. So when you draft your will, make sure it will be found easily.

Appendix
&
Glossary

Appendix

Here are three examples of estate plans, including the wills prepared for each plan. These plans are not designed to be representative of any particular reader's needs or estate plan. They have been deliberately simplified and are designed to give you some feeling for what an estate plan is and, especially, what a completed will looks like.

Sample Estate Plan #1

Mark and Linda are married, in their 30's, with two young children. Mark is employed as a carpenter, Linda works part-time as a proofreader for a publisher. They own real property (heavily mortgaged) "as community property." This is the only major asset of their estate. Otherwise, they own two cars, an old Ford and an older VW station wagon, the inexpensive (but tasteful) furnishings of their home, personal possessions like clothing, stereos, etc., and $6000 in a savings account in Mark's name.

Mark and Linda each want to leave their entire estate to the other. In determining their estate plan, they decide they need to purchase substantial amounts of life insurance for both Mark and Linda to protect their children. They purchase $200,000 worth of term life insurance of Mark's life and $100,000 on Linda's life. Since each person has an "insurable interest" on the other's life, each purchases and exclusively owns the life insurance policy on the other's life. Thus, the proceeds of either insurance policy will be excluded from both the taxable and probate estate (each makes gifts to the other of half the amount needed for the premium payments). They transfer the $6000 in the savings account into a joint bank account, so either can collect the amount on the death of the other. Their house will not have to go through probate since it can be transferred by the community property petition. The only assets that remain are their cars, home furnishings, personal clothes, etc. These can also be transferred outside of probate by using the community property petition.

Following is Mark's will:

Will of Mark P. Ceery

I, Mark P. Ceery, a resident of Marin County, California, declare that this is my will.

FIRST: I revoke all wills and codicils that I have previously made.

SECOND: I am married to Linda F. Foster and all references in this will to "my wife" are to her only. I was married once before, to Anita Moreau, which marriage was terminated by divorce. I have two children now living, whose names and dates of birth are:

James Ceery	October 12, 1973
Jennifer Ceery	March 4, 1977

The terms "my child" and "my children" as used in this will shall include any other children hereafter born to or adopted by me.

THIRD: I leave all my property, real and personal, to my wife, Linda F. Foster.

FOURTH: I nominate Linda F. Foster as executor of this will, to serve without bond. If Linda F. Foster shall for any reason fail to qualify or cease to act as executor, I nominate Don Curley, also to seve without bond.

I direct that my executor petition the court for an order to administer my estate under the provisions of the Independent Administration of Estates Act.

FIFTH: I declare that I have made arrangements with the Kidney Foundation of Northern California to donate my body and body parts for use in any transplant operation, procedure or need they deem necessary.

SIXTH: If my wife and I should die simultaneously, or under such circumstances as to render it difficult or impossible to determine who predeceased the other, I shall be conclusively presumed to have survived my wife for purposes of this will.

If my wife does not survive me and at my death any of my children are minors, I appoint Robert Mondoson of San Francisco, California, as guardian of the estate of my minor child or children, and recommend Robert Mondoson be appointed as guardian of the person(s) of those children.

If Robert Mondoson shall for any reason fail to qualify or cease to act as such guardian, I appoint Jessie Costeau of San Francisco, California as such guardian.

I request that no bond be required of any guardian named in this clause.

I subscribe my name to this will this _____ day of _____, 19_____, at _____, California.

_____

On the date last written above, Mark P. Ceery declared to us, the undersigned, that this instrument, consisting of three pages, including this page signed by us, was his will and requested us to act as witnesses to it. He thereupon signed this will in our presence, all of us being present at the same time. We now, at his request, in his presence, and in the presence of each other, subscribe our names as witnesses.

We declare under penalty of perjury that the foregoing is true and correct.

_____ residing at _____
_____

_____ residing at _____
_____

_____ residing at _____
_____

Sample Estate Plan #2

Barbara O'Reilly is a widow in her late 50's with no present plans to marry. She has three adult children, Andrew, Catherine, and Constance. Andrew is single, Constance divorced with one child, and Catherine is married with no children. Barbara has a well-paying job and estate consisting of a home worth $440,000 with $80,000 equity, many valuable antiques worth roughly $40,000, a Mercedes-Benz worth $15,000, savings of $80,000, for a total estate of $575,000.

Barbara wants to leave the bulk of her estate to her children, with several smaller bequests to friends. Barbara's estate would be subject to estate tax if she dies before 1987. Barbara decides she wants to avoid estate tax, so she commences a program of giving each of her children $10,000 per year. She trusts her children and knows that in the unlikely event that she comes into financial trouble, they will give back all the money she has given them. She will continue this gift program for years, thus eventually avoiding a significant amount of estate taxes.

To reduce probate costs, Barbara places her house in a revocable inter vivos trust naming her two daughters as equal beneficiaries of the trust. She also places half of her savings in three Totten trust savings accounts, one for each of her children. Her probate estate now consists of her car, some remaining savings and her antiques. She decides it is too much bother to set up inter vivos trusts or joint tenancies for these assets, so decides to pass this property by will.

Following is Barbara O'Reilly's will:

Will of Barbara O'Reilly

I, Barbara O'Reilly, a resident of Los Angeles County, California, declare that this is my will.

FIRST: I revoke all wills and codicils that I have previously made.

SECOND: I was married to Harry O'Reilly, who predeceased me. I have three children now living, whose names and dates of birth are:

Andrew O'Reilly	6/15/46
Catherine O'Reilly	3/1/48
Constance O'Reilly	9/1/50

The terms "my child" and "my children" as used in this will shall include any other children born to or adopted by me.

THIRD: I make the following gifts of money or personal property:

1. I give the sum of $1000 to Alicia McRae, if she survives me by 180 days. If she does not, to her issue who survive me by that period, by right of representation.

2. I give $500 to Joel Johnston, if he survives me by 180 days. If he does not, to his issue who survive me by that period, by right of representation.

3. I give my signed Tiffany lamp to Robin Smith, if he survives me by 180 days; if not, to his wife of she survives me by 180 days.

4. I give my oak roll-top desk to Marina Mills, if she survives me by 180 days; if not, to her sister Mora Mills.

5. I forgive and cancel the debt of $1347.66 owed to me by James Arthur Bennett IV.

FOURTH: I give all my jewelry, clothing and household furniture and furnishings, automobiles, (etc.), and other tangible articles of a personal nature, or my interest in all such property, not otherwise specifically disbursed by this will or in any other manner to Constance O'Reilly, if she survives me by 180 days; if not, to her children in equal shares, as they shall agree on, or as my executor shall in my executor's discretion determine if her children do not agree.

FIFTH: I give the residue of my estate as follows:

1. To Andrew O'Reilly, if he survives me by 180 days;

2. If not, to Catherine O'Reilly, if she survives me by 180 days;

3. If neither Andrew nor Catherine O'Reilly survive me by 180 days, to Constance O'Reilly.

SIXTH: I direct that all inheritance, estate, or other death taxes that may, by reason of my death, be assessed against my estate or any portion of it, whether passing by probate or not, shall be paid by my executor as follows: out of the residue of my probate estate.

SEVENTH: I nominate Catherine O'Reilly as executor of this will, to serve without bond. If Catherine O'Reilly shall for any reason fail to qualify or cease to act as executor, I nominate Constance O'Reilly, also to serve without bond.

I direct that my executor petition the court for an order to administer my estate under the provisions of the Independent Administration of Estates Act.

I authorize my executor to sell, either at public or private sale, any assets or property of the estate not mentioned in Sections 3 or 4 of this will 1) as she deems proper to pay for the costs of probating the estate, and maintaining my family after my death, **OR** 2) as she in her discretion deems necessary for the proper administration and distribution of my estate.

EIGHTH: If any beneficiary under this will in any manner, directly or indirectly, contests or attacks this will or any of its provisions, any share or interest in my estate given to the contesting beneficiary under this will is revoked and shall be disposed of in the same manner provided herein as if that contesting beneficiary had predeceased me without issue.

NINTH: I declare that I have made and paid for funeral arrangements with the Los Angeles Funeral Society, and I direct my executor to take all steps necessary to carry out such arrangements.

I subscribe my name to this will this _____ day of _____, 19_____, at _____, California.

_____

(Full Name)

On the date last written above, Barbara O'Reilly declared to us, the undersigned, that this instrument, consisting of four pages, including this page signed by us, was her will and requested us to act as witnesses to it. She thereupon signed this will in our presence, all of us being present at the same time. We now, at her request, in her presence, and in the presence of each other, subscribe our names as witnesses.

We declare under penalty of perjury that the foregoing is true and correct.

_____ residing at _____

_____

_____ residing at _____

_____

_____ residing at _____

_____

Sample Estate Plan #3

Robert and Edwina Speelcas are a prosperous married couple in their early 70's. Both have now retired and live comfortably off their savings, assets and retirement payments. Their estate consists of a house in San Francisco worth $250,000 (all equity), a summer home in Lake Tahoe worth $125,000 ($75,000 equity), stocks worth $300,000, art works valued at $90,000, jewelry valued at $50,000, savings of $60,000, and miscellaneous personal property worth a total of $45,000. The total net worth of their estate is $920,000. It is all community property so each spouse's share of the estate is $460,000.

The Speelcas have four children: Jessica (married, two children), Robert Jr. (divorced, four children), Deborah (single), Tommy (married, no children). Each wants to leave their share of their estate first to the surviving spouse, and then to their children in equal shares. They also wish to make several smaller bequests to friends and relations. After reviewing their alternatives, they decide they need to talk to a lawyer about establishing a testamentary trust to save estate taxes when the surviving spouse dies. They aren't sure of the exact amount of the trust they'll establish, or whether the money will be left in trust for their children, or their grandchildren in a "generation skipping" trust. But they do know what questions to ask the estate planner, and they have planned the rest of their estate. They can transfer any property to the surviving spouse outside of probate by using the community property petition. The surviving spouse will create revocable inter vivos trusts to transfer outside of probate their art works to the friend they want to receive them.

Following is a sample of the draft will Edwina takes to the estate planner. The final will won't be completed until she decides exactly how much she will leave in the testamentary trust.

WILL OF EDWINA SPEELCAS

I, Edwina Speelcas, a resident of San Francisco County, California, declare that this is my will.

First: I revoke all wills and codicils that I have previously made.

Second: I am married to Robert Speelcas, and all references in this will to my husband are to him. I have never been married before. I have four children now living, whose names and dates of birth are:

Jessica	11/5/37
Robert Jr.	10/2/38
Deborah	6/19/40
Tommy	3/29/43

Third: I make the following gifts of personal property:

1. I give the sum of $8000 to my butcher, Arthur Pedrozzi;

2. I give the sum of $5000 to my gardener, William Service;

3. I give the sum of $3000 to my friend, Betty Post;

4. I give the sum of $3000 to my friend, Mary Bale.

Fourth: I leave the following amounts in trust:

$ _____ in trust for my daughter Jessica;

$ _____ in trust for my son Robert Jr.;

$ _____ in trust for my daughter Deborah;

$ _____ in trust for my son Tommy.

(The terms of the trust will be spelled out in the final version of the will. The trust will provide its income to her husband Robert during his life.)

Fifth: I give the residue of my estate, all my real and personal property not specifically disposed of by this will or otherwise to my husband, Robert Speelcas.

Sixth: I direct that all death taxes due on either my taxable estate, whether the property is transferred by will or not, shall be paid by the beneficiaries of this will, pro-rata in proportion of the percentage of the total taxable estate they receive.

Seventh: I nominate Robert Speelcas as executor of this will, to serve without bond. If Robert Speelcas shall for any reason fail to qualify or cease to act as executor, I nominate Robert Speelcas Jr., also to serve without bond. (and so on)

I direct that my executor petition the court for an order to administer my estate under the provisions of the Independent Administration of Estates Act.

I authorize my executor to sell, either at public or private sale, any assets or property of the estate not mentioned in Sections 3 or 4 of this will 1) as he deems proper to pay for the costs of probating the estate and maintaining my family after my death, **or** 2) as he, in his discretion, deems necessary for the proper administration and distribution of my estate.

Eighth: If any beneficiary under this will in any manner, directly or indirectly, contests or attacks this will or any of its provisions, any share or interest in my estate given to the contesting beneficiary under this will is revoked and shall be disposed of in the same manner provided herein as if that contesting beneficiary had predeceased me without issue.

Ninth: I declare that I have made and paid for funeral arrangements with Our Lady of the Sorrows Funeral Parlor, and I direct my executor to take all steps necessary to carry out such arrangements.

Tenth: If my husband and I should die simultaneously, or under such circumstances as to render it difficult or impossible to determine who predeceased the other, I shall be conclusively presumed to have survived my husband for purposes of this will.

I subscribe my name to this Will this _____ day of _____ , 19 _____ , at _____ , California.

_____
(FULL NAME)

On the date last written above, Edwina Speelcas declared to us, the undersigned, that this instrument, consisting of four pages, including this page signed by us, was her will, and requested us to act as witnesses to it. She thereupon signed this will in our presence, all of us being present at the same time. We now, at her request, in her presence, and in the presence of each other, subscribe our names as witnesses.

We declare under penalty of perjury that the foregoing is true and correct.

_____ residing at _____

_____ residing at _____

_____ residing at _____

TEAR-OUT WILL

NOTE: California has just adopted a "statutory will" - a fill-in-the-blanks, check-the-boxes will form. This form cannot be changed and the options it provides are few, which means it is not desireable for many people. For example, essentially, property must be left only to a spouse or to children equally. No gifts can be made to any other person, except charities, nor can property be divided unequally. There is no real advantage to using a "statutory will" compared to the will forms provided here, which allow you to dispose of your property in any way you choose.

At the printing of this edition, actual "statutory will" forms are not available. If you are interested, contact the clerk of the probate court of your County Superior Court or check local stationery stores.

TEAR-OUT WILL INSTRUCTIONS

1. Before using this form, be sure you have read Chapter 12, Wills, and understand what you want to accomplish with your will and the rules for drafting a will in California.

2. Except for signatures, TYPE every word you use in this will. If you insert handwriting in this tear-out, the will may well be invalidated by a court.

3. There is space left on side two of the will for you to insert any particular additional clauses you want, such as a guardian for your children's estate, simultaneous death clause, prior marriages and children, etc.

4. If you have any confusion regarding what goes in the blanks, review the following sample short form will.

Sample Short Form Will:

LAST WILL AND TESTAMENT

I, Ilona Jane Wilson, a resident of Alameda County, California, declare this is my last will and testament.

1. I revoke all prior wills and codicils.

2. I leave $10,000 to Alma Johnson. I leave all the rest of my estate to my son, Don Wilson.

3. I appoint Don Wilson as my executor, and direct that no bond be required of him.

I subscribe my name to this will this 6th day of July, 1982, at Oakland, California.

_____

Ilona Jane Wilson

On this 6th day of July, 1982, at Oakland, California, Ilona Jane Wilson, declared to us, the undersigned, that this instrument, consisting of one page, was her will, and requested us to act as witnesses to it. She thereupon signed this will in our presence, all of us being present at the same time. We now, at her request, and in her presence, and the presence of each other, subscribe our names as witnesses.

We declare under penalty of perjury that the foregoing is true and correct.

_____

Mary Smith,   residing at   2077 Fairmont Ave, Oakland, California.

_____

Louise Brooks,   residing at   171 A Garden Lane, Oakland, California.

WILL OF

_____

I, _____ , a resident of

_____ County, California, declare that this is my will.

First: I revoke all prior wills and codicils.

Second: I leave my property as follows:

Third: I nominate _____, as executor of this will to serve without bond.

I subscribe my name to this will this _____ day of _____, 19____, at _____, California.

_____

On this _____ day of _____, 19____, at _____, California, _____, declared to us, the undersigned, that this instrument, consisting of one page, front and back, was _____ will, and requested us to act as witnesses to it. _____ thereupon signed this will in our presence, all of us being present at the same time. We now, at _____ request, and in _____ presence, and the presence of each other, subscribe our names as witnesses. We declare under penalty of perjury that the foregoing is true and correct.

_____ *residing at* _____

_____ *residing at* _____

Glossary

Part of the hold that the legal profession has over us has to do with their use of specialized language. It is easy to be intimidated and uncomfortable when we don't know what lawyers and judges are talking about. It is only beginning to dawn on many of us that legal language is consciously and often cynically used to keep us intimidated and that the concepts behind the obtuse language are often easily understandable. I wish I could throw out all semantic pettifoggery and use only simple terms in this book, but unfortunately we are stuck with a legal system that creaks into motion best when ''magic'' (often four-syllabic) words are used.

If I fail to include definitions for all confusing terms, try the dictionary, but be sure to read the entire definition, as specialized legal meanings are often listed last, or check *Black's Law Dictionary,* available in all law libraries. Words with a definition in quotes and the symbol (B.) following are definitions taken from Ambrose Bierce's *The Devil's Dictionary*.

Administration (of an estate) — The distribution of the probate estate of a deceased person. The person who manages the distribution is called the **executor** (male) or **executrix** (female) if there is a will. If there is no will, this person is called the **administrator** or **administratrix.**

Autopsy — Examination of the body of a deceased person to determine the cause of death.

Annuity — Payment of a fixed sum of money to a specified person at regular, periodic intervals.

Basis — This is a tax term which has to do with the valuation of property. If you buy a house or a poodle for $20,000 and later sell it for $35,000, your tax basis is $20,000. A stepped-up basis simply means that you have been able to raise this basic amount from which taxes are computed. A buyer of property takes the purchase price as his or her tax basis.

Beneficiary — A person or organization who is legally entitled to receive benefits; used to identify the person who benefits from a trust or under the terms of a will.

Bequest (in a will) — A provision in a will leaving certain property to a specified person or organization.

Codicil — A supplement to a will containing a modification, amendment, explanation, etc.

Community property — Property acquired during the course of a marriage from the earnings or efforts of either spouse.

Consideration — Something of value, given or done in exchange for something of value given or done by another. You need consideration from both, or all parties, to a contract in order to have a valid contract. A promise to do an act later on is valid consideration.

Contract — An agreement between two or more people to do something. A contract is normally written, but can be oral if its terms can be carried out within one year. A contract is distinguished from a gift in that each of the contracting parties pledges to do something in exchange (in consideration) for the promises of the other(s).

Creditor — As used in this book, this means a person to whom money is owed. A creditor may be the person who actually lent the money, or he may be a lawyer or bill collector who is (trying to) collect the money for the original creditor.

Custodian — A person appointed or selected to supervise the affairs of another, because that person is a minor, incompetent, etc.

Death taxes — Taxes levied at death. The federal government's death taxes are called ''estate taxes;'' California's are called inheritance taxes.

Debtor — A person who owes money.

Deed — The legal document by which one person or persons transfer title (recorded ownership) to real property to another person or persons. If the transfer is by a grant deed, the person transferring title makes certain guarantees or warranties as regards the title. If the transfer is by quitclaim deed, the person transferring does not make any guarantees, but simply transfers to the other persons all the interest he has in the real property.

Decedent — A person who has died. The physical body of a decedent is called the **remains.**

Descendant — A person who is an offspring, however remote, of a certain ancestor or family.

Dissolution — Legal jargon for divorce.

Donor — One who gives a gift. A **donee** is one who receives a gift.

Estate — All the property of a person who died. The **taxable estate** is all of the estate property subject to death taxes. The **probate estate** is all of the estate that passes by will (or intestate succession).

Estate planning — What this book is about.

Estate taxes — Taxes levied at death by the federal government.

Executor/trix — The man or woman named in a will to supervise the administration of the decedent's probate estate.

Equity — The dollar amount of your home or other property that you own. On a home, figure it by taking the sale value of your home and then subtracting the amount you still owe on your mortgage and the amount it would cost to make the sale. For example, if your home could be sold for $80,000 and you owe $60,000 on your mortgage and it would cost $2,000 to sell (realtor's commissions, etc.), then your equity is $18,000.

Funeral — "A pageant whereby we attest to our respect to the dead by enriching the undertaker, and strengthen our grief by an expenditure that deepens our groans and doubles our tears." (B.)

Future interest — A right to property which cannot be enforced in the present, but at some future time.

Gift — A present (you knew that). A gift "causa mortis" is one made in contemplation of imminent death.

Gift taxes — Taxes levied by the federal and California governments on gifts made during a person's lifetime.

Guardian—A person appointed or selected to supervise the affairs of another, because that person is a minor, incompetent, etc.

Hearse—"Death's baby carriage." (B.)

Heir—One who inherits property from a decedent.

Holographic will—A will that is completely handwritten.

Homestead—On the simplest level, a document you file with the County Recorder, and when you do it, you gain a lot of protection for your home. More specifically, if you file a declaration of homestead, then your equity in your home will be protected against forced sale by creditors. A **probate homestead** is a homestead created for the family home by the probate court, where no homestead had been recorded during the decedent's life.

Inherit—To receive property from one who dies.

Inheritance taxes—Taxes levied at death by the State of California.

Incidents of ownership—All (or any) control over a life insurance policy.

Insurance—"An ingenious modern game of chance in which the player is permitted to enjoy the comfortable conviction that he is beating the man who keeps the table." (B.)

Intestate—Without a will. To die "intestate" means to die without having a will. **Intestate succession** is the way property of a deceased person is distributed according to California Probate Law, if the deceased did not leave a valid will.

Inter vivos trust—A trust "among the living," i.e., one created while the trust creator is alive, not upon his or her death.

Joint tenancy — A form of shared ownership of property in which the surviving owner(s) automatically own the interest of a deceased owner; all joint tenants own an equal (undivided) interest in the joint tenancy property.

Lawful — "Compatible with the will of a judge having jurisdiction." (B.)

Lawyer — "One skilled in circumvention of the law." (B.)

Legacy — "A gift from one who is legging it out of this vale of tears." (B.)

Life estate — The right to use property, most often real property, during one's lifetime.

Lineal descendant — A person who is in the direct line of descent from an ancestor. A person's children, grandchildren and great grandchildren, etc. are his or her lineal descendants.

Liquidity — Cash or assets that can readily be turned into cash.

Mausoleum — "The final and funniest folly of the rich." (B.)

Minors — In California, anyone under age 18.

Next-of-kin — The closest living relation.

Personal property — All property other than land and buildings attached to land. Cars, bank accounts, wages, furniture, insurance policies, season basketball tickets, etc. are all personal property.

Primogeniture — Medieval rule of law that the eldest son inherited all land or all property.

Probate — The name for the court procedure designed to prove a will authentic, pay the decedent's debts and taxes, and distribute the property according to the will, or intestate succession law if there is no will.

Power of attorney — A document authorizing another person to act as attorney-in-fact for the signing person.

Quasi-community property — Property outside the state of California bought by a married couple which would have been community property had it been bought here.

Real property — Land and those items attached to the land, such as buildings, etc.

Residue — The property left in a probate estate after all specific bequests have been distributed.

Separate property — In states which have community property, all property which is not community property.

Settlor — The person who creates ("settles") a trust.

Siblings — Brothers and sisters.

Spouse — Either member of a married couple; one's husband or wife.

Tenancy-in-common — A form of shared ownership where there is no right of survivorship. Tenants-in-common can own property in unequal shares, unlike joint tenants who each own an equal share of the property.

Testate — Leaving a valid will.

Testator — The person who leaves property by his or her will; normally the person who drafts his or her (own) will.

Trust — A relationship in which one person (the trustee) holds title (often subject to a number of conditions) to property for the benefit of another person (the beneficiary). A trust is commonly used when money is left to people inexperienced in its management such as children or as a tax saving device. A testamentary trust is one established by a will.

Totten trust — A simple savings bank trust, revocable at any time before the death of the depositor/settlor.

Vest — To become legally in control; when a former future interest turns into a present right, it vests.

Will — A legal document in which a person states who he wants to inherit his property, etc.

ABOUT THE AUTHOR

Denis Clifford is a partner in an Oakland, California law firm. A graduate of Columbia Law School, where he was an editor of the Law Review, he has been a law clerk for a federal district judge, a law professor, a government legal consultant, and has practiced law in numerous ways, including working with Montgomery Street law firms specializing in financial affairs of wealthy clients to managing a neighborhood "legal aid" law office in East Oakland. He has done extensive research and work in the field of estate planning. Denis loves writing novels, playing basketball, and sleeping late.

ABOUT NOLO

We Americans have more money and property than ever before. At the same time many of us are fearful and insecure. As a society we have lost that "peaceful, easy feeling."

The chaos in our legal system is both a reflection and root cause of our anxieties. How can we be secure if we are surrounded by laws, legal procedures, courts, and administrative procedures which directly affect our lives, but over which we have little say, and no control? Even Jerry Brown and Jimmy Carter have recently discovered that we are often oppressed by laws and lawyers.

Many people who have given some thought to the roots of human behavior have concluded that survival is our most basic urge. Certainly there is evidence that, when pushed against a wall, most of us will either fight back as hard and viciously as we can, or try to escape. In a way, this is what many of us are forced to do when faced with a legal problem. While both running and fighting may be good for survival, they don't do much to create a decent society where we are secure in the knowledge that laws are truly understandable, reasonable and spring from a genuine consensus of the citizenry.

But there is something constructive we can do. This is to limit our dependence on legal professionals who have a financial stake in having us remain insecure and fearful and to take the time to understand how our laws and courts work. Behind the long words and convoluted procedures, the basic concepts are almost always simple. Our own knowledge will help us banish many devils, but there is a larger job. This is to be sensitive to ways that we, as a society, can gain the right to participate in, and be treated with respect by, our legal system. We need to expand Small Claims Courts, allow non-lawyers to serve as arbitrators, mediators and judges, to cut back on the number of lawyers in our legislatures, to teach basic laws and legal procedures in our schools, to simplify legal procedures and language, to teach people how to use the courts, etc.

Reform in the future sounds great, but today participation in our legal system depends on an understanding of many procedures and technicalities. This is where Nolo Press comes in. Our "do your own law" books are designed to provide the practical legal information that the average citizen needs in order to be able to fill out forms, serve papers, present himself/herself in court, and make the kinds of legal decisions that we normally turn over to attorneys. It has long been our belief that lawyers shroud information in a cloud of totally incomprehensible language so as to justify high fees and ''professional standing.'' Our books are an attempt to cut through the legal jargon of law books and judicial decisions and present clear, straightforward information to the layperson in a language we can all understand.

Our books have been written, illustrated, designed and printed by a group of friends headquartered in Berkeley and Occidental, California. Without ever planning to, we have created our own cottage industry. We hope you get as much out of reading our books as we did in making them, and we would be delighted to get any feedback you would care to send our way.

BOOKS BY NOLO

CALIFORNIA BOOKS

PLAN YOUR ESTATE: WILLS, PROBATE AVOIDANCE, TRUSTS & TAXES by attorney Clifford. Here in one place for the first time Californians can get information on making their own will, alternatives to probate, planning to limit inheritance and estate taxes, living trusts, and providing for family and friends. [August 1982] $15.95

HOW TO FORM YOUR OWN CALIFORNIA CORPORATION by attorney Anthony Mancuso. Provides you with all the forms, Bylaws, Articles, stock certificates and instructions necessary to file your small profit corporation in California. It includes a thorough discussion of the practical and legal aspects of incorporation, including the tax consequences. [October 1981] $17.95

THE NON-PROFIT CORPORATION HANDBOOK by attorney Anthony Mancuso. Completely updated to reflect all the new law changes effective January 1980. Includes all the forms, Bylaws, Articles and instructions you need to form a nonprofit corporation in California. Step-by-step instructions on how to choose a name, draft Articles and Bylaws, attain favorable tax status. Thorough information on federal tax exemptions which groups outside of California will find particularly useful.
[August 1981] $17.95

THE PARTNERSHIP BOOK by attorneys Clifford & Warner. This book supplies everything you need to establish a solid, legal partnership. Sample agreements are included to use "as is" or modify to fit your needs. Buy-out clauses, unequal sharing of assets, death or withdrawal of a partner, valuation of partnership assets, and limited partnerships are discussed in detail.
[November 1981] $15.95

BANKRUPTCY: DO IT YOURSELF by attorney Janice Kosel. Tells you exactly what bankruptcy is all about and how it affects your credit rating, your property and debts, with complete details on property you can keep under the state and federal exempt property rules. Shows you step-by-step how to do it yourself and comes with all forms and instructions necessary.
[March 1981] $12.00

BILLPAYERS' RIGHTS by attorneys Honigsberg & Warner. Complete information on bankruptcy, student loans, wage attachments, dealing with bill collectors and collection agencies, credit cards, car repossessions, homesteads, child support and much more.
[July 1981] $ 7.95

HOW TO DO YOUR OWN DIVORCE IN CALIFORNIA by attorney Charles Sherman. Now in its tenth edition, this is the original "do your own law" book. It contains tear-out copies of all the court forms required for an uncontested dissolution, as well as instructions for pauper's oath, lost summons, and publi-cations of summons.
[January 1982] $ 9.95

FIGHT YOUR TICKET by attorney David Brown. A comprehensive manual on how to fight your California traffic ticket. Radar, drunk driving, preparing for court, arguing your case to a judge, cross-examining witnesses are all covered in detail. If you have any thought of going into traffic court, you will want to have this book under your arm.
[March 1982] $12.95

CALIFORNIA TENANTS' HANDBOOK by attorneys Moskovitz, Warner & Sherman. Discusses everything tenants need to know in order to protect themselves: getting deposits returned, breaking a lease, getting repairs made, using Small Claims Court, dealing with an unscrupulous landlord, forming a tenants' organization, etc. Completely updated to cover new rent control information and law changes for 1981. Sample Fair-to-Tenants lease and rental agreement. [July 1982] $ 7.95

EVERYBODY'S GUIDE TO SMALL CLAIMS COURT by attorney Ralph Warner. Guides you step-by-step through the Small Claims procedure, providing practical information on how to evaluate your case, file and serve papers, prepare and present your case, and, most important, how to collect when you win. Separate chapters focus on common situations (landlord-tenant, automobile sales and repair, etc.).
[March 1982] $ 8.95

HOW TO CHANGE YOUR NAME by attorney David Loeb. Changing one's name is a very simple procedure. Using this book, people can file all necessary papers themselves, saving $200-300 in attorney's fees. Comes complete with all the forms and instructions necessary for the court petition method or the simpler usage method.
[January 1982] $10.95

PROTECT YOUR HOME WITH A DECLARATION OF HOMESTEAD by attorney Warner. Under the California Homestead Act, you can file a Declaration of Homestead and thus protect your home from being sold to satisfy most debts. This book explains this simple and inexpensive procedure and includes all the forms and instructions. Contains information on exemptions for mobile homes and houseboats. [1981] $ 5.95

AFTER THE DIVORCE: HOW TO MODIFY ALIMONY, CHILD SUPPORT & CHILD CUSTODY by attorney Joseph Matthews. Detailed information on how to increase alimony or child support, decrease what you pay, change custody and visitation, oppose modifications by your ex. Comes with all the forms and instructions you need. Sections on joint custody, mediation, and inflation.
[December 1980] $12.00

THE PEOPLE'S GUIDE TO MARRIAGE AND DIVORCE LAW by attorneys Ihara and Warner. This book contains invaluable information for married couples and those considering marriage on community and separate property, names, debts, children, buying a house, etc. Includes sample marriage contracts, a simple will, probate avoidance information and an explanation of gift and inheritance taxes. Discusses secret marriage and common law marriage.
[January 1981] $ 7.95

HOW TO ADOPT YOUR STEPCHILD by Frank Zagone. Shows you how to prepare
all the legal forms; includes information on how to get the consent of
the natural parent and how to conduct an "abandonment" proceeding.
Discusses appearing in court, making changes in birth certificates.
[1979] $10.00

SIXTY PLUS IN CALIFORNIA This Cragmont publication covers social security, retirement benefits, age discrimination, medicare, debt problems,
taxes, wills, housing problems and many other legal rights and remedies
of senior citizens and retired persons.
[1979] $ 6.95

THE CALIFORNIA PROFESSIONAL CORPORATION HANDBOOK by attorneys Mancuso
and Honigsberg. In California there are a number of professions which
must fulfill special requirements when filing a corporation. This book
contains detailed information on the special requirements of every
profession and all the forms and instructions necessary to file a professional corporation.
[Available Winter 1982] $19.95

NATIONAL BOOKS

CHAPTER 13 by attorney Janice Kosel. This book allows an individual to
develop and carry out a feasible plan to pay one's debts in whole over a
three-year period. Chapter 13 is an alternative to straight bankruptcy
and yet it still means the end of creditor harassment, wage attachments
and other collection efforts. Complete with all the forms and work-
sheets you need.
[June 1982] $12.95

LEGAL RESEARCH: HOW TO FIND AND UNDERSTAND THE LAW by attorney Stephen
Elias. A hands-on guide to unraveling the mysteries of the law library.
Shows exactly how to find laws relating to specific cases or legal
questions, interpret statutes and regulations, find and research cases,
understand case citations and Shepardize them.
[January 1982] $12.95

THE PEOPLE'S LAW REVIEW edited by Ralph Warner. This is the first
compendium of people's law resources ever published. It celebrates the
coming of age of the self-help law movement and contains a 50-state
catalog of self-help law materials; articles on mediation and the new
"non-adversary" mediation centers; information on self-help law programs
and centers (programs for tenants, artists, battered women, the disabled, etc.); articles & interviews by the leaders of the self-help law
movement, and articles dealing with many common legal problems which
show people "how to do it themselves"
without lawyers. [1980] $ 8.95

A LEGAL GUIDE FOR LESBIAN/GAY COUPLES by attorneys Curry and Clifford.
Here is a book that deals specifically with legal matters of lesbian and
gay couples. Discusses areas such as raising children (custody, support, living with a lover), buying property together, wills, etc. and
comes complete with sample contracts and agreements.
[1980] $10.95

THE <u>UNEMPLOYMENT</u> <u>BENEFITS</u> <u>HANDBOOK</u> by attorney Peter Jan Honigsberg. Comprehensive information on how to find out if you are eligible for benefits, how the amount of those benefits will be determined. It shows how to file and handle an appeal if benefits are denied and gives important advice on how to deal with the bureaucracy and the people at the unemployment office. [April 1981] $ 5.95

<u>MARIJUANA:</u> <u>YOUR</u> <u>LEGAL</u> <u>RIGHTS</u> by attorney Richard Moller. Here is the legal information all marijuana users and growers need to guarantee their constitutional rights and protect their privacy and property. Discusses what the laws are, how they differ from state to state, and how legal loopholes can be used against smokers and growers. [May 1981] $ 6.95

<u>SMALL</u> <u>TIME</u> <u>OPERATOR</u> by Bernard Kamoroff, C.P.A. Shows you how to start and operate your small business, keep your books, pay your taxes and stay out of trouble. Comes complete with a year's supply of ledgers and worksheets designed especially for small businesses, and contains invaluable information on permits, licenses, financing, loans, insurance, bank accounts, etc. Published by Bell Springs Press. [January 1982] $ 8.95

THE <u>LIVING</u> <u>TOGETHER</u> <u>KIT</u> by attorneys Toni Ihara and Ralph Warner. A legal guide for unmarried couples with information about buying or sharing property, the Marvin decision, paternity statements, medical emergencies and tax consequences. Contains a sample will and Living Together Contract. [1979] $8.95

<u>DON'T</u> <u>SIT</u> <u>IN</u> <u>THE</u> <u>DRAFT</u> by Charles Johnson. A draft counseling guide with information on how the system works, classifications, deferments, exemptions, medical standards, appeals and alternatives. [1980] $ 6.95

<u>LANDLORDING</u> by Leigh Robinson. Written for the conscientious landlord or landlady, this comprehensive guide discusses maintenance and repairs, getting good tenants, how to avoid evictions, recordkeeping, and taxes. [October 1981] $15.00

<u>IMMIGRATING</u> <u>TO</u> <u>THE</u> <u>U.S.A.</u> by Danilov. Covers all aspects of immigration: student visas, work permits, preference categories, requirements for U.S. citizenship, nonimmigrant visas, deportation laws, etc. Comes complete with all the forms and instructions necessary. [June 1980] $ 9.95

<u>MEN'S</u> <u>RIGHTS:</u> <u>A</u> <u>HANDBOOK</u> <u>FOR</u> <u>THE</u> <u>80s</u> by Wishard. This book discusses rights and issues with which men (and women) are concerned: living together, abortion, fatherhood, employment, child custody, support, visitation, etc. [1980] $ 6.95

<u>LEGAL</u> <u>CARE</u> <u>FOR</u> <u>SOFTWARE</u> by attorney Dan Remer. Here we show the software programmer how to protect his/her work through the use of trade secret, tradework, copyright, patent and, most especially, contractual laws and agreements. This book is full of forms and instructions that give programmers the hands-on information to do it themselves. Available Winter 1982. $19.95

WE OWN IT! by attorney Honigsberg and C.P.A.s Kamoroff and Beatty. This book provides the legal, tax and management information you need to start and successfully operate all types of coops and collectives.

$ 9.00

Nolo Press also publishes the following books in national editions:

THE PARTNERSHIP BOOK by Clifford & Warner $14.95

EVERYBODY'S GUIDE TO SMALL CLAIMS COURT by Warner $ 6.95

BANKRUPTCY: DO IT YOURSELF by Kosel $11.95

Some of our publications are designed specifically for Texas. They include:

HOW TO FORM YOUR OWN TEXAS CORPORATION by Mancuso, Simons
& Lehman $14.95

HOW TO DO YOUR OWN DIVORCE IN TEXAS by Sherman and Simons $ 9.95

PLAN YOUR ESTATE, TEXAS EDITION by Clifford and Simons $ 9.95

TEXAS TENANTS HANDBOOK by Simons, Warner & Moskovitz $ 6.95

Pacific Rim Series

CALIFORNIA DREAMING: THE POLITICAL ODYSSEY OF PAT AND JERRY BROWN by Roger Rapoport. Here for the first time is the story of the first family of California politics from the Gold Rush to the 1980s. Based on more than 200 interviews, access to papers previously unavailable to scholars, lengthy talks and travels with Pat and Jerry Brown and their family. $ 9.95

In a Lighter Vein

29 REASONS NOT TO GO TO LAW SCHOOL by attorneys Toni Ihara and Ralph Warner with illustrations by Mari Stein. A humorous and irreverent look at the dubious pleasures of going to law school. $ 4.95

Order Form

Quantity	Total		Unit Price	Total
	How to Adopt Your Stepchild			
	After The Divorce			
	Bankruptcy: Do-It-Yourself (Calif. Edition)			
	* Bankruptcy: Do-It-Yourself (Natl. Edition)			
	Billpayers' Rights			
	* Chapter 13: The Federal Plan to Repay Your Debts			
	* Computer Law			
	How To Form Your Own California Corporation			
	How To Form Your Own Texas Corporation			
	How To Do Your Own Divorce in California			
	How To Do Your Own Divorce in Texas			
	Plan Your Estate (Calif. Edition)			
	Plan Your Estate (Texas Edition)			
	Fight Your Ticket			
	* A Legal Guide for Lesbian/Gay Couples			
	Protect Your Home With A Declaration of Homestead			
	* Immigrating to the U.S.A.			
	* Landlording			
	* Legal Research: How To Find and Understand the Law			
	* The Living Together Kit			
	* Marijuana: Your Legal Rights			
	People's Guide to California Marriage & Divorce Law			
	How to Change Your Name			
	The Non-Profit Corporation Handbook (Calif. Edition)			
	The Partnership Book (Calif. Edition)			
	* The Partnership Book (Natl. Edition)			
	* People's Law Review			
	* Rights of the Elderly and Retired			
	Sixty Plus in California			
	Everybody's Guide to Small Claims Court (Calif. Edition)			
	* Everybody's Guide to Small Claims Court (Natl. Edition)			
	* Small Time Operator - Managing Small Businesses			
	California Tenants' Handbook			
	Texas Tenants' Handbook			
	* Men's Rights			
	* Don't Sit in The Draft			
	* The Unemployment Benefits Handbook			
	How To Form Your Own Professional Corporation (Calif. Ed.)			
	* 29 Reasons Not To Go To Law School			

* Applicable in all 50 states
prices subject to change

SUBTOTAL _____

Postage and handling
(see below) _____

TOTAL _____

Please total the amount owed, then include 85¢ postage and handling for the first book and 60¢ for each additional book. California residents add sales tax (6½% BART & Santa Clara Counties; 6% all others).

Name_____

Address_____

City, State, Zip_____

NOLO PRESS, 950 Parker St., Berkeley, CA 94710 (415) 549-1976

or

NOLO PRESS DISTRIBUTING, Box 544, Occidental, CA 95465 (707) 874-3105

UPDATE SERVICE & LEGAL DIRECTORY

Our books are as current as we can make them, but sometimes the laws do change between editions. You can read about any law changes which may affect this book in the **NOLO NEWS**, a 12 page newspaper which we publish quarterly.

In addition to the **Update Service**, each issue contains a directory of people-oriented lawyers and legal clinics available to answer questions, handle a complicated case or process your paperwork at a reasonable cost. Also featured are comprehensive articles about the growing self-help law movement as well as areas of the law that are sure to affect you.

To receive the next 4 issues of the **NOLO NEWS**, please send us $2.00.

Name _____

Address _____

_____

Send to: **NOLO PRESS, 950 Parker St., Berkeley, CA 94710**